Sport, Physical Activity, and the Law

Neil J. Dougherty
Alan S. Goldberger
Linda Jean Carpenter

Second Edition

Sagamore Publishing
WWW.SAGAMOREPUBLISHING.COM

10 9 8 7 6 5 4 3 2 1

ISBN
1-57167-492-6
LIBRARY OF CONGRESS CARD CATALOG NUMBER
2002101305
PRODUCTION MANAGER
Janet K. Wahlfeldt
BOOK DESIGN, LAYOUT
Jennifer L. Polson
COVER DESIGN
Michelle R. Dressen

SAGAMORE PUBLISHING
804 North Neil Street
Champaign, IL 61820

Visit us on the Web at www.sagamorepublishing.com

CONTENTS

PREFACE

I t's virtually impossible to exist within organized society without having your actions affected and controlled—at least to some degree—by elements of law. The laws of society dictate the rights and responsibilities of individuals as well as procedures for redress when the actions or inactions of others infringe upon those rights.

Although sport, as an institution, and the individuals who deliver and participate in programs of sport and physical activity are subject to the same legal principles as the rest of society, sometimes the nature of the activity and the attitudes of those involved creates a subculture in which the authority of the coach is overestimated and, thus, the rights of the participants are perceived as depending primarily on the coach's desires and decisions. Questions concerning eligibility to participate and disqualifying conditions or circumstances sometimes become a matter of local or league preference. Injuries may be considered "part of the game" and, although unfortunate, certainly not matter for litigation. In all aspects of team discipline and control, the decision of the coach in the eyes of some is, in effect, law.

In fact, however, legislation case law and the growing legal sensitivity of the populace have pulled sport from its protected cocoon squarely into the mainstream of legal practice. Issues such as the right to participate and compensation for injuries are frequently the subjects of lawsuits and other formal legal proceedings. Coaches, administrators, game officials, and even players are the target of legal action based on their alleged commissions or omissions.

These developments make it essential that all persons involved with creating and delivering programs of amateur sport and physical activity clearly understand the fundamental legal principles that most directly affect their actions and activities. *Sport, Physical Activity, and the Law* has been developed to meet this need. Because the dimensions of legal considerations in professional sport are different from those of amateur sport and physical activity, and because the legal aspects of professional sport affect a comparatively small number of practitioners, we have elected to focus on amateur sports in this text.

This, the second edition of *Sport, Physical Activity, and the Law* has been revised to reflect the ever-expanding body of statutory and case law, to address additional topics of concern to the practitioner, and to further enhance the clarity and readability of the writing. New to this edition are chapters on Risk Management and Contracts. The material on inclusion vs. exclusion and the rights of participants has been entirely reorganized and expanded to better reflect the historical pattern of development, the interrelationship of the applicable statutory controls, and the pattern of current case precedent.

The common organizational pattern of the chapters facilitates study and review. First we present a brief scenario to illustrate the nature of the chapter's main topic. This is followed by a list of objectives that articulate the key elements of the chapter. As new, important terms are introduced, they appear in bold print. Many chapters contain management sections that show the sports administrator how to turn the legal concepts and requirements discussed into proactive tools that build better programs. At the end of the discussion portion of each chapter is a summary of the key concepts followed by several case studies that demonstrate real-world applications of the legal concepts addressed. The cases have been presented in simple narrative form rather than a formal, legal reporting style.

Although all are based on actual situations, not all have been adjudicated and reported at the appellate level. Case studies based on lower court decisions are identified and, for the most part, use fictitious names and places. We chose this format, as opposed to the more common reporting of appellate decisions only, to maximize readability and interest for readers and to allow us to base cases on matters adjudicated in the lower courts or in some instances settled before trial. This practice lets students develop a better understanding of the day-to-day application of legal principles than if examples were limited to the relatively rare instances in which formal legal precedent has been established. The case studies are followed by a list of key terms and several questions to aid in review and self-evaluation. Finally, we list the references cited in the chapter and, in many chapters, suggest additional readings for those who want to explore further the material presented.

We have written this book to help current and future practitioners and administrators develop safe and legally sound sport and physical activity programs. This text is not intended to substitute for the advice of an attorney when it is called for, nor can it necessarily forestall lawsuits—no text can make such claims. But we're convinced that the principles and guidelines in *Sport, Physical Activity, and the Law* can form a foundation for a program that complies with both the letter and the spirit of the law, which in turn minimizes the likelihood of lawsuits and maximizes the likelihood of winning any that may occur. Even more important, participants in such programs will be given maximum opportunities and options in a safe and effectively regulated environment.

PART I

UNDERSTANDING AND DEALING WITH LAWS AND LEGAL SYSTEMS

CHAPTER 1

OVERVIEW OF THE LEGAL SYSTEM

Ladies and gentlemen of the jury: We are here today because a young athlete has suffered severe and permanent injury as a result of her coach's failure to exercise the degree of care that she owed to the members of her team. The coach was negligent. Because of this negligence, Margaret Quinn has been made to suffer physical and mental discomfort, extensive medical bills, and severe and permanent disability. Only you can compensate Margaret Quinn for the needless damage that she has suffered as a result of the unprofessional and improper actions of her coach, Jean Sharp.

These words are typical of an all-too-familiar and sad occasion: an opening statement to the jury by the attorney for a plaintiff. The question is, how does a successful, highly regarded coach land in a courtroom, being labeled by the plaintiff's attorney as negligent and thus responsible for the injuries suffered by one of her athletes? Although the scenario is fictitious, it represents an ever-increasing occurrence in the field of sport and physical activity. More and more, people are turning to the courts as a means of correcting or seeking compensation for wrongs which they claim to have suffered because of the actions of others.

Our society has reached a level of complexity whereby much of our day-to-day functions are controlled by law. The legal process is designed to protect the rights of every person. In so doing, the process establishes the limits of individual rights and responsibilities not only for those who participate in sport but for the leaders and administrators as well. Therefore, thorough understanding and application of the law as it applies to sport and physical activity have become essential components of the planning and delivery of all activities.

LEARNING OBJECTIVES

Upon completion of this chapter, the student will be able to:
1. distinguish between matters that are normally subject to criminal laws and those that are normally subject to civil law,
2. name and explain the steps in the process of a civil suit,
3. describe the nature and application of the primary forms of pretrial discovery, and
4. recognize the value of the law as a managerial tool.

DEFINITION OF LAW

Reduced to simple terms, law is a system of principles or rules that are established and enforced to regulate human behavior. This regulation is accomplished by establishing obligations and rights and by imposing a system for redress that allows the court to require or prohibit the doing of a particular act; to provide compensation for losses; and/or to impose penalties for violations. Elements of law can be found in virtually every aspect of American society. This is certainly no less true in the field of sport and physical activity, where issues such as who may participate, who may assume leadership roles, and the rights and responsibilities of each are often prescribed by law. In order to fully understand one's legal rights and responsibilities, it is necessary to identify the three sources of law: common law, codified law, and case law.

COMMON LAW

The written pronouncements of the law are preceded historically by the development of the **common law,** a somewhat amorphous framework of principles and strictures dating back to ancient times, refined and preserved by the courts of England, and subsequently accepted and applied in American courts. Concepts of common law have been discussed, refined, defined, codified, and sometimes nullified by courts, legislatures, and Congress throughout the history of those institutions. In essence, the common law is comprised of legal principles originally based upon judicial decree which through time and usage have become accepted by the courts. Though largely ancient, elements of common law continue to be legally applicable unless and until they are supplanted by appropriate codified or case law.

CODIFIED LAW

Codified law refers to specific laws and regulations promulgated by the legislative branches of government. Laws enacted by Congress and state legislatures are commonly referred to as **statutes.** Laws enacted at the lower levels of government are normally referred to as **ordinances** or **codes.** Many of our day-to-day activities fall within the bounds of federal, state, and local law. Laws affecting discrimination against individuals because of sex, race, or handicapping condition, for instance, have been enacted at the federal level, in every state, and by local governments.

The question of whether federal or state law would take precedence in any given situation is often fairly clear-cut. Federal law takes precedence unless the requirements of the state are stricter. The state law takes precedence if it is more restrictive than, and not in conflict with the intent of, the federal law. Federal law, for instance, excludes contact sports from the prohibitions against sex discrimination in federally funded educational programs. However, a state law that requires all sports, whether contact is involved or not, to be accessible to both sexes would take precedence, because the state law would be seen as a more restrictive interpretation of the legal equality of the sexes. Indeed, some states have enacted legislation to that end.

The same principles apply to laws enacted at the local level. That is, the laws enacted by a given municipality may not contravene those of the state or federal governments. It is important, therefore, to be aware of applicable state and local laws as well as federal laws.

Much of the day-to-day operation of governmental organizations is controlled by **administrative regulations.** Various governmental agencies have the authority to develop and enforce policies, rules, and regulations for activities under their control. In addition, legislative bodies frequently relegate many of the details of the application of statutes to administrative codes. These have the force of law and thus play important roles in the organization and management of many sport and physical activity programs. For example, the New Jersey Administrative Code contains guidelines established by New Jersey's state Department of Education regarding the educational qualifications of coaches employed by public schools. The athletic programs of every New Jersey public school district are bound by these regulations.

CASE LAW

Case law is the terminology used to refer to judicial decisions of matters in controversy between parties to a legal proceeding.

Legal precedent constitutes a major element in establishing the day-to-day application of the law. This concept is embodied in the legal doctrine of *stare decisis*, which means literally "to stand by things decided." In practice, this means that courts called upon to adjudicate disputes customarily consider case **precedent** (that is, the courts will consider how other courts have ruled on similar cases) as well as existing statutes. When a court issues a decision, it establishes a precedent that ordinarily guides the subsequent actions of all courts of equal or lower stature within its jurisdiction on cases in which the facts and circumstances are essentially similar to the previously decided case.

CONTRACTS

Under the American legal system, parties are free to define their legal relationships, including the rights and obligations of the participating individuals or groups, through the use of formalized agreements known as contracts. Contracts are, in general, legally enforceable, and a failure to fulfill the demands of a contract that results in damages to one of the parties involved may result in legal action (see Chapter 10).

One of the most visible examples of such formalized agreements in the area of sport and physical activity may be found in league and organizational rules. Virtually all sport and physical activity programs establish rules and regulations regarding competition, organizational structure, and the conduct of their members. Generally speaking, all members of a given group are bound by its rules and regulations. However, when such rules are in conflict with existing law, or when the organization takes actions that conflict with its own rules, the aggrieved party can seek redress through the courts. Chapter 12 details the complex nature of these interactions.

CIVIL OR CRIMINAL?

Laws are divided into two major categories: criminal laws and civil laws. **Criminal laws** regulate public conduct and are enforced by the government body that enacted them. Violations of criminal laws result in action by the government aimed at imposing some form of **punishment**. Criminal acts are classified according to their level of severity. **Felonies** are the most heinous crimes and include murder, rape, assault, and robbery. Such offenses are punishable by monetary fines, imprisonment in a state or federal penitentiary, and, in extreme cases, capital punishment. **Misdemeanors** are lesser criminal offenses such as driving while under the influence of alcohol, disorderly conduct, and vandalism. Persons found guilty of misdemeanors may be subject to short-term imprisonment, fines, or both.

The overwhelming majority of legal actions involving sport and physical activity focus on alleged violations of civil law. **Civil laws** regulate interactions between individuals or groups. A civil action may be brought when one person feels wronged by another. The purpose of the civil action or lawsuit is to seek compensation for or to right an alleged wrong. Unlike criminal cases, the primary objectives of civil suits are to compensate someone for damages and/or to correct the an alleged wrong.

Since the civil and criminal law systems have different objectives, the rules and procedures differ for each system. For instance, in a civil lawsuit, a party must prove a claim by a "reasonable preponderance" of the evidence. (In other words, the claim must be "more likely than not"). In a criminal proceeding, on the other hand, the government must prove its case against the defendant beyond any reasonable doubt.

Finally, it is also possible for a given situation to result in both criminal charges and a civil action. The results of such criminal and civil actions are not normally dependent on one another. That is why we have sometimes seen individuals acquitted of criminal charges while, nevertheless, being held responsible for civil damages (e.g., O.J. Simpson).

THE BUSINESS OF THE COURTS

Under common law, a person has a legal right to bring a lawsuit against another under two separate and distinct legal theories: contract and tort. Actions for violations of contracts were based upon the concept of *assumpsit,* or the notion that a failure to fulfill the requirement of a contract may subject one to liability for damages caused by one's actions or inaction. A **tort**, on the other hand, is a legal wrong for which one may, under certain circumstances, seek compensation through the courts. Most civil cases brought against programs of sport or physical activity involve an alleged tort.

A person who believes that he or she has suffered an injury or a loss because of the actions of another, or because of that person's failure to act in a prescribed manner, has the following three legal or quasi-legal options to choose from:

1. Do nothing. Many people are unwilling to get involved with the legal system, are unaware of their rights, or are unsure of the validity of their complaints. These and numerous other personal factors lead some individuals simply to accept a situation rather than to pursue any legal remedy.
2. Attempt to obtain satisfaction without professional aid. Depending upon the nature of the grievance, an individual could contact school or program administrators or insurers and set forth the elements of his complaint. Then the officers of the organization or their insurers would either offer to correct or compensate for the problem or would deny such support, depending upon their assessment of the circumstances and of the potential legal outcome if the **grievant** (the individual seeking compensation for an alleged loss) chooses to pursue the matter through the courts.
3. Seek the services of an attorney who, upon reviewing the matter, would either refuse the case or agree to represent the client, by acting as the grievant's official representative in attempting to negotiate a settlement with the organization and/or its insurer, or by instituting a lawsuit or other formal claim.

Legal proceedings may be commenced in a variety of venues, depending on local law and the objectives one seeks to achieve. While specific applications vary from state to state, civil actions by aggrieved persons may be brought in local, state, or federal courts or in administrative tribunals. In some states, for example, municipal courts or justice courts may have jurisdiction over disputes involving small sums of money. In other states, county courts are the place to litigate claims for contracts regardless of the amount involved. Other claims are allowed to be brought in federal courts. These cases usually involve a right secured by federal law or lawsuits between residents of different states. Some other disputes between those involved in sport are properly directed to administrative agencies that employ judicial officers to hear certain types of disputes. In some states, for instance, complaints may be heard by an administrative law judge who will conduct fact-finding and adjudicate the matter without empaneling a jury. Still other relationships may allow or require that claims and disputes be submitted to arbitration or mediation as a prerequisite to prosecuting legal proceedings.

If an attorney decides to seek compensation through the court system, he or she would file a **complaint** or **petition** in the appropriate court. A **complaint** is a formal document that initiates a civil suit. The complaint would enumerate the basic legal theories and facts put forth by the injured party (the **plaintiff**). The complaint would also state the damages or other form of relief the plaintiff seeks from the **defendant** (the individual against whom the complaint is filed). Figure 1.1 (pages 9-11) shows portions of a sample complaint. After a complaint has been filed and served on the defendants, their attorneys normally file an **answer**. The answer normally denies all or some of the allegations made in the complaint and puts forth legal arguments on behalf of the defendants. Figure 1.2 (pages 12-13) is an example of an abbreviated answer to a complaint filed by a Figure 1.2 plaintiff.

After these initial pleadings have been filed, the case moves into what is commonly called the discovery phase of the proceedings. The **process of discovery** encompasses the period between the commencement of the lawsuit and the commencement of the trial. During this time, the attorneys exercise a number of legal options to find and develop all the pertinent facts that bear upon the case. The primary forms of pretrial discovery are interrogatories, depositions, and requests for production of physical evidence.

Interrogatories are written questions sent by the attorney representing one party involved in a lawsuit to one of the adversarial parties. These questions must be answered truthfully and under oath. They may be introduced as evidence at the time of trial and should be answered with the advice of an attorney. Figure 1.3 provides examples of questions frequently found on interrogatories.

A **deposition** is pretrial testimony of a witness that is taken in response to a legal order. Attorneys for all parties are usually present at a deposition, and a court stenographer is present to administer oaths of truthfulness to the witnesses and to make a verbatim recording of the testimony. As with interrogatories, the transcript of a deposition may be used as evidence at the trial. This procedure serves a dual function: It allows the discovery of a great deal of factual information about the case,; and, no less importantly, it allows the attorneys to assess the manner in which witnesses conduct and present themselves under the pressure of adversarial questioning.

The wide availability of videotape equipment has led to its increasing use in the judicial process. Sometimes, for instance, the attorneys for all parties to a suit agree to

FIGURE 1.1
COMPLAINT OF THE PLAINTIFF

Jones, Smith & Brown, P.A.
9 South Avenue
Point Pleasant, New Jersey 08742
ATTORNEYS FOR PLAINTIFF

PLAINTIFF(S)	)	SUPERIOR COURT OF NEW JERSEY
MARGARET QUINN	)	LAW DIVISION: OCEAN COUNTY
vs.	)	DOCKET NO.: OCN-L-3200-90
DEFENDANT(S)	)	Civil Action
JEAN SHARP AND CITY OF	)	AMENDED COMPLAINT
WELDON, BOARD OF	)	AND
EDUCATION, a public	)	DEMAND FOR TRIAL BY JURY
entity of the State of	)	
New Jersey	)	

The Plaintiff, Margaret Quinn, residing at 12 Banks Street, in the
City of Weldon, County of Ocean, and State of New Jersey, by way
of Complaint against the Defendants, says:

/A/**FIRST COUNT**

1. On or about February 9, 1992, Plaintiff, MARGARET QUINN,
was a high school student enrolled in Weldon High School, located
at 121 St. Johns Avenue, Weldon, New Jersey and a member of the
Weldon High School Girls' Track and Field Team.
2. On or about February 9, 1992, and at all times
hereinafter relevant, the Defendant, JEAN SHARP, was an employee
of the Defendant, CITY OF WELDON, BOARD OF EDUCATION, and was
specifically employed as a physical education teacher and coach at
said Weldon High School.
3. On or about February 9, 1992, and at all times
hereinafter relevant, the Defendants, JEAN SHARP and CITY OF
WELDON, BOARD OF EDUCATION, were directly responsible for the
instruction, control and supervision of students enrolled at
Weldon High School, including, but not limited to, members of the
Weldon High School Girls' Track and Field Team, of which Plaintiff
was a member.
4. On or about February 9, 1992, and at all times
hereinafter relevant, the duties, obligations, and
responsibilities of the Defendants, included, among other things,
the proper, reasonable and careful supervision of all students
involved in organized practices of any and all athletic teams,
including the Weldon High School Girls' Track and Field Team,
conducted upon school premises and the protection of said students
from injuries while being involved in said practice sessions.
5. On February 9, 1992, Plaintiff, MARGARET QUINN, was a
student properly and lawfully enrolled in Weldon High School, and
a proper and lawful member of the Weldon High School Girls' Track

FIGURE 1.1 CONTD.

COMPLAINT OF THE PLAINTIFF

and Field Team, involved in team practice.

6. On February 9, 1992, while the Plaintiff was present and in attendance in the aforesaid team practice, she was injured as a direct and proximate result of the negligence of the Defendants, JEAN SHARP and CITY OF WELDON, BOARD OF EDUCATION, in failing to properly supervise and control the aforesaid practice session of the Weldon High School Girls' Track and Field Team.

7. As a direct and proximate result of the aforesaid negligence of the Defendants, the Plaintiff, MARGARET QUINN, was caused to sustain, and did sustain, serious, severe and permanent personal injury; she did and has continued to experience great pain and suffering; she has and will continue to be obliged to seek medical treatment as a result of her injuries; she has and will continue to incur medical expenses substantially in excess of $1,000.00; she has and will continue to be unable to engage in her routine activities and affairs; and she has otherwise been damaged.

8. On or about March 14, 1992, Plaintiff filed a notice of claim on Defendant CITY OF WELDON, BOARD OF EDUCATION, in accordance with N.J.S.A. 59:8-9. Six months have elapsed since the filing of said notice of claim and no disposition of this case has yet been made as to Defendant, CITY OF WELDON, BOARD OF EDUCATION.

WHEREFORE, the Plaintiff, MARGARET QUINN, demands judgment against the Defendants, JEAN SHARP and CITY OF WELDON, BOARD OF EDUCATION, jointly, severally or in the alternative, in the amount of her damages, together with interest and cost of suit.

/A/SECOND COUNT

1. Plaintiff, JEAN SHARP, repeats and realleges all the allegations contained in the First Count of the Complaint and incorporates the same herein by reference.

2. The Defendant, CITY OF WELDON, BOARD OF EDUCATION, is liable for the negligence of its public employee, Defendant JEAN SHARP, in accordance with the doctrine of **respondeat superior** and pursuant to **N.J.S.A.** 59:2-2 of the New Jersey Tort Claims Act, **N.J.S.A.** 59:1-1 **et seq.**

WHEREFORE, the Plaintiff, MARGARET QUINN, demands judgment against the Defendant, CITY OF WELDON, BOARD OF EDUCATION, a public entity of the State of New Jersey, in the amount of her damages, together with interest and cost of suit.

/A/DEMAND FOR TRIAL BY JURY

Plaintiff hereby demands a trial by jury as to all issues.

/A/CERTIFICATION

The undersigned hereby certifies that the matter in controversy is not the subject of any other action presently pending in any Court or of any pending arbitration proceedings and that no other actions or arbitration proceedings are presently contemplated.

FIGURE 1.1 CONTD.

COMPLAINT OF THE PLAINTIFF

The undersigned further certifies that there are no other parties of which he is presently aware who should be joined in the action.

/A/**NOTICE OF TRIAL COUNSEL**

Please take notice that NANCY R. JONES, ESQ., is hereby designated as trial counsel in the above captioned matter for the firm of Jones, Smith & Brown, pursuant to Rule 4:25 et seq.

JONES, SMITH & BROWN, P.A.
Attorneys for Plaintiff

By:_____
NANCY R. JONES

DATED: October 23, 1992

videotape the testimony of a witness prior to trial. The procedure is conducted under oath, with all parties having the opportunity to question the witness. The videotape can then be shown to the jury at the trial. This is particularly useful when circumstances beyond reasonable control would prevent a key witness from appearing at the trial.

During the process of discovery, attorneys for each side also make requests for various types of physical evidence to be produced. It is not uncommon, for instance, for attorneys or their representatives to examine equipment that was being worn or used at the time of an injury, or written items such as lesson plans, accident reports, attendance records, and medical records.

Although the pretrial process itself is conducted by the attorneys for each party according to clearly prescribed procedures, its eventual outcome can be greatly affected by factors within the defendant teacher's or coach's control. The completeness and availability of written materials such as lesson plans, diagnostic test scores, accident reports, or documents used in employer screening and evaluation can provide persuasive evidence of the propriety of one's actions. Moreover, the confidence, poise, and professionalism one displays during depositions can greatly influence both the likelihood and the nature of one's appearance before a jury at the time of trial. Simply put, a plaintiff's attorney would not be anxious for a jury to listen at length to a poised professional who displays thorough subject matter knowledge, honest concern for the athletes in her care, and a clear understanding of the nature and the reasoning behind the actions that are at issue.

Once all the pertinent facts have been disclosed and each side has had the opportunity to assess the relative strengths and weaknesses of its case, a pretrial conference is

FIGURE 1.2
ANSWER TO THE COMPLAINT OF THE PLAINTIFF

/A/Figure 1.2
/A/Answer to the Complaint of the Plaintiff

LLOYD JAMES, ESQ.
85 Livingston Avenue
Tidewater, New Jersey 08745
Attorneys for Defendants, JEAN SHARP AND CITY OF WELDON BOARD OF
EDUCATION

		SUPERIOR COURT OF NEW JERSEY
		LAW DIVISION - OCEAN COUNTY
		Docket No.: OCN-L-3200-90
MARGARET QUINN,	:	
	:	Civil Action
Plaintiff,	:	
	:	ANSWER, SEPARATE DEFENSES,
vs.	:	DEMAND FOR STATEMENT OF
JEAN SHARP and CITY OF:	:	DAMAGES AND JURY DEMAND
WELDON, BOARD OF EDUCATION,:		
a public entity of the	:	
State of New Jersey,	:	
Defendants.		

The Defendants, JEAN SHARP and CITY OF WELDON, BOARD OF
EDUCATION, by way of Answer to the Complaint of the Plaintiff, say
that:

/A/FIRST COUNT

The Defendants, JEAN SHARP and CITY OF WELDON BOARD OF
EDUCATION deny the allegations contained in Paragraphs 6 and 7 of
the First Count of the Complaint.

/A/SECOND COUNT

The Defendants, JEAN SHARP and CITY OF WELDON, BOARD OF
EDUCATION repeat their answers to all allegations contained in all
paragraphs of the First Count of the Complaint as though set forth
at length herein and makes them their answer to paragraph 1 of the
Second Count.

/A/FIRST SEPARATE DEFENSE

These Defendants were guilty of no negligence which was the
proximate cause of the injuries and damages alleged.

/A/SECOND SEPARATE DEFENSE

Any injuries of damages allegedly sustained by the Plaintiff
were the result of the contributory negligence of said Plaintiff.

/A/THIRD SEPARATE DEFENSE

Any injuries or damages allegedly sustained by the Plaintiff

FIGURE 1.2 CONTD.

ANSWER TO THE COMPLAINT OF THE PLAINTIFF

were the result of the sole negligence of a third party or parties over whom this Defendant had no control.

/A/**FOURTH SEPARATE DEFENSE**

The Plaintiff is barred by contributory negligence, which negligence was greater than that of this Defendant.

/A/**FIFTH SEPARATE DEFENSE**

The Plaintiff is not entitled to recover for pain and suffering, pursuant to N.J.S.A. 59:9-2(d).

/A/**SIXTH SEPARATE DEFENSE**

Any amount the Plaintiff may recover shall be reduced in proportion to the amount of negligence attributable to the Plaintiff.

/A/**DEMAND FOR STATEMENT OF DAMAGES**

Please take notice that the defendants, JEAN SHARP and CITY OF WELDON, BOARD OF EDUCATION, request within the time provided by the Rules of the Court that the Plaintiff serves a written statement of the amount of damages claimed in the within action.

/A/**JURY DEMAND**

The Defendants, JEAN SHARP and CITY OF WELDON, BOARD OF EDUCATION, hereby demand a jury trial on all triable issues.

/A/**CERTIFICATION**

I hereby certify that the within Answer has been served and filed in accordance with the provisions of the Rules of the Court.

LLOYD JAMES, ESQ.
Attorney for Defendants,
JEAN SHARP and CITY OF WELDON,
BOARD OF EDUCATION

Dated: December 12, 1992   By:_____
                                        Lloyd James, Esq.

FIGURE 1.3

EXAMPLES OF QUESTIONS FOUND ON INTERROGATORIES

/A/Figure 1.3
/A/Examples of Questions Found on Interrogatories

1. State: (a) your full name, (b) present address, (c) address at the time cause of action arose, (d) date and place of birth, (e) date and place of any marriages or termination of marriages, and if a corporation, (f) date and state of incorporation, (g) names and addresses of officers and registered agent, and, (h) whether or not corporation is authorized to do business in New Jersey.

2. State: (a) the date and place on which these interrogatories were answered, (b) whether you were ever convicted of a crime, and, if so, (c) the nature of the offense, (d) the date and place of conviction.

3. State: (a) the names and addresses of all insurance or surety companies that insure or guarantee any possible liability on your part for occurrences set forth in the pleadings, (b) which of said insurers or sureties have primary, excess or concurrent coverages, (c) the policy or bond limits with respect to each category of coverage, (d) set forth in detail the carrier's names, policy numbers, and coverages for each insurance policy owned by you or any relative residing in your household at the time of the said occurrences.

4. With respect to all expert witnesses, including treating physicians and experts who have conducted an examination, inspection, investigation, or been consulted with respect to the facts of the instant litigation, whether or not said expert is expected to testify, state: (a) such expert's name, address, and area of expertise, (b) date and place of examination, inspection, investigation, or consultation; (c) what or who was inspected or examined, (d) names of experts expected to testify at trial, (e) annex a true copy of all written reports rendered to you, (f) if no written report has been submitted, supply a summary of any oral reports rendered to you or the essence of such testimony as is anticipated will be given by said experts.

5. Set forth the names, addresses and all alleged knowledge of all persons having knowledge of relevant facts; (a) respecting the cause of action, (b) surrounding the happening of the occurrence set forth in the pleadings, (c) as to the damages claimed, (d) who were eye-witnesses to said occurrences.

6. State with regard to the track practice during which Margaret Quinn was injured on February 9, 1992:
  (a) the number of athletes on the team
  (b) the names of the athletes on the team
  (c) the present addresses of the athletes on the team
  (d) any other persons who might have been present at said practice, listing names and current addresses if known.

7. Please state the view of the Weldon Board of Education as to how the incident occurred which gave rise to the cause of action of this suit.

8. Was any accident report, to either the Weldon High School Authorities or to any municipal or law enforcement

FIGURE 1.3 CONTD.
EXAMPLES OF QUESTIONS FOUND ON INTERROGATORIES

```
authority made with reference to the incident which is the subject
of the complaint?  If so, state:
            (a) name and address of the person making the
                report;
            (b) name and address of the person to whom
                the report was made;
            (c) attach a copy of each such report to
                these answers.
        9.  Was Jean Sharp the only coach or supervisory person in
charge of the track and field team on February 9, 1992?
            If not, state the names and addresses of the other
persons in charge on that date.
```

usually scheduled. At this conference, the attorneys attempt to reach agreement on certain undisputed facts such as the date, time, and location of the incident in question.

By this time, each side will have had an opportunity to establish a dollar figure that they feel would satisfactorily conclude the litigation; therefore, pretrial conferences frequently include negotiations leading to **settlement.** During these negotiations, the judge or some judicially appointed individual frequently acts as a **mediator** or **arbiter** and tries to facilitate an equitable settlement to avoid the relatively costly and time-consuming process of a trial. Alternatively, the parties may agree to submit the dispute to an arbitrator or mediator whom they jointly engage. Services of this type are provided by both commercial enterprises and non-profit organizations. The decisions of arbitrators are binding upon the parties, while mediators simply seek simply to broker an agreed-upon resolution. It is important to recognize that the overwhelming majority of civil cases are settled prior to the conclusion of a trial. Such settlements are financial agreements between the parties involved and carry no connotation of guilt or innocence. Both parties simply agree that the advantages of accepting the negotiated financial agreement in order to end the legal process outweigh the advantages of continuing. However, if no such agreement can be reached, the case normally proceeds to trial.

At the trial, the plaintiff is required to prove the elements of his case by the greater weight of evidence. Both parties present **physical evidence** such as incident reports, lesson plans, the equipment involved in the incident, and game films as well as testimony from the witnesses who appear in court. **Fact witnesses** are called to testify concerning what they saw, felt, or heard regarding the incident or situation in question. **Expert witnesses,** on the other hand, are called to share their knowledge. These witnesses are persons who, as a result of training and experience, have greater knowledge in a given field than the general populace. Expert witnesses are frequently asked to testify on the professional standards that apply to the incident in question and the degree to which the actions of the defendant complied with those standards.

It is not necessary for the jury in a civil case to return a unanimous verdict. Normally the agreement of any five of the six voting jurors constitutes an acceptable majority.

A party to a civil suit who is not satisfied with the outcome of the trial has the right to file an initial **appeal** to the appellate court of the state. Subsequent appeals are granted at the discretion of the higher courts only in cases in which the interests at stake or the disputed issues of law are considered significant enough to warrant their determination.

It is important for people involved in developing or delivering physical activity programs to recognize the possibility that they may be sued. They should prepare themselves for such an occurrence by developing a thorough background in the law as it applies to their day-to-day activities. They must then translate this knowledge into action by planning and documenting their activities in a manner that minimizes the risk of lawsuits and maximizes the likelihood of successfully defending themselves in any that may arise.

MANAGEMENT GUIDELINES

The impact of law on physical activity and sport is without question a major concern for teachers, coaches, and administrators. It would, however, be a serious professional error to view the law only as a source of problems or additional paperwork. Although ignorance or breach of applicable law can create problems, and effective documentation to prepare for or to avoid the possibility of a lawsuit will likely require at least a qualitative change in your usual level of paperwork, there are real advantages to be gained from applying the law effectively.

The law is in fact a kind of managerial tool. Like any tool, its value depends upon the skill and efficiency with which you use it. The more you know about the day-to-day application of the law, the easier it will be for you to apply it and the less likely you will be to misuse it. Moreover, like any other skilled person, you will begin to find ways in which elements of law can be creatively applied to become positive forces in program development and improvement.

For instance, consider the plight of an athletic director to whom a coach has presented a request for the purchase of new equipment, which the coach claims is necessary in order to meet acceptable safety standards for the sport. Can the director really afford to deny the request and risk the potential liability of an injury attributable to substandard equipment? Although the answer to this question would vary based upon the level of risk, the nature of the program, and many other factors, clearly the legal ramifications of the decision can be used as a persuasive point of argument.

One of the most readily observable examples of the benefits of creatively applying law can be seen in programs that have sought to guarantee equal opportunities to individuals regardless of gender. Although some individuals view the prohibitions against gender-biased programming as a major problem, others have seized upon it as a virtually unassailable argument for developing and improving their programs. They have implemented elective programs of physical education, reduced class sizes, individualized the instructional content, and instituted skill-referenced ability grouping and many other procedures that maximize the instructional potential and interest while reducing the difficulty of coping with heterogeneous class groups. As a result, they have been able to redesign or modify their programs in ways that have enhanced opportunities for all students regardless of gender while, at the same time, guaranteeing that no student is denied access without a legally valid reason. Remember: The same legal principles that can be used to condemn poor programs can often be used by the wise professional to develop and improve both programs and personnel.

CHAPTER SUMMARY

Laws are the formal means by which a society regulates the behavior of its members. Violations of civil laws, which regulate the interactions between individuals or groups, represent the majority of cases involving sport and physical activity. People who believe they have been wronged by the actions of others can seek compensation for their losses through the courts. This process, known as **litigation,** is prescribed by law and involves extensive pretrial discovery and negotiations aimed at accomplishing an amicable settlement. If a settlement cannot be reached, the case proceeds through a formal trial and possibly even through a process of appeals.

The more knowledgeable you are about the law and the manner in which it is applied, the better able you will be able to work effectively within the law and to use it as the productive managerial tool it should be.

KEY TERMS

Administrative regulations
Answer
Appeal
Arbitrator
Case law
Civil laws
Codified law
Common law
Complaint
Criminal laws
Defendant
Deposition
Expert witnesses
Fact witnesses
Felonies
Grievant
Interrogatories
Legal precedent
Litigation
Mediator

Misdemeanors
Physical evidence
Plaintiff
Precedent
Process of discovery
Punishment
Settlement
Stare decisis
Statutes
Tort

QUESTIONS FOR DISCUSSION

1. Give sport-specific examples of criminal and civil law violations. What are some alternative methods by which one might reasonably seek to remedy each of the cited examples?
2. The process of discovery effectively removes much of the element of surprise from a civil trial. How is this accomplished?
3. Create a situation in which one person feels that she has been harmed by the actions of another. Explain how she would pursue the matter through the process of litigation and appeal. What is the nature of each step in the process, and what alternatives might be possible?
4. Give specific examples of situations in which a knowledgeable or creative professional might use the law as a tool for program improvement. Can you think of positive changes in the nature of particular sports or activities that are largely due to the influence of the legal system?

ADDITIONAL READINGS

Clement, A. (1988). *Law in sport and physical activity.* (chap. 1 & 9). Indianapolis: Benchmark Press.

Keeton, W. (Ed.). (1984). *Prosser and Keeton on the law of torts.* St. Paul: West.

van der Smissen, B. (1990). Legal aspects overview. In *Legal liability and risk management for public and private entities.* Cincinnati: Anderson.

CHAPTER 2

RISK MANAGEMENT

John was a fitness devotee and the first in his family to attend college. Two years ago when he graduated with an M.S. in physical education, his parents used their home as collateral on a loan to finance John's lifelong dream. Six months later he opened Fit Forever, a small but well-equipped fitness club catering to well-to-do clients.

Six months ago, while John was out of the club on an errand, one of his clients suffered a seizure. The incident occurred on a weekday morning when there were only three clients in the club. The employee was a recent high school graduate who John himself had trained to manage the facility and service clients. Unfortunately, the employee had panicked in the face of the obvious medical emergency. This led to considerable confusion and delay in the administration of first aid as well as the summoning and arrival of emergency medical personnel.

The client never fully recovered from the seizure and has instituted a negligence suit seeking three million dollars in compensatory damages for present and future medical costs and loss of wages and future income.

John has liability coverage in the amount of one million dollars. While he holds certification as a Health/Fitness Director from the American College of Sports Medicine, his employee, on the other hand, has no certification or training beyond that which John provided, and John cannot provide documentation in support of that training. Neither can John provide an incident report documenting the accident, copies of emergency plans for the club, client screening information, or proof that the injured client had been effectively prepared for the activity in question or warned of the risks involved.

John is a talented, concerned young professional, and in time he would probably have developed a successful business. The prospects for a successful defense of this lawsuit, however, are extremely dim. While there's no guarantee that a careful and thorough approach to risk management would have prevented the injury, it almost certainly would have made an enormous difference in his defensibility in the subsequent lawsuit.

LEARNING OBJECTIVES

Upon completion of this chapter, the student will be able to:

1.   enumerate the benefits of the risk-management process,
2.   identify the components of a risk-management plan,
3.   conduct a risk analysis for a variety of activities,
4.   develop risk-management policies and implement procedures for assigned programs, and
5.   explain alternative procedures that might be used to transfer the risk of financial loss.

RISK MANAGEMENT

When pressed to explain risk management in the simplest possible terms, many sports administrators will say that it is a process of determining the circumstances in which losses are most likely to occur, and then designing and implementing policies to minimize the likelihood of their occurrence. While this is fundamentally correct, it fails to recognize a third component of the risk management process which is of particular importance in programs of sport and physical activity. We must acknowledge the fact that, regardless of how carefully we develop and deliver our programs, some losses will still occur. Uncontrollable performance errors, the effects of the weather, and equipment breakdowns are but three of many factors which can result in unexpected losses despite the very best efforts to the contrary. Accordingly, a sound program of risk management must not only identify and reduce the potential occurrence of losses, it must include appropriate steps to minimize the impact of those losses that cannot be prevented.

WHY RISK MANAGEMENT?

Inherent in programs of sport and physical activity is the risk of bodily injury. Risk-management planning allows one to maximize the benefits of these programs while minimizing the risks of physical injury to the participants and financial loss to the organization. Most risk-management programs are designed to provide one or more of the following benefits:

1.   Careful risk-management planning allows program administrators to maximize the number and variety of programs offered. While the very nature of physical activity gives rise to a degree of risk, few activities are so dangerous in and of themselves that they cannot be adapted and controlled in a way that renders them reasonably safe for inclusion in a given program.
2.   A well-designed and implemented risk-management plan helps protect the financial stability of the organization by reducing the potential for injuries and by transferring the financial burden of those losses that may occur. Thus, operating costs can be more easily predicted and controlled.

3. To varying degrees, all programs of sport and physical activity depend on facilities and equipment. Through risk-management planning, the administrator can minimize time lost due to breakdowns in the equipment or the facilities, in order to maximize their usable lifespan, and to avoid (as much as possible) concomitant losses to participants.

4. Equipment breakdowns and participant injuries tend to result in negative publicity, feelings of concern and reticence among the participants and, eventually, diminished participation. By effectively controlling the risks of any given program, the administrator can better maintain participant satisfaction and support.

5. Over and above the legal and financial justifications for risk-management planning, most program administrators recognize a moral responsibility to provide the safest experience possible for their patrons. They enter the field of sport and physical activity because of a sincere belief in the benefits of an active lifestyle and because they enjoy and care about people in general. This usually leads to honest concern for the well-being of the participants and a dedication to effective risk management.

6. Finally, good risk-management planning encourages the active involvement of all staff members and the integration of all aspects of the program. As a result, a good risk-management plan has a unifying and synthesizing effect that tends to result in better, more balanced programs as well as greater staff confidence and cohesiveness.

RISK-MANAGEMENT PLANNING

A well-designed risk-management plan includes a systematic analysis of the services or activities offered, an assessment of the potential for loss, and practical approaches to deal with the loss potential. To be effective, the plan must be tailored to the particular organization. You cannot take a plan developed for the Sunnyvale Fitness Club and implement it into the fitness center at Branden Tolley High School. Differences in program objectives, legal regulation, facilities, staffing, and clientele require differences in the plans. While the general underlying principles may be shared, the details of application must be individualized. Finally, the risk-management plan, no matter how well designed, requires ongoing review and modification.

COMPONENTS OF THE PLAN

RISK ANALYSIS

The first task in the development of a risk-management plan is to conduct a detailed analysis of the program or activity to identify potential human and economic losses. This requires a careful study of the particular activity, including such details as the environmental conditions; nature, skill levels, and number of clientele; supervisory structure, and the extent and duration of the program. The program data is then analyzed in light of the applicable professional standards and guidelines. In the event of a lawsuit, your program will almost certainly be measured against the established standards of practice applicable to the activity in question. The prudent administrator will make these comparisons early in the risk-management planning process and well before activities are initiated or injuries occur.

Several resources can and should be pursued in seeking the best and most current professional standards applicable to any given activity. Most notable among these include:

1. Rules of the sport. If the activity in question is an athletic contest, it's almost certainly the subject of a set of rules promulgated by an organization such as the NCAA or the National Federation of High School Associations or by one of the National Governing Bodies (see Chapter 13). Rules dictate matters related to the playing area, officiating, conduct of the activity, equipment, and a host of safety-related issues. While not the sole source of information, the rules are certainly an indispensable first stop where competitive activities are involved.

2. Professional Associations. Many professional associations provide standards and guidelines relative to activities within their areas of interest. For instance, the American Association for Active Lifestyles and Fitness (AAALF) has published *Facilities Planning for Physical Activity and Sport,* The National Association for Sport and Physical Education (NASPE) has published *Principles of Safety in Physical Education and Sport,* and the American College of Sports Medicine (ACSM) has published *Health Fitness Facility Standards and Guidelines.* While resources of this type are not official rules or binding standards, they do represent the carefully considered recommendations of recognized leaders in the profession and, thus, constitute an important component of risk assessment. See Chapter 14 for a more complete resource list.

3. Statutes and Codes. Seek legal counsel regarding the impact of federal, state, and local legislation and administrative codes that affect broadly divergent aspects of athletic and recreational programs. Everything from general requirements for building occupancy and fire safety to the details of teacher or coach certification, volunteer immunity, and the requirements for swimming pool operations may be reflected in statutes or administrative codes. These *must* be reflected in all risk-management planning. It's very difficult to defend programs conducted in violation of law.

4. Case Analysis and Court Decisions. Watch the newspapers and the professional literature to stay abreast of the most current information regarding the nature and frequency of lawsuits affecting programs or activities similar to those under analysis. While this information will probably not provide clear guidelines with regard to applicable standards of practice, it may provide a fairly clear indication of the type of injuries suffered and the allegations of negligence that resulted. Such information should thus be used to identify areas or conditions that you might wish to examine more closely.

5. Common Practice. Sometimes, particularly in the case of new or unique activities, little information can be gleaned from the above sources. At this point, the appropriate question becomes, "How are other quality programs handling this activity?" Seek out and consult with other well-respected programs in your area and across the country. If they are conducting a similar activity, what risk-reduction procedures have they implemented? What problems have they encountered? Is there a pattern

of practice developing? These are often precursors to the development of more formalized standards and guidelines and can provide valuable guidance until the literature catches up with the ongoing practice.

After comparing the program data to the available standards and guidelines, the risk manager should estimate the potential extent of the identifiable losses in terms of the following parameters:

1. Frequency. How many losses are likely to be encountered in a given season or fiscal year? This estimate should be based on historical data from the program at hand as well as predictive data provided by organizations such as the National Safety Council who publish *Injury Facts*,[1] an annual report on the characteristics and costs of medically treated unintentional injuries, including those related to many sports and recreational activities. Other resources of this type are listed at the conclusion of the chapter.

2. Severity. How serious are the potential losses likely to be both in terms of the magnitude of the injury and the impact upon the program? Obviously, as the level of exposure rises, whether in terms of the impact on the program or the level of injury which might reasonably occur, both the importance and the nature of the risk management approaches will be affected.

3. Predictability. How comfortable can you be with your predictions of the frequency and severity of losses? Where a program has been in existence for some time and subject to good record keeping, the interpolation of accurate program data with national statistics and trends should result in fairly reliable predictions. On the other hand, where there is a new program or activity and neither local nor national data are available for guidance; frequency and severity predictions will be based primarily on the record of the overall program and comparisons to other activities that bear some degree of similarity to the one in question. A far greater margin of error must be accepted in the latter situation.

ALTERNATIVE CONTROL APPROACHES

The simplest method of reducing a risk in an activity is to eliminate the risk from the program. Certainly there will be no injuries associated with activities that are avoided. Neither will there be any learning, enjoyment, or physical development. We who work in the field of sport and physical activity do little to advance the causes of active lifestyles and fitness by exercising the approach of **elimination**. There are, unquestionably, times when the wisest course of action is to eliminate an activity or a program. Keep in mind, however, that very few activities are regarded as so dangerous in and of themselves that they cannot, with proper planning, be effectively delivered. Furthermore, how often do you want to tell your superiors or clients that you can't or won't provide activities in which they have an interest?

For all activities that are conducted there must be **program and operational controls** that focus on the reduction of risks through program management and financial controls that minimize the financial impact of any losses that might occur.

Program and operational controls are best accomplished through the development and implementation of effective policies and procedures. **Policies** are position statements through which upper-level managers define the limits of the powers and responsibilities of their subordinates. **Procedures** are the detailed instructions of the plan through which the manager describes the authorized method(s) of dealing with situations within the limits of accepted policy. Each policy, therefore, should be supported by a set of detailed procedures through which it will be implemented. Figure 2.1 provides examples of common risk-management policy topics.

As we mentioned earlier in this chapter, not all losses can be prevented. Thus, risk managers must take steps to minimize the effect of these losses by transferring some or all of the resulting financial obligations to another party or by making provisions whereby it can be retained within the sponsoring organization.

Transfer is an economic approach to risk management that seeks to reduce the potential for financial loss away from the association by shifting the financial risk to another party. The transfer may be accomplished by legislative means or through contracts and agreements. Figure 2.2 illustrates common options for transferring financial risks associated with program losses.

When an organization has sufficient funds, it will often elect to **retain** some portion of the financial loss potential via one or more of the following ways: (1) through **self-insurance** or **funded reserve,** whereby the organization sets aside sufficient funds to provide their own insurance up to a predetermined level; (2) through **current expensing,** whereby financial losses below a predetermined level are paid through the annual operating budget; or (3) through **insurance deductibles,** whereby the organization will bear the first XXX dollars of each loss, and the insurer will bear the remainder. **Aggregate deductible** policies set a maximum annual amount on the deductible losses borne by the insured after which all losses will be covered by the insurer.

IMPLEMENTATION

The first step in the implementation process is to select and apply the operational and financial approaches to be used. Each activity must be carefully assessed in terms of operational and financial risk-management procedures, and both should be applied. More than one operational approach will almost certainly apply and, in fact, several may be chosen for simultaneous application. Remember, too, that operational approaches frequently involve behavioral and attitudinal adjustments as well as the prescribed policies themselves. Designating the individuals responsible for facility inspections and the procedures by which they will be accomplished, for instance, will have a far more positive impact if the individuals involved are concerned with safety, committed to reducing risks through careful inspection procedures, and able to recognize potentially hazardous conditions when they encounter them.

MONITOR AND MODIFY THE PLAN

No one can think of everything on the first try. Even if someone could, over time elements of the program, the nature of the participants, and the standards of the profes-

FIGURE 2.1

EXAMPLES OF COMMON RISK MANAGEMENT POLICIES

Personal needs
- When? Where? How many?
- Job requirements
- Duties
- Screening and certification
- In-service training
- Evaluation
- Use of volunteers

Facility Safety Inspection Policies
- What will be inspected
- When
- By whom
- Reporting and documentation
- Remediation and follow-up

Medical Information Policies
- Preparticipation examinations
- Client-answered checklists
- Clearance to resume activity after injury or illness

Medical Emergency Policies
- Appropriate first-aid
- Nature of the emergency medical response system
- Activation of the emergency medical response system
- Follow-up

Spectator Management Policies
- Where spectators will or will not be permitted
- Time constraints
- How spectators will be controlled

Postponement and Cancellation Policies
- Reasons for postponement or cancellation
- Decision-making authority
- Timelines
- Notification of appropriate individuals

Emergency Evacuation Policies
- When facilities will be evacuated
- How evacuation will be accomplished
- Decision-making authority
- Reporting requirements

Transportation Policies
- Acceptable methods of transportation
- Who may operate vehicles
- Insurance requirements
- Time and distance restrictions

Telecommunication Policies
- Method of communication
- Access to equipment
- Circumstances requiring communication plans
- Notification chains
- Equipment backup procedures

FIGURE 2.2: COMMON TRANSFER OPTIONS

Basis	Method	Shifts some or all of Financial burden to	How
Contract	Waiver	Participant	Participant assumes certain risks of Participating, including those related to ordinary negligence of the provider and agrees not to sue for related losses.
	Hold harmless	Equipment/facility renter	User assumes financial responsibility for agreed-on losses associated with participation.
	Indemnification	Participant/renter	Participant or renter agrees to reimburse the provider for agreed upon losses associated with the activity or event.
	Informed consent	Participant	Participant acknowledges understanding and acceptance of the risks and responsibilities of participation. Constitutes evidentiary support for comparative/contributory negligence defense.

FIGURE 2.2: COMMON TRANSFER OPTIONS CONTD.

Basis	Method	Shifts some or all of Financial burden to	How
	Rental agreement	Equipment/facility renter	User of the facility/equipment acknowledges and accepts responsibility for use. When a hold harmless clause is included, the user, rather than the owner, accepts financial responsibility for associated losses.
	Insurance	Insurer	In return for an agreed-on premium, the insurer agrees to assume financial responsibility for covered losses and associated expenses up to a specified maximum.
	Allocation of Responsibility	Independent contractor	Employer is normally not liable for tort or responsibility workers compensation associated claims with the programs and activities conducted independent contractor-employer liability limited to selection of contractor.
Legislation	Immunity	Participant	Removes certain forms of negligence from common law liability.
	Tort statutes	Participant	Place limits on the right to sue and/or the amount of recovery.

sion would almost certainly change. Constant review and modification of the program and plan is thus essential to effective risk management.

MANAGEMENT GUIDELINES

The development and implementation of an effective risk-management plan is best accomplished by managers who focus on the four Ds: determination, deliberation, details, and documentation.

1. **Determination.** Risk-management planning is relatively difficult and time consuming. Unless you're committed to the process and determined to make it an important and ongoing part of your managerial activities, your likelihood of success is compromised.
2. **Deliberation.** Good risk management does not occur by chance but is a function of careful investigation and analysis that lay the foundation for wise planning choices.
3. **Details.** Few administrative functions so dramatically depend on attention to details. In fact, in risk management it's best to invert an old saying: *Always* sweat the small stuff. The assistance of an attorney in reviewing recurring liability situations as part of program and operational controls as well as negotiating and reviewing financial control devices can be invaluable.
4. **Documentation.** Anything that is not well documented tends to be more easily forgotten and more difficult to prove in a court of law. A policy carefully expressed in writing and that includes provisions for the ongoing documentation of procedural activities tends to be more closely followed and, if necessary, more convincing to a jury than vague recollections of what was "supposed to be done."

CHAPTER SUMMARY

A carefully developed and conscientiously applied program of risk management is essential to the financial stability of a program or activity and to the safety of its participants. The risk-management plan should begin with an analysis of the services offered in light of the applicable professional standards. From this the manager can develop policies and procedures for the safe and effective conduct of the program as well as strategies to handle the financial burden of losses that may arise. The manager should monitor the risk-management program to identify weaknesses and problem patterns and to ensure compliance with changing standards of professional practice. Finally, all noted discrepancies should be analyzed and should lead to appropriate program modifications.

KEY TERMS

Aggregate deductible
Current expensing
Determination
Deliberation
Details
Elimination
Financial controls
Insurance deductibles
Loss frequency
Loss predictability
Loss severity
Policies
Procedures
Professional standards and guidelines
Program and operational controls
Retention
Risk analysis
Risk management
Self-insurance or funded reserve
Transfer

QUESTIONS FOR DISCUSSION

1. Review the *Health Fitness Facility Standards and Guidelines of the American College of Sports Medicine.* Arrange to visit a fitness center either on your campus or nearby. Discuss the policies and procedures through which the fitness center manages such things as staffing, client screening and readiness, facility inspections, and emergencies. Identify strengths and weaknesses of the risk-management program and make suggestions for change as necessary.

2. You are the Director of Recreation for a small four-year college. A student service organization has requested your help in conducting a one-day mud volleyball marathon to raise money to fight cancer. Discuss the steps you would follow in developing a risk management plan. Research the relevant issues and lay out appropriate policies and procedures for the conduct of this event.

REFERENCES

Injury Facts—National Safety Council, Itasca, Illinois

ADDITIONAL RESOURCES

Dougherty, N.J. (Ed.) (1993) *Principles of safety in physical education and sport.* Reston, VA: AAHPERD.

Sawyer, T.H., Goldfine, B., Hypes, M.G., LaRue, R.L., & Seidler., T. (1999). *Facilities planning for physical activity and sport—Guidelines for development.* Dubuque, IA: Kendall/Hunt Publishing Company.

Tharett, S.J., & Peterson, J.A. (1997) *ACSM's health/fitness facility standards and guidelines,* 2nd edition. Champaign, IL: Human Kinetics.

PART II

ON THE BENCH OR IN THE GAME: EXCLUSION V. INCLUSION

CHAPTER 3

SOURCES OF THE LEGAL RIGHT TO BE TREATED FAIRLY

C hris and Lee, highly skilled athletes and excellent students, lived in a community with two high schools: North High and South High. Each school had substantially equal facilities, equipment, and faculty but the two schools were racially segregated. Chris and Lee were expected to attend South High, their race's school, but Chris and Lee wanted to attend North High. The school district had no rules, other than those based on race, which prohibited Chris and Lee from attending North High.

On the first day of school, Chris and Lee walked up the front stairs of North High but were turned away by the school's principal. Each day for a week the two students attempted to enter North High, and each day they were turned away. Finally, the two frustrated students brought a lawsuit in state court contesting the state law that permitted "separate but equal" educational programs based on race. The students argued that the 14th amendment of the United States Constitution promised them that no agency of a state government, such as a public school, could treat them unequally because of their race and that the state law violated that promise and was thus unconstitutional.

Ultimately, the case found its way to the United States Supreme Court, where the issue was framed in question form as, "Does segregation of children in public school solely on the basis of race, even though the physical facilities and other "tangible" factors may be equal, deprive the children of the minority group of equal educational opportunities?"[1] [*Brown* I, 1954, at 493] The Supreme Court decision was unanimous as it struck down segregation in public schools and said, "in the field of public education, the doctrine of 'separate but equal' has no place."[2] [*Brown* I, 1954, at 493] On the next school day after the Supreme Court had issued its ruling, Chris and Lee again tried to attend North High but were again turned away by the principal. A law passed by a legislature had been interpreted by the judiciary as being unconstitutional, but how could the winning students enforce the decision? Could they ask the state legislature that originally passed the now unconstitutional law to enforce the court's decision so they could attend North High? Could the students ask the court to enforce its own decision? Where could the students turn next? [The facts in this scenario are loosely based on *Brown v. Board of Education*, 394 U.S. 294 (1955).

LEARNING OBJECTIVES

Upon completion of this chapter, the student will be able to:
1. differentiate between constitutional provisions and statutory laws,
2. describe the purpose of the United States Constitution and the purpose of the inclusion of the Bill of Rights, and
3. discuss the unique roles of each of the three branches of government: legislative, judicial, and executive.

"That's not fair" is a phrase intended to elicit change. Once something is labeled "unfair," we hope that the unfair circumstances will change automatically and the treatment will become fair. "The test isn't fair." "The official's call wasn't fair." "It's not fair to keep me on the bench; I have just as much right to play as Pat." "It's not fair that I am paid less than Lee." All these are said with the hope that something will change, but we are frequently disappointed. Still, our hope for fair treatment is well founded in our nation's statutory and constitutional law.

The **Constitution** of the United States was created, in no small measure, to limit the power available to the **federal** government rather than to simply itemize its powers. Those who drafted and adopted the constitution on behalf of their constituents did so having previously endured forms of central governments that included no safeguards on the limit of power or the fairness with which such governmental power was wielded. Indeed, the limited power of our federal government is further limited by being partitioned into three parts: legislative, executive and judicial.

The **legislative** branch (Congress) has the power to enact **laws** but may do so only on subjects over which it has been given jurisdiction by the Constitution. For instance, Congress has been given power by the Constitution to enact laws about interstate commerce. It has also been given power to enact laws relating to Congress' ability to spend the federal budget. However, Congress has not been given power to enact laws that relate to areas solely under the control of individual states nor in subject areas not specifically enumerated within its jurisdiction by the Constitution. The Constitution determines what is Congress' business and what is not.

Laws that have been rightfully enacted by Congress must still satisfy all additional requirements of the Constitution and its **amendments** in their form and in their scope. If a federal statute doesn't satisfy those requirements, the law may be subject to claims of unconstitutionality and thus be found unenforceable and void.

Although the body of the Constitution reserved for the people and their state governments all powers not specifically granted to the federal government, the framers of the Constitution wanted to make absolutely sure that the federal government would never and could never engage in the particularly heinous and fearful violations of basic human **rights** the framers had experienced as citizens of other countries. So the first 10 amendments were added to the Constitution to be certain from the outset that those enumerated basic human rights could never be violated by the federal government. The first 10 amendments are known collectively as the **Bill of Rights**, and they protect us from the federal government violating our basic human rights. Among the rights protected by the Bill of Rights are holding religious beliefs of our choice (1st amendment, separation of church and state), meeting with whomever we wish (**1st amendment**, right of assembly), saying whatever we like, including criticizing our federal government (1st amendment, freedom of speech), keeping the FBI out of our homes (**4th amendment**, warrantless searches), and refusing blood tests in search of illegal substances (**5th amendment**, incriminating testimony against self).

There are more than 10 amendments to the Constitution but few of the additional amendments have a direct impact on the allied fields of sport and physical activity. One significant exception is the **14th amendment**.

Until the ratification of the 14th amendment just after the civil war, only the federal government was barred from infringing on the rights highlighted in the various amendments to the Constitution. For instance, if you ever drive from town to town in Massachusetts, you'll notice that most towns have a big white, steepled church in the center of town. If you look more closely, you'll notice that the church is almost always a Congregational Church. Indeed, taxpayer money was used to build and maintain those churches for a number of decades after the adoption of the Bill of Rights. Doesn't the 1st amendment say that church and state are separate and that the government cannot establish or support any church with tax payer money? Yes, however, the beautiful white churches of the Massachusetts countryside were not supported by the federal government but rather by the Commonwealth of Massachusetts. When ratified, the Bill of Rights applied only to the federal government, not the state government.

Until the passage of the 14th amendment, protections guaranteed by the Constitution and its amendments were only guaranteed in relation to the *federal* government and its agents. The distinction is important if you are to understand the historical development of the protections guaranteed by the Constitution and its amendments. So, until the 14th amendment was ratified, the **state** or town government where you lived could have searched your home legally without a warrant, or if you worked for a state university, could have paid you an unfairly low salary just because your boss didn't like you, or could have arrested you if you had dinner with a few of your friends that the state didn't like. The 14th amendment, important for many reasons, expanded the group of people who have to observe your basic human rights as enumerated in the Constitution and its amendments. The 14th amendment in substance says that any person acting on behalf of any governmental entity including town, state, and federal governments must abide by the rights guaranteed by the Constitution and its amendments. So, after the 1868 ratification of the 14th amendment, a school teacher at the local high school, an employee of the department of motor vehicles, and a dean at the state university must all honor your rights just as the *federal* government has always had to do.

The 14th amendment also added very important rights to the list, including the right to due process (fair procedures whenever life, liberty, or property are being removed or restricted) and equal protection (fair treatment when compared to how other people are being treated in the same circumstances).

In addition to the existence of the rights guaranteed by the Constitution and its amendments, Congress has enacted **statutes** (laws) that sometimes give us additional specifications with which to define fairness. For instance, Title VII is a law that prohibits employers from treating female and male, black and Asian, old and young, and religious and atheist employees and job applicants differently from one another. Title VII and its regulations give the employer and employee a better understanding of what is fair treatment in the eyes of Congress. The Equal Pay Act is another federal statute enacted by Congress that helps to define what's fair in the realm of salary equity. Title IX, another federal statute, has provided very specific direction concerning what is fair in educational settings. All of these statutes and others will be discussed in greater detail in Chapter 4, but it's important here to understand that the power Congress has to enact such statutes comes from specific grants of power found in the Constitution and that Congress is the only entity, on the federal level, given the power to enact laws.

Sometimes Congress enacts laws that either exceed its power or concern subject matter not within its jurisdiction. Such laws might be ruled unconstitutional. Sometimes Congress words laws in a manner so vague as to need interpreting. In any of these cases, it's up to the judicial branch of government, when a case is presented to it, to review the constitutionality or to interpret the wording of the law. Only the judicial branch (court) has the power to review and interpret statutes.

Having a law on the books or a judicial decision/interpretation of the law in hand is one thing— enforcing the law or decision is another. Do the members of Congress and the Senators carry handcuffs and have the power and duty to arrest someone who violates a federal statute or a court's decision concerning the statute? No, the power to enforce federal law or a court's ruling on that law is, according to the Constitution, only granted to the executive branch (the president and all the president's various enforcement agencies such as the Department of Justice). In the scenario at the beginning of this chapter, two students won their case in the U.S. Supreme Court but were still being denied access to a racially segregated school. The Constitution gives enforcement power solely to the executive branch, and so, in the case that served as the factual basis for the chapter-opening scenario, the President of the United States finally used troops to enforce the court's decision so that the students could attend the formerly segregated school. The executive branch of government is the only branch that has enforcement power.

MANAGEMENT GUIDELINES

Legal rights arise from many sources, but the primary sources are the Constitution of the United States and federal statutory law. Because the majority of managers within sport serve in institutions or programs that function as "state actors" (defined in Chapter 4), they need to comply with the rights promised to their employees and clients by these two sources. Thus a thorough understanding of the source of those rights as well as their enforcement and interpretation mechanisms is central to an ability to comply with those rights. A manager who doesn't understand the rules of the game will not long remain an effective manager.

CHAPTER SUMMARY

Each of the three branches of government has its own unique set of powers that is not given to any other branch. The legislative branch enacts the laws; the judiciary interprets/reviews the laws; and the executive branch enforces the laws.

The pattern of three branches of government is substantially mirrored by each state government. Similarly, many provisions of the U.S. Constitution and its amendments as well as federal statutory law are often found in similar form within state constitutions and statutory laws. Although simplistically stated, the overriding purpose of the Constitution and statutes is to structure government so that it and its citizens act in ways that are fair.

CASE STUDY

CASE 3.1

A small private college in Pennsylvania refused to comply with a federal statute (legislative branch) that required it to sign a letter acknowledging its compliance with antidiscrimination legislation known as **Title IX**. The Departments of Justice and Health, Education, and Welfare (executive branch) sought to enforce the statute by removing all federal funding from the college. The college sued the government for the reinstatement of federal funding, and the case ultimately arrived at the U.S. Supreme Court (judicial branch).

One of the issues of the case revolved around terminology in the statute and the question of whether the terminology referred to the entire institution or only the sub-units that actually received federal funding. The answer to the question would determine whether the federal statute was applicable to the entire college. The court interpreted the statute's wording and decided that the term "program" meant "subunit of the institution." The court's interpretation meant that at other colleges, programs such as athletics and physical education that receive no federal funding would not be within the jurisdiction of Title IX.

Congress (legislative branch) had not intended the interpretation of the word "program" to mean "subunit" but rather intended it to refer to the entire institution. Congress could either reshape its original intent to the interpretation of the court or, in the alternative, exercise its legislative powers and pass legislation that would formally remove or alter the previous vague language. Congress chose to exercise its legislative powers and in 1988 passed the **Civil Rights Restoration Act of 1987** over presidential veto. The Civil Rights Restoration Act in substance made it clear that the language of Title IX, and other similar antidiscrimination legislation, was to apply on an institution-wide basis.

Thus, this case, *Grove City College v. Bell*, 104 S.Ct. 1211 (1984) and Congress' response to the court's decision in the form of legislation known as the Civil Rights Restoration Act, 20 USCS Section 1687, demonstrate the source of a right and take us through a complete cycle of actions by each of the three branches of government.

1. Initially, Congress exercised its legislative powers by passing the federal statute known as Title IX, a legislative source of right to be treated fairly in federally funded educational programs without regard to gender.
2. Title IX's provisions were then enforced by the executive branch.
3. The judiciary entered the scene by interpreting language found in the original legislation.
4. Congress then again exercised its legislative powers to more clearly define its intent.

KEY TERMS

Amendment
Bill of Rights
Civil Rights Restoration Act of 1987
Constitution
Executive
Federal
Interpretation
Judicial
Law
Legislative
Review
Right
Sources of right
State
Statute
Title IX

QUESTIONS FOR DISCUSSION

1. Differentiate between the three branches of government and discuss the unique duties/powers each has.
2. If the Constitution of the United States fails to mention a power, who "owns" the power and why?
3. Articulate examples of rights found in at least four different constitutional amendments.
4. How did the ratification of the 14th amendment affect the application of the Bill of Rights *vis a vis* state governments and their agents?
5. Why is it important for a teacher, coach, administrator, or sports manager to understand the source of constitutional rights?
6. Read and react to the legal logic used in the decision in *Brown v. Board of Education*.

REFERENCES

Brown v. Board of Education, 349 U.S. 294 (1955), *Brown I,* and 347 US 483 (1955), *Brown II.*
Civil Rights Restoration Act, 20 USCS Section 1687 (1988)
Grove City College v. Bell, 104 S.Ct. 1211 (1984)

CHAPTER 4

CONSTITUTIONAL GUARANTEES
AND THEIR ANALYSIS

Jamie, born in Mexico but a citizen of the United States, has worked as the sports information director, a temporary staff position, at Prestigious University, a public institution, and has just been reappointed for a fourth year. A written policy at Prestigious University states that if a staff member is reappointed for three years in a row, the staff member will be classified as a permanent employee and thereafter will be eligible for three-year rather than one-year contracts.

A few weeks into the fourth year of employment, Jamie questioned the fact that the new contract was for a "temporary" employee and was for one year rather than three. Jamie's supervisor responded that P.U. was pleased with the work Jamie was doing and that Jamie should not worry about the technicalities of the contract. A few weeks later, Jamie was speaking with another P.U. staff member of Hispanic background and learned that no Hispanic staff member had ever been granted a "permanent" position. Angry and frustrated, Jamie again approached the supervisor. The supervisor gently but firmly told Jamie that because the student body at P.U. was almost entirely white and the university's administration believed that the racial makeup of faculty and staff should mirror the racial makeup of the student body. The supervisor denied that the policy was discriminatory and promised that when the racial makeup of the student body included more Hispanic students, Jamie might be considered for a "permanent" position. *[This scenario is fictitious but presents legal issues characteristic of many constitutional claims.]*

LEARNING OBJECTIVES

Upon completion of this chapter, the student will be able to:

1. apply constitutional analysis techniques to real-life situations,
2. differentiate between fundamental and nonfundamental rights,
3. define "state actor" and provide at least five examples from professional organizations, and

4.   enumerate and define the levels of judicial scrutiny applied to constitutional issues.

When circumstances seem unfair or discriminatory or appear to violate rights enumerated in the Constitution or its amendments, it's time to take a close look at the circumstances. The legal review of the circumstances proceeds in a step-by-step fashion. The first step is to determine the nature of the person or entity who is the alleged violator of the right. There are only two categories into which the violator can fall: state actor and nonstate actor. Constitutional rights are mandated to be free of violation only by state actors. Nonstate actors have no such obligation to honor the rights guaranteed by the constitution or its amendments. So, who is a state actor?

STATE OR NONSTATE ACTOR?

Many state actors are easy to recognize. **State actors** are those who act in the furtherance of their positions as employees of governmental agencies. Public school teachers, police officers, IRS employees, county government employees, staff at the Department of Motor Vehicles, and athletic administrators at a community college are all state actors and thus, in their jobs, must act in ways that do not violate the constitutional rights of others.

The same people who are state actors in relation to their jobs are not state actors when they come home after a long day at work and interact with their neighbors and local shop keepers. The mantel of state actor status rests on the aegis and circumstances under which an activity is taking place rather than the personal identity of the violator. So, if you work for a state college department of athletics, at work you would be a state actor but at home you could legally decide to socialize only with members of your ethnic group or religion. You could legally tell your friends that they will be asked to leave your house if they utter words containing the letter "E." In sum, in your personal, nonstate actor life you have no constitutional obligation to be free of discriminatory behavior and no constitutional obligation to allow free speech among your friends. But in your role as a state actor, you do have these constitutional obligations and more.

Not all violators are easy to categorize into either state actor or nonstate actor. Sometimes a violator is considered a state actor for one activity and a nonstate actor for another. For instance, the NCAA has, in lawsuits related to different functions, been categorized as a state actor and in others as a nonstate actor (see Case 4.1). The courts must often deal at length with the issue of state actor versus nonstate actor before even beginning to deal with the merits of the case. [See *Brentwood Academy v. Tennessee Secondary School Athletic Association.* 531 v.s. 288, 121S. Ct. 924 (2001) for a good discussion of this issue.]

If a nonstate actor is the violator, there's no constitutional violation because there's no obligation on the part of nonstate actors to uphold the constitutional rights of others. On the other hand, if a state actor is the violator, the constitutional analysis proceeds to the second step: identification of the right allegedly violated.

WHAT RIGHT HAS BEEN VIOLATED?

Let's take a look at some constitutionally guaranteed rights that are commonly the subject of litigation from sport-related venues.

The 1st amendment carries with it rights relating to freedom of speech (including symbolic speech such as arm bands and raised fists) and freedom of assembly (including associating with off-campus teams). The 1st amendment also separates church and state (including issues of pregame prayers and team membership requirements of "morality" relating to particular religious tenets).

The 4th amendment safeguards our personal security from warrantless searches (including drug testing of athletes and locker room searches).

The 5th amendment provides for **due process** (including procedural safeguards against whimsical firings, athlete suspensions for misbehavior, and removal of athletic financial aid). This amendment also protects people from being compelled to give incriminating testimony against themselves (including providing urine for drug tests searching for illegal drugs).

The 14th amendment adds to the due process protections of the 5th amendment as well as giving the right to expect **equal protection** under law (including prohibitions against treating people differently based on gratuitous classifications, such as differential scholarships for male and female athletes.)

The right being violated must be identified, as well as the **source of that right**. Is the 1st amendment right of free speech violated when athletes are suspended for wearing arm bands protesting an increase in tuition on campus? Is the 5th amendment violated when the results of a random drug test showing illegal drugs are shared with the police? Is the 14th amendment violated when black candidates for coaching positions are never hired? If no right is identified, there is no point in proceeding with a constitutional analysis. However, once a right is identified, it then needs to be categorized into one of two possible categories: fundamental right and nonfundamental right.

IS THE RIGHT FUNDAMENTAL OR NONFUNDAMENTAL?

There is no exhaustive list of **fundamental** and **nonfundamental rights.** Instead, federal case law has created a fluctuating list and continues to add and subtract from the list on a case-by-case basis. Nonfundamental rights are much more likely to be violated with impunity than are fundamental rights. Nonfundamental rights, although important, may be violated if the state actor who violates them has a "good reason." The term "good reason" is nebulous, so the courts have settled on a term which, even if it gives no greater guidance than "good reason," is at least consistently used to indicate a specific level of mild scrutiny when reviewing an activity. The term of art used is "rationally related to a legitimate state interest."

We'll talk more about the mild scrutiny known as "rationally related to a legitimate state interest" used for reviewing violations of nonfundamental rights in later paragraphs, but first we must discuss what are nonfundamental rights. The fluctuating list could be endless, but the courts have made it clear in many cases that at least the following are nonfundamental rights: the right to receive welfare, the right to have the housing of your choice, the right to an education, and the right to be treated equally when you apply for or have a government job. If nothing additional is added to the mixture, violations of nonfundamental rights are reviewed with the mild scrutiny of the "rationally related to a legitimate state interest" test.

Among fundamental rights are the 1st amendment rights, the right to travel from state to state, the right to vote, the right to due process before being sent to jail, privacy rights, and the right to choose whom you decide to marry. The list is fluid, and sometimes a right solidly believed to be a fundamental right is sometimes switched to the nonfundamental list. [The Supreme Court cast doubt on the fundamental nature of the 4th amendment right to be free of warrantless searches in an athletics drug testing case known as *Veronia School District v. Acton*. 515 v.s. 646 (1995).] Fundamental rights are so important and central to the meaning of being an American that they cannot be violated with impunity unless the violator has a "very good reason." The term of art used to define "very good reason" is the strict **scrutiny** of "necessary to accomplish a compelling state interest." Again, we'll talk more about scrutiny in later paragraphs, but you can see that the specific right and the type of right being violated must first be identified before we can determine what level of scrutiny the courts will use.

LEVEL OF SCRUTINY

When state actors are accused of violating nonfundamental rights, the courts use mild scrutiny, **rationally related to a legitimate state interest** to evaluate if the intrusion on the right is legally justifiable. The mild scrutiny test has two parts: (1) rational relationship and (2) legitimate state interest. For example, the health and safety of students is a legitimate state interest and so is maintaining a disciplined and reasonably quiet learning environment in schools. The legitimate state interest then needs to be combined with a method of accomplishment that is rationally related to accomplishing the goal. So, sending rowdy students who refuse to sit quietly in their seats throughout class to the assistant principal for discipline may appear to violate the students' right to an education (nonfundamental right), but the method of removing the students from class is easy to argue as being rationally related to accomplishing the state interest of creating an effective learning environment. If the argument is successful, the apparent violation of the right to an education is allowable. Our constitutional rights are not guaranteed against all intrusions—only against intrusions that do not meet the appropriate level of scrutiny.

When state actors are accused of violating a fundamental right, the courts use strict scrutiny, **necessary to accomplish a compelling state interest**, to evaluate if the intrusion on the right is legally justifiable. The strict scrutiny test has two parts: (1) necessary methodology (least restrictive, effective, least intrusive, etc.) and (2) compelling state interest. Preventing excess noise in classrooms is not as compelling as, for instance, keeping drunk drivers from killing innocent bystanders. But just because the state interest is compelling doesn't mean the state actor has license to attain the goal through any method. For instance, shooting anyone who enters a bar or who purchases alcoholic beverages elsewhere would certainly be effective at keeping drunk drivers off the road, but the first part of the strict scrutiny, **necessary,** test would not be met. "Necessary" means that the method, in addition to being effective, must be the least restrictive, least invasive effective method. Breathalizer tests of suspected drunk drivers may appear to violate both the 4th amendment (search of the body) and 5th amendment (incriminating testimony against self—the breath sample is testimony). Both the 4th and 5th amendments are historically considered to be fundamental. Breath analyzer tests have been determined to be necessary to accomplish a compelling state interest and thus are allowable.

Now that we have it clear in mind that fundamental rights use the "necessary to accomplish a compelling state interest" test and nonfundamental rights use "rationally related to a legitimate state interest" to evaluate if their intrusion is allowable by state actors, let's add a few complications.

The 5th and the 14th amendments both include due process clauses. The 5th amendment's due process clause applies to federal state actors, and the 14th applies to all other state actors. Thus between the two clauses, all state actors must protect our due process rights. We'll talk a bit more about due process in Chapter 7, but for now, just remember that state actors must do whatever they do with fair procedures. The 14th amendment also includes a clause that state actors must treat everyone the same under the law; they can't classify people and then treat them differently based on that classification. The clause is called the "equal protection clause," and we'll talk more about its application to sport and physical activity in Chapter 8. For now however, it's necessary to understand that certain classification schemes alter the level of scrutiny used to review the action. Remember, if whatever right is being infringed is a fundamental right, strict scrutiny is used. On the other hand, if the right is a nonfundamental right and the review would otherwise involve mild scrutiny, but the classification scheme is based on one of three "**suspect**" classes, the scrutiny automatically shifts from mild to strict.

If someone's right to an education (nonfundamental) is infringed, you would expect mild scrutiny to be used. If, however, the person being denied access to school is being denied because of membership in one of three suspect classes, the scrutiny becomes strict. The three suspect classes are race, alienage, and national origin. The additional consideration of the classification scheme used in 14th-amendment claims creates complications. An example is found in our chapter-opening scenario on Jamie. Jamie's right to employment at a public education institution (state actor) is only subject to mild scrutiny because employment is a nonfundamental right. However, when the right to employment is infringed upon because of membership in a suspect class (Mexican birthplace) the scrutiny level jumps up to strict scrutiny.

A second complication relates to a middle area of scrutiny. The middle area has no formal name nor even a term of art which describes how much scrutiny is used by the courts. The lack of details comes from the lack of specificity by the courts. We know that some few classification schemes such as age, gender, and disability will be reviewed with something more than mild scrutiny and something less than strict scrutiny. Again, you'll be reading more about this in Chapter 8, but we needed to mention it here so that you understand the application of various levels of scrutiny when constitutional issues are reviewed.

MANAGEMENT GUIDELINES

If you're a manager, you must recognize that there is more to be aware of than federal and state statutes. The overriding principles of equity, fair play, and inclusion flow from the U.S. Constitution and its amendments. In order to act with flexibility rather than fear but also with fairness under the Constitution, you must understand the following:

1. the sources of the rights,
2. the fact that the rights are not without possibility of intrusion if the reason is good enough, and
3. the techniques used by the courts to review actions alleged to violate those rights.

The smart administrator practices reviewing constitutional issues from all angles. Select even the slightest intrusion on rights—uniforms, attendance, suspensions, removal of scholarships, selection of personnel and their retention, or rules about who can use and who can't use the copy machine—and then evaluate those intrusions through a constitutional review process. This will make you a much more constitutionally aware manager who is more sensitive to constitutional rights. You'll also know what is and what is not an area that can be intruded upon.

CHAPTER SUMMARY

Only state actors must uphold and honor our constitutional rights. The source of our constitutional rights comes mainly from amendments to the constitution. In the sport and physical activity arena, the most frequently involved rights come from the 1st, 4th, 5th, and 14th amendments.

Constitutional review is a complex activity, although the rules seem simple. Intrusion upon fundamental rights and classifications based on the suspect classifications of race, alienage, and national origin are reviewed using the strict scrutiny test, which is stated to be "necessary to accomplish a compelling state interest."

Intrusion upon nonfundamental rights and most nonsuspect classifications are reviewed using the mild scrutiny test which is stated to be "rationally related to a legitimate state interest."

There is a growing middle level of scrutiny that's frequently applied to classifications based on gender, age, and discrimination. The Virginia Military Institute case below defined this middle ground as it applies to gender-based classifications as being an exceedingly persuasive level of scrutiny. More specifically, this middle-level test is stated to be "substantially related to an **important state interest.**"

CASE STUDIES

CASE 4.1

Jerry Tarkanian, a high-profile coach at the University of Nevada, Las Vegas, had apparently violated several NCAA regulations while coaching at the university. As part of its sanctions against the university for the violations, the NCAA insisted that Coach Tarkanian be removed from the university's program. The university fired Tarkanian, and Tarkanian sued the university, which was later joined by the NCAA, for, among other things, violation of his 14th-amendment due process rights. One of the main issues of the case was whether the NCAA was a state actor. If it was determined that the NCAA was a state actor for its actions relating to the removal of Tarkanian, the NCAA would need to uphold Tarkanian's constitutional rights, including those found in the 14th amendment. If the NCAA was held not to be a state actor, the NCAA would not need to uphold any constitutional rights relating to Tarkanian.

The Supreme Court of Nevada supported the lower court's grant of an injunction prohibiting UNLV from removing Tarkanian in response to the request to do so by the NCAA and ruled that the NCAA's action constituted state action.

The case eventually arrived at the United States Supreme Court, which granted *certiorari* (agreed to hear the case). In a 5-4 decision, the U.S. Supreme Court ruled that the NCAA, for this particular action, was not a state actor. Among its reasons were that "(a) neither the university's decision to adopt the association's [NCAA] standards, nor the university's minor role in their formulation supplied a sufficient state action basis, (b) the association [NCAA], which enjoyed no governmental powers to facilitate its investigation, did not, and could not, directly discipline the coach or any other university employee, while the university had options other than suspending the coach, such as retaining the coach and risking additional sanctions, or withdrawing voluntarily from the association, (c) even if, as alleged, the university had no practical alternative other than compliance, and even if it were assumed that a private monopolist can impose its will on a state agency by a threatened refusal to deal with the agency, it did not follow that such a private party was therefore acting under color of state law, (d) the university delegated no power to the association to take specific action against any university employee, (e) the association [NCAA], instead of being a joint participant with the university, was more properly viewed as a private actor at odds with the state, when the association [NCAA] represented the interests of its entire membership in the investigation of one public university, and (f) there was no suggestion of any impropriety or corruption in the agreement between the association [NCAA] and the university." [*NCAA*, 2001 at 179]

The dissent, however, thought that the NCAA was indeed a state actor for the purposes of this case because, "the suspension of the coach, a public employee at a public university, was state action [by the university]; and (2) the association [NCAA] acted jointly with the university in suspending the coach, and thereby also became a state actor, where the university suspended the coach because the university embraced the association's rules governing the conduct of the university's athletic program and adopted the results of the hearings conducted by the association concerning the coach, as the university had agreed that it would." [*NCAA*, 2001 at 179]

Which side would you be on, the majority or the dissent?

CASE 4.2

Virginia Military Institute (VMI), a public higher education institution, refused to allow females to be students at the historically all male school. A 14th-amendment lawsuit was brought against it, and although VMI's status as a state actor is much easier to determine than in the *Tarkanian* case above, the level of scrutiny to be used to evaluate the constitutionality of the rejection of females provides precedent-setting issues.

The decision held that "parties who seek to defend gender-based government action must demonstrate an 'exceedingly persuasive justification' for that action. . . Neither federal nor state government acts compatibly with equal protection when a law or official policy denies to women, simply because they are women, full citizenship stature—equal opportunity to aspire, achieve, participate in, and contribute to society based on their individual talents and capacities. To meet the burden of justification, a State must show "at least that the [challenged] classification serves 'important governmental objectives and that the discriminatory means employed' are 'substantially related to the achievement of those objectives." [*United States,* 1996.]

The U.S. Supreme Court in the 1996 VMI case described a level of scrutiny that trades the term "*rationally* related" for "*substantially* related" when dealing with gender discrimination. The Court also traded the term "*legitimate* state interest" for "*important* state interest." The increase in scrutiny, although not to the level of strict scrutiny (necessary to accomplish a compelling state interest) reserved for fundamental rights and suspect classifications, elevates gender classifications above the norm and signals that the Court is viewing gender discrimination as a more serious issue than before. Why do you think the change in level of scrutiny is happening for gender classifications?

KEY TERMS

1st, 4th, 5th, 14th amendments
compelling state interest
due process
equal protection
fundamental right
important state interest
legitimate state interest
necessary
nonfundamental right
rational relationship
substantially related
suspect classes
scrutiny
sources of rights
state actor
unconstitutional

QUESTIONS FOR DISCUSSION

1. What would you include in an in-service training meeting for your coaching/teaching staff members to help them understand what constitutional issues might need to be considered if a coach removed a student from the team simply because the athlete refused to come to an added practice held on Sunday?
2. Race, alienage, and national origin all trigger strict scrutiny. Gender, age, and disability classifications trigger something less. Why do you think the classification schemes included in the three suspect classes trigger strict scrutiny and the others don't? Can you also find some basis for the difference in the history of the 14th amendment?
3. Have you ever felt that any of your constitutional rights have been violated? If so, analyze the circumstances from the point of view of the person or entity who was responsible for the apparent violation. Was the violator a state actor? What right was being violated?
4. Reread the chapter-opening scenario involving Jamie. Review the situation from a constitutional analysis basis, determining if a state actor is involved, the source of right, the level of scrutiny and, if you were a Supreme Court Justice, what you think the outcome should be if Jamie sued Prestigious University.

REFERENCES

United States Constitution and Amendments 1, 4, 5, and 14

Brentwood Academy v. Tennessee Secondary School Athletic Association. 531 US 288, 121 S. Ct. 924 (2001).

National Collegiate Athletic Association v. Jerry Tarkanian. 488 U.S. 179, December 12, 1988.

United States v. Virginia, et al. 518 U.S. 515, June 26, 1996.

Vernonia School District v. Acton. 515 U.S. 646 (1995).

CHAPTER 5

FEDERAL LEGISLATION

TIMELINE

1868 *14th Amendment is ratified.*

1870 Utah women are the first women in the United States to vote in a statewide election.

1876 General Custer dies at Battle of Little Bighorn.

1883 Brooklyn Bridge, the largest suspension bridge in the world at the time (1,594 feet long) costs $15 million to complete.

1898 United States declares war on Spain and invades Puerto Rico.

1900 Paper clip is invented by Johann Vaaler; air conditioning is invented by Willis Carrier.

1903 Orville and Wilbur Wright accomplish first successful powered flight of 120 feet in 12 seconds.

1905 Albert Einstein develops theory of relativity.

1908 First Ford Model T is sold for $850.

1912 Diesel locomotive is invented.

1913 13th Amendment to the U.S. Constitution authorizes income tax.

1920 Commercial radio broadcasts begin.

1920 *19th Amendment to the U.S. Constitution is ratified, giving women the right to vote.*

1921 Insulin is discovered.

1928 Penicillin is discovered by Alexander Fleming.

1929 Stock market crashes.

1934 Jesse Owens wins four gold medals at the Olympic Games in Berlin.

1941 United States enters World War II.

1945 World War II ends.

1947 First supersonic flight takes place.

1952   Brooklyn Dodgers lose World Series to New York Yankees.

1953   Brooklyn Dodgers lose World Series to New York Yankees again.

1954   Dr. Jonas Salk develops an injectable vaccine for polio.

1955   *U.S. Supreme Court declares segregated "separate but equal" public schools unconstitutional in* Brown v. Board of Education.

1955   Brooklyn Dodgers finally beat the New York Yankees in the World Series.

1956   Brooklyn Dodgers lose yet another World Series to the New York Yankees.

1958   Russian satellite, Sputnik, is launched.

1961   Alan Shepard is the first man in space.

1963   *Equal Pay Act is enacted by Congress.*

1964   *Title VII of the Civil Rights Act of 1964 is enacted by Congress.*

1964   *24th Amendment ends the use of poll taxes to prohibit voting by the poor.*

1967   *Age Discrimination in Employment Act (ADEA) is enacted by Congress to prohibit employment age discrimination.*

1968   *Amateur Sports Act is enacted by Congress to provide for Olympic Committee authority.*

1969   Astronaut Neil Armstrong is the first human to step on the moon.

1971   *Amendment 26 extends the right to vote to 18-year-olds.*

1972   *Title IX of the Education Amendments of 1972 is enacted to bar sex discrimination in schools.*

1973   *Rehabilitation Act of 1973 is enacted, section 504 of which applies Title IX wording to handicapped individuals.*

1975   *Individuals with Disabilities Education Act (IDEA) is enacted by Congress to increase educational opportunity for handicapped children.*

1980   Mt. St. Helens in Washington State erupts, killing 57.

1981   Association for Intercollegiate Athletics for Women ceases operations and files an antitrust lawsuit against the NCAA.

1984   First female marathon is held in the Olympic Games.

1984   Grove City v. Bell, *U.S. Supreme Court decision removes college athletics from Title IX.*

1985   Volcano Nevado Del Ruiz erupts in Columbia, killing 23,000.

1987   *President Reagan vetoes Civil Rights Restoration Act.*

1988   *Congress passes Civil Rights Restoration Act over veto and thereby returns college athletics to Title IX jurisdiction.*

1990   *Americans With Disabilities Act (ADA) is enacted by Congress.*

1992   Franklin v. Gwinnett, *U.S. Supreme Court decision declares availability of compensatory and punitive damages for intentional violations of Title IX.*

1992   NCAA releases its first gender equity study and declares that men's and women's athletics programs are grossly inequitable.

1998   *Ted Stevens Amateur and Olympic Sports Act is enacted by Congress.*

2000   Y2K fizzles.

LEARNING OBJECTIVES

Upon completion of this chapter, the student will be able to
1. identify legislation that protects employees from discrimination,
2. identify legislation that protects students from discrimination,
3. identify legislation that protects solely against sex discrimination,
4. differentiate the various triggers for jurisdiction for federal antidiscrimination legislation, including the EPA, Title VII, Title IX, Section 504, and the ADA,
5. discuss the impact and limitations of federal antidiscrimination legislation such as the EPA, Title VII, Title IX, Section 504, and the ADA,
6. discuss the meaning of "reasonable accommodation" in a sport scenario,
7. discuss the relationship between the United States Olympic Committee and Congress,
8. outline the enforcement agencies/mechanisms for at least the EPA, Title VII, Title IX, Section 504, and the ADA, and
9. define "qualified" and "disability" in the context of the ADA or Section 504.

EQUAL PAY ACT, TITLE VII, AND TITLE IX

Federal legislation relating to equity proceeded slowly in the first 100 years following ratification of the 14th Amendment (equal protection and due process) to the United States Constitution. In many ways, the enactment of federal legislation reflects the development of society and indicates what society considers valuable.

Less than a decade after federal troops left Little Rock upon the completion of their task of enforcing desegregation of schools, two very strong statutes affecting equity in the workplace were enacted by Congress: The Equal Pay Act (1963) and Title VII (1964). Only eight years after Title VII, Title IX (1972) was enacted. As reflected in its legislation, society was strongly rejecting a broad range of discriminatory practices. Let's take a look at how the few sentences of several of those federal statutes, such as the EPA, Title VII, and Title IX, are fleshed out to define their jurisdiction and enforcement procedures. In Chapter 8 we'll review more of the laws' specific requirements and prohibitions.

The EPA and Title VII have comparable jurisdictions that are limited to employees. For either the EPA or Title VII to apply, an employer must have at least 15 employees who work 20 or more calendar weeks. There is *no* requirement that the employer be a state actor. There is *no* requirement for federal funding. Jurisdiction of the EPA and Title VII hinges only on the existence of the required number and type of employees.

Title VII prohibits a broader range of discrimination than does the EPA. The EPA prohibits only sex discrimination, whereas Title VII prohibits sex discrimination plus discrimination based on race, color (e.g., based on light skinned/dark skinned rather than ethnology), religion, and national origin.

Title VII reads,

"It shall be an unlawful employment practice for an employer to discriminate against any individual with respect to . . . compensation, terms, conditions or privileges of employment because of a person's: race, color, religion, national origin or sex." [Title VII, 1964]

The **Equal Pay** Act states,

"No employer having employees subject to any provisions of [the EPA] shall discriminate, within any establishment in which such employees are employed, between employees on the basis of sex by paying wages to employees . . . at a rate less than the rate at which [wages are paid] to employees of the opposite sex in such establishment for equal work on jobs the performance of which requires equal skill, effort, and responsibility, and that are performed under similar working conditions." [Equal Pay Act, 1963]

You might be thinking, wouldn't it be simpler if *one* statute said simply, "Thou shalt not discriminate anywhere against anyone"? Unfortunately, our federal statutory fabric is created on a thread-by-thread basis, with laws enacted only as society is ready for them. The patchwork quilt effect of antidiscrimination laws reflects society's progress, but the warp and weave of the fabric's pattern is confusing. Perhaps most confusing is the variety of enforcement methods. For instance, individuals who believe their employer has violated the EPA may either file a private lawsuit or file a complaint with the Equal Employment Opportunities Commission (**EEOC**), which is part of the executive branch of the federal government. The same employee may also wish to enforce Title VII rights. The administrative enforcement of Title VII resides, as with the enforcement of the EPA, with the EEOC. However, unlike the EPA or Title VII, the employee who wants to file a lawsuit rather than a complaint cannot simply file a Title VII lawsuit in the courts. Instead, the employee must first either file a complaint with the EEOC or, if the employee resides in a state that has an antidiscrimination law and an agency authorized to grant or seek relief, the employee must first file a complaint with that state or local agency.

Let's add another federal statute to the list of those that protect employees. **Title IX** protects employees as do both the EPA and Title VII. However, unlike the EPA and Title VII, Title IX also protects students, and also unlike EPA and Title VII, Title IX requires the presence of **federal money** and an educational program within which the discrimination takes place. There is no minimum number of employees required to trigger Title IX's jurisdiction; instead, three elements—sex discrimination, federal money, and an educational program—are all that are required.

Title IX reads,

No person in the United States shall, on the basis of sex, be excluded from participation in, be denied the benefits of, or be subjected to discrimination under any education program or activity receiving Federal financial assistance. [Title IX, 1972]

Title IX's protection is limited to sex discrimination, as is the EPA. Unlike both the EPA and Title VII, the agency charged with **administrative** enforcement of Title IX is not the EEOC but the **Office for Civil Rights**, which is found within the Department of Education. Also unlike either the EPA or Title VII, someone who is using Title IX to protect rights against sex discrimination has a greater choice of method. The victim of alleged Title IX violations may elect to go directly to court and file a lawsuit. Lawsuits are expensive even when the attorney is working on a contingency basis, so the victim may instead choose to file a complaint with OCR. OCR is then obligated to investigate and reach a determination without any financial cost to the complainant. A negative determination doesn't preclude the victim from then filing a lawsuit, although the chances of winning a lawsuit after a negative determination is made by OCR are substantially reduced. The same victim may not want the notoriety of being associated with either a complaint or a lawsuit and may elect to have someone else file an OCR complaint without the victim's name being included as a complainant.

Although any **lawsuit** requires the plaintiff to be someone with **legal standing**, OCR complaints don't require legal standing and so a victim may, but doesn't have to, use a surrogate to sign the complaint, thus masking the victim's involvement in the complaint and thereby retaining a better chance of being free of retaliation. If neither of these choices is selected, one or more enforcement options is available to the victim using Title IX; in-house complaints may be filed with the institution's designated Title IX officer. According to Title IX's Regulations, each institution must have a designated Title IX officer whose duties include receiving and investigating complaints. Although filing an **in-house complaint** is a legal choice, it's seldom an effective one, partly because most institution's Title IX officers are employed at the will of the principal/president and are thus unlikely to investigate diligently for the presence of illegal acts on campus, since their job may depend on their support of the principal's/president's actions.

FIGURE 5-1
JURISDICTION AND ENFORCEMENT OF THE EPA, TITLE VII AND TITLE IX

EPA

Applies to:	Enforcement	Discrimination	Jurisdiction requires:
Employees	EEOC and courts	Sex	15 or more employees working 20 or more calendar weeks, impact on interstate commerce

Title VII

Applies to:	Enforcement	Discrimination	Jurisdiction requires:
Employees	EEOC and courts	Sex, race color, religion, national origin	15 or more employees working 20 or more calendar weeks, impact on interstate commerce

Title IX

Applies to:	Enforcement	Discrimination	Jurisdiction requires:
Employees and Students	OCR and courts	Sex	Federal money and Education and program

FIGURE 5.2
INITIAL ENFORCEMENT REQUIREMENTS FOR THE
EPA, TITLE VII AND TITLE IX

First Step in Enforcement Procedure

EPA	Victim may choose to complain to EEOC or file a lawsuit
Title VII	Victim must complain to EEOC first (or state/local agency if any)
Title IX	Victim may choose in any order: in house complaint, OCR complaint, lawsuit

The EPA, Title VII, and Title IX are very useful, strong statutes, but unless a victim understands their varied jurisdictions and enforcement mechanisms, it's difficult to use them effectively. See Figures 5.1 and 5.2.

REHABILITATION ACT OF 1973 SECTION 504 AND THE AMERICANS WITH DISABILITIES ACT

A year after the enactment of Title IX in 1972, discrimination on the basis of disability began to be an issue for legislative consideration. In 1973, Congress enacted the Rehabilitation Act. **Section 504 of the Rehabilitation Act of 1973** substantially, but not completely mirrors the language found in Title IX.

Section 504 reads,

> No qualified handicapped individual shall, on the basis of handicap, be excluded from participation in, be denied the benefits of, or otherwise be subjected to discrimination under any program or activity that receives or benefits from federal financial assistance. [Americans With Disabilties Act, 1990]

As with Title IX, Section 504 of the Rehabilitation Act of 1973 requires three elements in order to trigger jurisdiction. Title IX's three elements are sex discrimination, education program and federal funds. Section 504's three elements are discrimination based on a handicap, federal funds, and **qualified** individual. Section 504's jurisdiction

FIGURE 5.3

Building facilities such as this one with no steps to the entrance of the pool or locker room make physical activity accessible to all.

extends to realms beyond those bounded by the phrase "education program" but is limited to "qualified handicapped person[s]" instead of Title IX's broad proclamation protecting any "person."

What is a "qualified handicapped person" according to Section 504? The term means first that the person needs to be qualified and second that the person must meet the statute's definition of "handicapped." "Qualified" in the context of Section 504 means that the person, once given reasonable accommodation, must be able to do the job or activity. If a wheelchair-bound job applicant at a place of employment having federal funding had the computer skills demanded by the job but could not fit the wheelchair underneath the computer terminal, the individual would be "qualified" if the **reasonable accommodation** of providing a wheelchair accessible desk were provided. On the other hand, if a deaf student were seeking admission to a college but lacked the minimum GPA, the provision of a sign language interpreter as a **reasonable accommodation** would still not make the student "qualified."

The second issue in the term "qualified handicapped person" means that the person must fit within the statute's definition of "handicapped." Section 504's regulations tell us that the term "handicapped" refers to "any person who (i) has a physical or mental impairment which substantially limits one or more major life activities, (ii) has a record of such impairment, or (iii) is regarded as having such an impairment." Major life activities include "caring for one's self, performing manual tasks, walking, seeing, hearing, speaking, breathing, learning, and working." [These definitions and other material useful in understanding the ADA are found at Title I, section 12111 (Sec. 101, (8) of the ADA].

If Section 504 of the Rehabilitation Act of 1973 prohibited discrimination of handicapped/disabled people, why would Congress need to have the **Americans With Disabilities Act (ADA)**, signed into law on June 16, 1990? A closer reading of Section 504 reveals that its jurisdiction is limited to programs that receive federal funding (or that receive benefit from federal funding, such as programs using federally funded buildings or federally funded equipment). Thus Section 504 would not protect individuals in most private sector situations, such as private employers, airports, bakery shops, and super markets. The ADA significantly expands the scope of the protections first brought by Section 504. In school settings, however, it has had little impact, because Section 504 already applied in school settings.

Both the ADA and Section 504 are enforced by the Office for Civil Rights (OCR), as is Title IX, and both apply to students and employees (the ADA has an even broader constituency). Also both the ADA and Section 504 use similar definitions for "qualified" and "handicap/disability."

AMATEUR SPORTS ACT

Not all federal legislation that has an impact on sport and physical activity relates to equity issues as do the Equal Pay Act, Title VII, Title IX, Section 504 of the Rehabilitation Act of 1973, and the Americans With Disabilities Act. The Amateur Sports Act was created to strengthen Olympic participation in the United States and to end organizational bickering about which governing body was actually in charge. In the late 1960s, the AAU, the NCAA, and the United States Olympic Committee were overlapping each other in their drive for enhancing their various jurisdictions and expanding their constituencies. The nation's athletes were often caught in the middle, losing eligibility with one organization because of competing in meets and tournaments sanctioned by another. So, in 1968 the Amateur Sports Act (ASA) became the charter for the U.S. Olympic Committee (**USOC**) and, among other things, gave exclusive use of the word "Olympic" to the USOC. The notion of "amateur" changed significantly over the following 30 years, and so in 1998 the ASA was significantly altered to better suit the perceived needs of the USOC, and the ASA became the **Ted Stevens Olympic and Amateur Sports Act**.

Can federal legislation (or for that matter, state legislation, regulations, or case law) restrict constitutional rights? Certainly, and the ASA did just that. When the ASA reserved the exclusive use of the word "Olympic" for the USOC, Congress intruded into our first amendment free speech rights. Opening a business called "The Olympic Gold Sport Center" or "The Olympic Ice Cream Shoppe," would be prohibited because of the provisions of the ASA. Yes, you can drive around town and see signs using the word "Olympic," but if the USOC chose to pursue the issue, and it often does, it could enforce its exclusive right to "Olympic" through the courts.

The ASA is the source of the USOC's right and power to govern the Olympic program in the United States. With the power comes specific obligations and limitations. For instance, the constitution and bylaws of the USOC must not contain any provisions that conflict with the ASA. The ASA sets out the purposes and defines major parameters on the business procedures of the USOC. For more information on the USOC as a governing body, see Chapter 11.

MANAGEMENT GUIDELINES

As sport managers and professionals in the area of physical activity and sport, the best mindset is one of inclusion rather than exclusion, because such a mindset is the best protection against claims of discrimination. Adding to that mindset an understanding of the rights and responsibilities of the major antidiscrimination federal laws is even more helpful, both in protecting your agency from controversy and in assisting your clients and participants.

Develop policies that demonstrate a familiarity with the requirements and prohibitions of the Equal Pay Act, Title VII, Title IX, Section 504, and the ADA. Disseminate those policies and adhere to them.

Develop a pay scale format known by all employees. Adhere to the pay scale when hiring and promoting employees.

CHAPTER SUMMARY

Federal legislation influences the functioning of sport in America. The Ted Stevens Olympic and Amateur Sports Act sets out the power and responsibilities of the United States Olympic Committee.

Other federal legislation adds to the basic protections and rights found in the United States Constitution and its amendments. The Equal Pay Act, Title VII, Title IX, Section 504, and the ADA are all examples of federal legislation that have a strong impact on programs in sport and physical activity. Because of such legislation, discrimination on the basis of sex, disability, race, color, religion, and national origin are prohibited in the workplace. In addition to the workplace protections, some of the same laws protect against discrimination on the limited basis of sex and disability in education programs, and some are broadly applicable as prohibitions against discrimination based on disability in places of public accommodation. The laws have similarities and distinctions in their jurisdiction, filing, and enforcement procedures, but it's difficult to create a scenario that includes a program in sport or physical activity that is beyond the reach of some or all of these laws.

CASE STUDIES

CASE 5.1

San Francisco Arts & Athletics, Inc. (SFAA) promoted the "Gay Olympics Games" and used those words on its letterhead and publicity. The games were patterned on the more traditional Olympic Games and thus included such activities as an extravagant opening ceremony, a plan to have 2000 runners across the United States pass a torch from New York to Kezar Stadium in San Francisco, and the gift of gold, silver, and bronze medals to the winners of each of 18 events.

According to the Amateur Sports Act, 36 U.S.C. section 380 sub section 110, the use of the word "Olympic" "without the consent of the [USOC] . . . for the purpose of trade, to induce sale of any goods or services, or to promote any theatrical exhibition, athletic performance or competition. . . .shall be subject to suit in a civil action by the [USOC]." [Before that enactment of the Amateur Sports Act, the unauthorized use of the word 'Olympic' was a criminal offense.]

Later in the ASA is found, "The [USOC] shall have exclusive right to use the name 'United States Olympic Committee'; the symbol described [of the 5 rings] . . . and the word 'Olympic,' 'Olympiad,' 'Citius Altius Fortius,' or any combination thereof subject to the preexisting rights [described earlier].

The SFAA argued that the USOC was trying to block the SFAA's use of the word "Olympic" in a discriminatory manner because it was being used in connection with an event for gay individuals, yet the USOC did not enforce its exclusive rights to the word against all others who use it. The U.S. Supreme Court (in its decision favoring the USOC) determined that the USOC was not a state actor and therefore had no obligation to protect the SFAA's 14th amendments right for equal protection.

The SFAA also argued that Congress violated SFAA's 1st Amendment right to free speech by denying them the use of the word "Olympic." The Court decided that it didn't. What arguments support the Court's decision?

CASE 5.2

Golfer Casey Martin suffers from a congenital degenerative circulatory disorder that produces atrophy and severe leg pain that makes walking long distances impossible; if he were to try to do so, he would risk hemorrhage and fracture of the leg. Casey requested the use of a golf cart for tournament play. The PGA Tour, Inc., which is in charge of the tournaments, refused. Casey believed that he was "qualified" as a professional golfer if the "reasonable accommodation" of a golf cart were to be provided. There is no dispute that Casey is "profoundly disabled." Casey sued the PGA for violating his rights under the Americans With Disabilities Act. What do you think should be the outcome? After you've decided, take a look at the U.S. Supreme Court's decision at *PGA Tour, Inc., v. Casey Martin,* 121 S. Ct. 1879, 149 L.Ed. 2d 904 (2001).

CASE 5.3

Mynne, a female college athlete, graduated but still had a year of competitive eligibility remaining. The graduate program of her choice was not offered at her undergraduate college, so she enrolled in another institution for her graduate work. She wanted to continue competing through her graduate school's athletics program but was denied that right based on NCAA rules prohibiting her from doing so anywhere except at her undergraduate institution. She appealed to the NCAA for a waiver but was denied. She did a bit of research and found that, in her opinion, the NCAA was more likely to grant such waivers—and in the past had indeed granted such waivers more frequently—to males than to females who requested them.

Mynne, with great courage, and without the assistance of an attorney, filed a Title IX lawsuit in federal court against the NCAA alleging that it discriminated against her request for a waiver on the basis of sex. Mynne knew that three elements are required for Title IX to have jurisdiction: allegations of sex discrimination, education program, and federal funding. The first two elements were easy; the third was not. Mynne alleged that the member institutions of the NCAA (at least the majority of them) receive federal funding, and when the institutions pay their dues to the NCAA that the federal funds are passed along to the NCAA, thereby bringing the NCAA under the jurisdiction of Title IX.

When Mynne's case worked its way up to the U.S. Supreme Court, the use of institutional members' dues as a method of triggering Title IX jurisdiction was rejected, but the door was left open for other sources of federal funding to the NCAA to be used as a Title IX trigger. Can you think of any potential sources of federal funding that might be used to trigger Title IX's jurisdiction over the NCAA? Why do you think the NCAA fought Mynne so hard?

(This case study is loosely based on the facts of *NCAA v. Smith,* 119 S.Ct. 924 [1999].)

KEY TERMS

Amateur sports act
Americans with Disabilities Act
Administrative complaint
EEOC
Equal Pay Act
Federal funding
In-house complaint
Jurisdiction
Lawsuit
Legal standing
OCR
Qualified
Reasonable accommodation
Rehabilitation Act of 1973, Section 504
Ted Stevens Olympic and Amateur Sports Act
Title VII
Title IX
USOC

QUESTIONS FOR DISCUSSION

1. Read the *Casey Martin* case, including the decision from the U.S. Supreme Court. Create arguments for both sides. Do you think a golf course is a public accommodation? Do you think the provision of a golf cart creates unfair competition? Do you think the PGA, whether it was victorious or not, has created a negative or positive impact on its public perception? What would you have done if you were in charge of a golf tournament and Casey Martin asked you for reasonable accommodation of his disability?

2. What are the laws discussed in this chapter that are applicable to employees?

3. What are the laws discussed in this chapter that are applicable to students?

4. What are the laws discussed in this chapter that require the presence of federal funding in order for the law to have jurisdiction?

5. Assume that you have a particularly dark complexion for your ethnic group. You are seeking a job as a program administrator of a fitness center in an all-white neighborhood. Your friend also wants the job. Your friend, also of your ethnic group, has a particularly light complexion. You have all the experience, degrees, and training required for the job; your friend does not. Your friend is offered the job. What federal legislation might be of assistance to you if you wanted to pursue the issue? What are the jurisdictional requirements of that legislation?

REFERENCES

Amateur Sports Act, 36 U.S.C. section 374 (13)), now known as the Ted Stevens Olympic and Amateur Sports Act, 36 U.S.C.S. section 220501, following extensive revision in 1998.

Americans With Disabilities Act of 1990, 42 U.S.C.A. § 12101 et seq.

Brown v. Board of Education, 349 U.S. 294 (1955).

PGA Tour, Inc. v. Casey Martin, 121 S. Ct. 1879, 149 L.Ed. 2d 904 (2001).

Civil Rights Restoration Act, 20 USCS Section 1687 (1988).

EEOC's "Guidance on Application of Anti-Discrimination Laws to Coaches' Pay at Education Institutions, issued on October 31, 1997, is available via the internet at www.eeoc.gov/press/10-31-97.html or by writing EEOC's Office of Communications and Legislative Affairs, 1801 L Street, N.W., Washington, D.C. 20507

Equal Pay Act, 29 USC section 206d(1).6. (1963).

Internet: ADA home page: USDOJ.GOV/CRT/ada/adahom1

Internet: EEOC home page: eeoc.gov/policy/guidance

Internet: OCR home page: ed.gov/offices/ocr

Rehabilitation Act of 1973, Section 504, 29 U.S.C. 794, 1973 (Supp. V. 1993).

San Francisco Arts & Athletics, Inc. et al v. United States Olympic Committee, et al; 483 US 522 (1987).

NCAA v. Smith, 119 S.Ct. 924 (1999).

Title VII of the Civil Rights Act of 1964 (Pub, L, 88-352) (USC 42 section 2000e et seq.)

Title IX of the Education Amendments of 1972, P.L. 92-318, 20 USCS section 1681 et seq.

PART III

BY THE RULES:
PERSONAL RIGHTS AND EXPECTATIONS

CHAPTER 6

FIRST AMENDMENT ISSUES IN SPORT AND PHYSICAL ACTIVITY

Most of the students attending Devout Public High School attended church regularly, so it didn't seem particularly odd for a member of the student government to offer a prayer before each assembly, graduation, and athletic event. Most of the prayers were general and along with offering thanks asked for safety and guidance. Some of the student-led prayers invoked the name of a deity, but most were nonsectarian. Lee, a member of the school board, was concerned that the prayers might be an infringement of the 1st amendment rights of those few people in town who were agnostic, atheist, or members of religions other than Christianity. Lee suggested to the board, and the board agreed, that a vote should be taken to determine (1) if the practice of pre-event prayers should be continued and, if yes, (2) who should lead the prayers. Overwhelmingly, those polled voted to continue the practice of pre-event prayers and selected the student body president as the leader of such prayers. A policy reflecting the outcome of the election was adopted.

Two students disagreed with the policy, and although both were themselves active members of their respective churches, they believed that the school board's policy on prayer violated their first amendment rights against government involvement in the establishment of religion. They argued that in order to fit in with the majority of the student body at school events, they felt obligated to participate in the prayer, which they equated to religious worship.

The president of the student body argued that first amendment right of free speech would be violated if a student was denied the opportunity of saying a prayer of the student's own choosing at pre-event activities. The student body president also argued that most of the events at which prayers were given were voluntary in nature. "If someone doesn't want to hear the prayer, they can stay home or put their hands over their ears," said the student body president.

The two students who disagreed with the policy filed a lawsuit in federal court. As might be expected, the majority of students didn't understand why and ostracized the two students as being antireligion. [This scenario is fictitious but presents legal issues characteristic of many school prayer cases, including *Santa Fe Independent School District v. Jane Doe et al.* 530 U.S. 290, 120 S. Ct. 2266, (2000).]

LEARNING OBJECTIVES

Upon completion of this chapter, the student will be able to

1.   explain the various rights protected by the 1st amendment and give an example of each within a sport or physical activity context,
2.   use appropriate techniques of constitutional analysis to review bans on "trash talk," political arm bands, and symbolic speech in general,
3.   discuss the balance between free speech rights and the religion-based Establishment Clause, and
4.   outline legal issues involved whenever pre-event prayers are contemplated.

THE FIRST AMENDMENT

The first amendment reads, "Congress shall make no law respecting an establishment of religion, or prohibiting the free exercise thereof; or abridging the freedom of speech, or of the press; or the right of the people peaceably to assemble, and to petition the Government for a redress of grievances."

[The 1st Amendment of the United States Constitution was ratified in 1791 along with the remaining Bill of Rights amendments.]

ESTABLISHMENT CLAUSE

In 45 words, the 1st amendment to the United States Constitution provides a great breadth of protections. The first protection relates to governmentally sanctioned or assisted support for a particular religion. This first protection is sometimes referred to as the **"Establishment Clause."** In the introductory scenario, when Devout Public High School, a state actor, provided assistance or sanctioned pre-event prayers, it was "establishing religion" in the view of the 1st amendment. This is true even though the prayers were often general and nondenominational because even general prayers presuppose the existence of a deity and thus may be interpreted as imposing deity-based religion on those present.

Some who support school prayer, often with goodwill rather than cunning, have proposed that selecting prayer-givers from a variety of faiths and belief structures "averages out" the offensive nature of school prayer. However, to do so doesn't reduce the discomfort of those present whose faith or lack thereof is not being served. Neither do such plans meet the constitutional criteria required by the 1st amendment.

Many teachers have participated in graduation ceremonies year after year and have heard an opening "invocation" offered by a local Jewish rabbi and a closing "benediction" offered by a local Catholic priest or *vice versa*. Although the notion of taking turns is popular, the practice of school prayers still contravenes well-settled constitutional law.

Does the prohibition on school prayer mean that all references to scriptures or deity are prohibited on school grounds? No. A Comparative Religion class, a Bible as Literature class, and other mentions of deities that are part of secularized traditions, such as the Pledge of Allegiance, are permissible as long as they are not an advancement of religion, such as would be the case in a school prayer. *[However, compelling students to recite the Pledge of Allegiance may conflict with rights guaranteed under the Free Exercise Clause. For instance, students with religious beliefs that prohibit pledging allegiance to anything other than a deity would need to be accommodated in situations where the Pledge of Allegiance is required to be recited.]*

The prohibition against school prayer may be more easily understood if viewed in light of the extremely narrow circumstances where even the smallest amount of governmental financial assistance is permitted for religious schools, particularly on the primary and secondary school level. Governmental aid is limited to:

1. police and fire protection, water, and sewer service,
2. reimbursement for student transportation, but only if similar support is provided to public schools and the religious schools enjoy no preference,
3. textbooks of purely secular content if public school students also receive textbooks,
4. property tax exemptions that are part of nonprofit exemptions offered to others,
5. released time for religious instruction off campus, and
6. limited health and remedial education services if also available for public school students.

Anything provided by the government in excess of the six areas above would involve too great an entanglement of the government and the recipient religious school to be in compliance with the Establishment Clause of the 1st amendment. So, if government funding is so narrowly restricted, it's logical that prohibitions on prayer are similarly strict. [*The Lemon v. Kurtzman,* 403 U.S. 602 (1971) case, I and II, set out specific tests concerning the nature of governmental entanglement when governmental funding and other forms of assistance find their ways into religious school settings.]

Don't be in doubt: pregame prayers that are anything more than individual students thinking or saying prayers for and to themselves are not permissible. The legal reasoning can get a bit complicated, but the end result is very well settled: no pre-event, school-sponsored or supported prayers, no matter how fully cloaked in sportsmanship goals, solemnization goals, or student-led formats, are permissible. "Thus, nothing in the Constitution as interpreted by this Court prohibits any public school student from voluntarily praying at any time before, during, or after the school day. But the religious liberty protected by the Constitution is abridged when the State affirmatively sponsors the particular religious practice of prayer." (*Santa Fe,* 2000 at 317)

FREE EXERCISE CLAUSE

The 1st amendment also contains a "**Free Exercise Clause.**" No, this clause doesn't mean that all commercial fitness gyms must stop charging their clients. Rather it means that the government is absolutely prohibited from interfering with ANY religious belief. Having a belief and practicing a belief are sometimes two different things. While the government is absolutely barred from prohibiting anyone's religious beliefs, no matter how unique, the government may, if the reason is good enough (i.e., meets strict scrutiny), prohibit or limit the practice of the belief. [See Chapter 4 for a full discussion of the Strict Scrutiny Test.]

When the government's actions inadvertently make the practice of a belief more difficult, the government must make some, but not great, accommodation to the practice requirements. It is the job of the person whose religious practice is being infringed upon to prove that the burden of the infringement is substantial (i.e., inhibits the practice and pressures the adherent to forego the practice). If the person successfully shows that the infringement is substantial, the burden then shifts to the government whose regulation/ law/policy is causing the infringement to show that there is a compelling secular reason not to accommodate the religious practice.

Consider a scenario where attendance at a public college's graduation is a requirement and those who don't attend don't graduate. Graduation is held on Saturday. Certain religious students, including orthodox Jews, would be forced to choose between practicing their religious beliefs concerning the Sabbath and graduating. It would probably be easy for the students to demonstrate that the Saturday graduation attendance requirement is a substantial infringement on the practice of their religion. Would it be easy for the school's administration to show that there is a compelling secular reason not to accommodate the religious practice by waiving the graduation attendance rule? Probably not.

The Establishment and Free Exercise Clauses sometimes conflict with each other. If the student body president wants to exercise personal belief in deity by offering a pregame prayer over the loudspeaker at a football game, a prohibition against school prayer might seem to be a violation of the president's free exercise rights. However, if the prayer were permitted by the school, other students' rights would be violated under the Establishment Clause. So who wins? The Establishment Clause wins. As in many other areas of the law, the balancing of several rights often determines which right will be upheld at the expense of the other. In the balancing of the rights found in the Free Exercise and Establishment Clauses of the 1st amendment, the Establishment Clause generally takes precedence. Indeed, the Establishment Clause's prohibitions don't generally interfere with a person's belief but rather the practice of that belief. Thus, the courts have viewed violations of the Establishment Clause to be more critical.

A person's religious beliefs, in themselves, do not affect other people. Religious practices, such as prayer in the schools, may affect another person with the strength of coercion.

Peer pressure is seen in the brand of shoes, backpacks, or toys children "must" have simply because their friends have them. Peer pressure is an extremely powerful motivation that often overcomes familial pressure or personal beliefs. It is not surprising then that the courts view allowing peer-led prayer within the realm of governmental functions such as schools to be a subtle but potentially strong coercive activity that violates the Establishment Clause.

Some people might say, "What's the difference between coercive pressure presented within schools and coercive pressure found on television, advertising, or religious pamphlets? The difference in the eyes of the Constitution is found in where the potential religious coercion takes place. If it takes place in the forum of a state actor's purview, it is forbidden as a violation of the 1st amendment.

To those of us who share the religious beliefs being exercised, a prayer in a state actor's domain may seem comfortable and noncoercive. But to those of us who have different religious beliefs or no religious beliefs at all, such prayers may carry with them either the subtext of exclusion or imprimaturs of state sponsorship.

It's often difficult for school children to "just say no" to drugs when some of their peers seem to approve of drug use. It's therefore logical that the subtle pressure to belong, to be the same as one's peers, can be quite coercive, even when many would suggest that the coercion is intended to move someone toward good rather than ill. If peer pressure can exert great power, consider how much greater the power can be when exerted by teachers and administrators. For example, consider the pressure to conform placed on a nonreligious athlete whose coach leads voluntary pregame prayers in the locker room. Those athletes who don't want to be present are invited to get up and leave for the field, to be followed later by the coach and participating athletes. If you were one of the athletes who did not share the desire to pray, would you , as a middle school or high school athlete have felt any pressure to stay with your teammates and coach in the locker room anyway?

"The principle that government may accommodate the free exercise of religion does not supersede the fundamental limitations imposed by the Establishment Clause. It is beyond dispute that, at a minimum, the constitution guarantees that government may not coerce anyone to support or participate in religion or its exercise, or otherwise act in a way which 'establishes a [state] religion or religious faith or tends to do so.'" [*Lee*, 1992 at 587]

FREE SPEECH

In addition to the Establishment Clause and the Free Exercise Clause, also included in the 45 words of the 1st amendment is a clause with nothing to do with religion but rather with words. The **Free Speech Clause** protects our right to say whatever we want without government intervention. We can criticize the government, we can say that the school principal or president is inept, and we can even passionately advocate via a radio interview the termination of football at all Division I colleges. The government may not make a law that requires us to say only nice things about it. The principal/president of the public school/college cannot prohibit all speech that isn't complimentary. If a radio station is willing to air our antifootball remarks, the government can't say, "Don't do that or you'll lose your broadcasting license."

If we can say nasty things about the government, principals, and football, why can't we say prayers? Isn't a ban on prayers also an infringement of the third part of the 1st amendment, the Free Speech Clause? Yes, but once again the Free Speech Clause loses the balancing test against the Establishment Clause.

In addition to the Free Speech Clause often losing the balancing argument with the Establishment Clause, it's important to remember that not all speech is protected by the 1st amendment. For instance, the government may enact a law that prohibits the yelling of "Fire!" in a crowded theater without unconstitutionally violating the 1st amendment Free Speech protection of the speaker. Similarly, legislation may be enacted that provides penalties, enforced by civil lawsuit, for those found guilty of speaking defamatory statements, but, on the other hand, those penalties need to be narrowly construed to avoid stifling debate on issues of public concern or about public figures. [*New York Times v. Sullivan*, 376 US 254 (1964) is a landmark case which makes it harder to be found guilty of defaming public figures, thereby reducing restrictions on free speech.]

DEFAMATION

Libel (written) and slander (spoken) are generally dealt with in modern law under the generic rubric of "defamation." Long before television and the internet, the written word had a much greater impact and life span than the spoken word. However, today's media explosion may, arguably, reverse that to some extent. So, little distinction, if any, between libel and slander remains in most jurisdictions. Defamation is not a favored cause of action and so has only a one-year statute of limitations.

Four elements are required to prove defamation:

1.   *False* statement
2.   Published to a *third party*
3.   Holds the plaintiff up to public *ridicule*
4.   Causes *financial loss.*

If the defamatory statement falls into one of these four categories, it's considered to be defamation *per se:*

1.   Loathsome disease
2.   Unchastity
3.   Crime of moral turpitude
4.   Professional misdeeds

If the defamatory statement falls into one of the four categories above, it's considered defamation *per se,* and the plaintiff no longer has to prove the fourth element of financial loss.

This is because the courts believe that false statements on one of the four categories is so outrageous as to be financially damaging automatically. In effect, the court is saying that defamation *per se* is bad enough to warrant a heavier restriction on the defamer's 1st amendment free speech rights.

At the other end of the defamation continuum is the public figure. Public figures (e.g., President of the United States, Margaret Thatcher, George Steinbrenner and Julia Child) have stepped into public view and thereby have submitted themselves to public rhetoric, even if false. Free speech, as a doctrine, developed out of a desire to protect the right of the people to comment on the lives and actions of individuals in the limelight without fear of legal retribution except when the defamer defames with either reckless disregard for the truth or with malice. Public figures must prove five elements (four basic plus reckless disregard or malice) to win a defamation suit. It's not easy to do. The protections for free speech when a public figure is the focus are much stronger than when a private figure is defamed concerning one of the four *per se* topics.

With increasing frequency, case law says that principals and school boards can place restrictions on what employees say publicly, even about topics of **public concern**. When the courts support these limitations, they bolster their ruling by weighing the maintenance of order more heavily than the value of open debate.

Remember, not all speech is equally "free."

TRASH TALK

"Fighting words" are not protected by the 1st amendment. However, the definition of "fighting words" has been consistently narrowed by the Court. Is trash talk within the definition of "fighting words"? Trash talk conveys very little information to the hearer. Rather, the words are often solely intended to be provocative and inciting rather than informative. One might arguably regard trash talk as nonsymbolic action rather than speech (and thus not protected by the Free Speech Clause) because the words lack intellectual content. Trash talk often produces an immediate reaction in the hearer, unfettered by the thought process, which might include violence. Does trash talk rise to the level of "fighting words" and thus lose 1st amendment protection as speech that encourages dialogue and debate or enlarges the marketplace of ideas? The matter is not yet totally clear in the courts, but it's unlikely that trash talk rises to the level of "fighting words."

One major problem arises when someone asks for a definition of "trash talk." Does trash talk become unprotected fighting words just because it contains four-letter words or demeaning descriptions of the hearer? No. Just because the context of the speech or the selection of wording is offensive or abusive to the hearer or tends to produce a negative or even violent reaction by the hearer, there's no automatic removal of the speech from the protected realm. Nor is the offensive speech removed from 1st amendment protection just because the audience is hostile. A few recent lower court cases have faced the issue of trash talk, but their decisions have not yet withstood the scrutiny of review, so there's no reason to believe that what sport professionals call "trash talk" will move into the legal realm of "fighting words," thereby losing its 1st amendment protections.

The law is evolving, but it seems clear that several factors need to be considered before speech loses its protections because it fits into the unprotected category of fighting words. These factors include the reaction of the hearers, the length of the speech, and the wording of specific legislation that seeks to limit such speech. Additionally, the pattern of decisions concerning "fighting words" demonstrates an increasing unwillingness to remove protection from speech, even nasty trash talk. Game officials may decide to penalize actions coinciding with or triggered by trash talk but from a legal standpoint, trash talk remains protected speech under the 1st amendment. So, just because you don't like what your public institution's students or their opponents are saying, it's not easy to constitutionally limit their speech. If the school, as a state actor, imposes speech codes upon its constituency, it does so at the peril of the rule being found unconstitutional.

SYMBOLIC SPEECH

Not all speech is heard by the ears—some is seen by the eyes. Symbolic speech, such as the use of arm bands to protest or support a particular cause, may be included within the 1st amendment Free Speech protections. In 1968, at the height of the Vietnam debate, the U.S. Supreme Court was asked to determine if burning a draft card was symbolic speech of a nature that would allow the action to be protected by the 1st amendment. [*United States v O'Brien*, 391 US 367 (1968) involved a statute which provided for penalties for burning draft cards. O'Brien asked the Court to interpret his actions as symbolic speech within the protections of O'Brien's 1st amendment rights.] In response, the Court developed a four-part test to determine if a particular act of symbolic speech was within the 1st amendment protections.

1. Is the regulation of the symbolic speech within the Constitutional power of the government?
2. Is the regulation furthering an important or substantial governmental interest?
3. Is the government's interest unrelated to the suppression of free expression?
4. Is the restriction on speech as minimal as possible in the furtherance of the government's interest? (*United States,* 1968)

Let's consider a scenario involving an athletic director who failed to reappoint a popular assistant basketball coach. The basketball team members met with the athletic director to express their displeasure with the AD's decision but couldn't change the AD's mind. Frustrated, the students decided to show their disagreement with the personnel decision by wearing red arm bands with a caricature of the AD and the words "Get Lost." The AD contacted the college president, who agreed that the arm bands, which would no doubt appear on national TV during the week's basketball games, would bring negative public attention to the college. They also believed that the controversy might get heated between the basketball players and other students who didn't like the non-reappointed coach. The president therefore drafted a new policy that said, "As of today, no arm bands may be worn on campus. If any student breaks this prohibition, the student will be suspended for a period of two weeks following a due process hearing." How would the new policy stand up to the four-part *O'Brien* test? Try to create arguments for and against each of the four parts.

The *Tinker v. Des Moines School District* (*Tinker,* 1969) case was also decided during the Vietnam era. The *Tinker* case involved arm bands, and the U.S. Supreme Court determined that wearing arm bands such as found in our scenario was an act "closely akin to pure speech" and thus entitled to 1st amendment protection (*Tinker,* 1959 at 505). In our scenario, the new policy forbade the wearing of arm bands but not all political symbols and therefore would fail the third part of the *O'Brien* test: "government interest is unrelated to the suppression of free expression." So, once the policy in our scenario fails the *O'Brien* test, the circumstances should next be evaluated using regular 1st amendment principles of balancing the restriction of free speech with the need for maintaining appropriate discipline on campus. It is likely the Court, as it did in *Tinker,* would find that the arm bands "were a silent, passive expression of opinion without any indication that the school's functioning would be disrupted" (*Tinker,* 1969 at 508). Tattoos, hair length, and clothing decisions and their relationship to symbolic speech are issues yet to be fully addressed by the Supreme Court.

There are times when we would prefer that protests would not involve us or our programs. At such times we're often too close to the situation to see the bigger picture of extremely valuable rights that are at risk if we exercise our authority to prohibit the protests. However, the Court in *Tinker* eloquently reminds us that,

[I]n our system, undifferentiated fear or apprehension of disturbance is not enough to overcome the right to freedom of expression . . . Any word spoken, in class, in the lunchroom, or on the campus that deviates from the views of another person may start an argument or cause a disturbance. But our Constitution says we must take this risk . . . and our history says that it is this sort of hazardous freedom—this kind of openness— that is the basis of our national strength and of the independence and vigor of Americans who grow up and live in this relatively permissive, often disputatious society."

—[*Tinker,* 1969 at 508]

DRESS CODES

Sometimes articles of clothing take on the significance of symbolic speech and are therefore protected by the 1st amendment. Certainly pink hair, creative tattoos and artistic makeup seldom rise to the level of symbolic speech thereby garnering 1st amendment protections. Dress codes are adopted for many reasons that would seldom withstand strict scrutiny in the courts but which, nonetheless, have pedagogical value. In sport, dress codes often are adopted so that the participant's attire promotes safety. Codes prohibiting jewelry and requiring sneakers are adopted to promote safety. Other codes stress uniformity of dress and are often adopted so that disparity between students with substantial financial resources and those without is made less visible. Other codes ban the wearing of trademarked goods because experience has shown the teachers/administrators that the likelihood of theft and violence is increased when one student covets the trademarked shoes or sport clothes of another. Still other codes are adopted to promote the easy classification into class or skill grouping (or to avoid gang colors) by the color of the uniform.

Most dress codes were originally adopted, even if in some instances now out-of-date, for positive pedagogical purposes. These reasons do not rise to the level needed to survive strict scrutiny but neither do they need to. They are not interfering with a fundamental right such as would be the case with bans on symbolic speech. On the other hand, political arm bands, protest buttons, and similar attire may rise to the level of protected symbolic speech. Thus a state actor's blanket rule prohibiting, for instance, a political arm band from being worn in class would have to be based on a reason that could withstand strict scrutiny (necessary to accomplish a compelling state interest). See Chapter 4 for more information on the levels of scrutiny and the meaning of "state actor."

MANAGEMENT GUIDELINES

Discipline and order are two characteristics for which many sport professionals have a special affinity. If you work for a "state actor" (see Chapter 4), carefully review the potential constitutional issues before you impose rules of behavior or speech on your employees or athletes.

Find positive ways to end trash talk. Set examples. Set goals. Encourage coaches to respond negatively when their athletes engage in trash talk. Discuss the many problems of trash talk; but if you're a state actor, don't suspend students or otherwise punish trash talk unless you're sure you can define trash talk explicitly enough to have it fall within the narrow legal definition of "fighting words."

Preventing trash talk might best be accomplished, without worrying about constitutional issues, if you focus on prohibiting and punishing **reactions** to trash talk. If there's no reaction to trash talk, the talk often disappears from the lexicon of an athlete's game behavior. Remember Mom's advice: "Just ignore your sibling. If you don't react, the teasing will stop." Sometimes it works . . . and it's constitutional.

Symbols of protest such as arm bands are often considered to be protected symbolic speech. Before banning such expressions, carefully evaluate the potential of violating your participants' 1st amendment rights.

Not all speech is protected by the 1st amendment. If you work for a "state actor," your speech on issues of personal concern rather than public concern may be, in some situations, limited or prohibited without infringing on your 1st amendment rights. For instance, expressing your thoughts at a board meeting about the personal sexual preferences of the school district's superintendent's private life may often be successfully prohibited by your employer without violating your 1st amendment rights. Personnel actions can be based on your employer's reasonable belief about your remarks, even if they are incorrect, without violating your rights. So, if you work for a state actor, be careful if you speak as an employee on matters of private concern. The distinctions are vague, but the impact on your job may be significant.

Resist the impulse to add pregame prayers to your program. The Supreme Court has made it quite clear that there are very few circumstances in which pregame or school prayers in public institutions would be in compliance with the 1st amendment rights of your participants and staff.

CHAPTER SUMMARY

The rights guaranteed by the 1st amendment are not absolute, but they are complex. The Establishment Clause bars **state actors** from any activity that fosters religion or supports one religion over another. Prayer in public school programs is almost always a violation of the Establishment Clause, and the smart administrator should avoid the issue by avoiding the inclusion of prayer in any form within the school program. Alternating types of prayer, using student led prayers, allowing students the right to select the type of prayer, using team prayers before a game—have all been shown to be ineffective attempts for circumventing the provisions of the 1st amendment.

When the Establishment Clause conflicts with rights guaranteed by the Free Exercise Clause, the Establishment Clause (prohibiting among other things, school prayer) takes precedence.

Trash talk is unlikely to rise to the level of "fighting words," and thus trash talk generally remains protected speech (though objectionable speech) in most situations. Thus, a public institution's rules banning trash talk often run counter to the provisions of the 1st amendment Free Speech Clause.

Remember that only state actors are obligated to honor 1st amendment rights. Programs that are not state actors have no obligation to avoid sanctioning prayers or banning objectionable forms of speech.

CASE STUDIES

CASE 6.1

Coach Chris believed that the use of caffeine as found in caffeinated sodas was an effective ergogenic aid. When Coach Chris' public high school contract was renewed, the school board made it clear that Chris was not to discuss the use of caffeine with athletes. The community as well as parents had expressed concern about the coach's discussion of caffeine use with students and pressured the school board into placing a ban on speech relating to caffeine. Part way through the season, Coach Chris reportedly suggested that a student athlete should drink a soda before the race. In response, the school board placed Chris on administrative leave for violating the board's ban on caffeine-related speech. Later, the board refused to renew Chris' contract. Chris sued the board, alleging that the board had infringed on her 1st amendment rights. What do you think? [This scenario is loosely based on *Schul v. Sherard,* 102 F. Supp. 2d 877 (2000). The *Schul* case is from the U.S. District Court for the Southern District of Ohio and as such does not represent any sort of national precedent but does make interesting reading.]

CASE 6.2

Coach Pat believed that the team needed a calming, solemnizing influence before each game. Not wanting to impose a religion on the nonreligious members of the team, Coach Pat invited those team members who wanted to join in a team prayer to remain in the locker room a few minutes while those who did not wish to participate in the prayer could go out to the field and begin preparing for the game. Coach Pat said the prayer to make sure there was no reference to a specific deity and that the prayer remained nonsectarian. Basically, the prayer asked for safety and good sportspersonship. It had been Coach Pat's experience over the years that the pregame prayer calmed the team and helped players keep their athletic participation in proper perspective.

There was no penalty imposed against athletes who elected to exit the locker room before the prayer. Indeed, one of the assistant coaches was always assigned to accompany the nonparticipating athletes to provide appropriate supervision on the field during the prayer in the locker room.

The community in which the school was located was quite religious and yet tolerant of its nonreligious members. What are the constitutional issues involved with the pregame prayer? Do you think the prayer is legally appropriate? [This scenario is fictitious but presents legal issues characteristic of many school prayer cases including, *Santa Fe Independent School District v Jane Doe et al.* 530 U.S. 290, 120 S. Ct. 2266 (2000.]

KEY TERMS

Establishment Clause
Fighting words
Free Exercise Clause
Free Speech Clause
Protected speech

Public concern, issues of
State actor
Symbolic speech
Trash talk

QUESTIONS FOR DISCUSSION

1.   Read the *Santa Fe v. Jane Doe* case and discuss the arguments made in the dissenting opinion. Do you agree with the dissenting opinion, or would you have been supportive of the majority opinion? Why?

2.   The courts typically give greater importance to the Establishment Clause than to the Free Exercise Clause when the two come into conflict with each other. Do you agree? Discuss the logic of your preference.

3.   Assume you're an athletic director and your soccer coach wants to include a pregame prayer before each game. You have told the coach that prayers are not allowed. The coach, who was born in South America and so doesn't come from a tradition of freedom of religion doesn't fully understand the 1st amendment. The coach asks you to explain your reasons and the supporting data for them. What do you say to the coach?

4.   Half of your team belongs to an Evangelical Christian church. A fourth is comprised of atheists, and a fourth is of an Islamic sect. The Evangelical church members ask if they may lead the team in prayer before the big game. The Islamic students remind you of their need to fulfill their religion's requirement to pray at specific times during the day. The atheist students haven't said anything to you about religion. You want to accommodate your students' needs while also being sensitive to their variety of beliefs. How do you respond to each group's request? Support your decisions with legal principles.

REFERENCES

First amendment of the United States Constitution

Holford, Elyzabeth Joy, "Praying Before the Game", *Strategies,* November/December, 1990 pp 17-18.

Lee v. Weisman 505 U.S. 577 (1992)

Lemon v. Kurtzman, 403 U.S. 602 (1971)

New York Times v. Sullivan, 376 U.S. 254 (1964)

Santa Fe Independent School District v. Jane Doe et al. 530 U.S. 290, 120 S. Ct. 2266, (2000).

Tinker v. Des Moines School District, 383 F.2d 988, rev.d 393 U.S. 503 (1969)

United States v. O'Brien, 391 US 367 (1968)

CHAPTER 7

FOURTH AND FIFTH AMENDMENT
ISSUES IN SPORT AND
PHYSICAL ACTIVITY

Families, hoping to find a safe community in which to raise their children, moved to a suburban Oregon town. The high school facilities were new, and the school had a good reputation for maintaining discipline and providing a good education. The town's newspaper seldom carried stories about teen drinking or drug use, and crime was amazingly low. The weather was mild and the scenery green and peaceful.

Following formal discussions involving the community, PTA, and law enforcement officials, the school initiated a policy requiring drug testing for any student who wished to participate in athletics. In brief, the testing program required all prospective athletes to sign a form permitting the school officials to perform drug tests of the athlete's urine. The drug tests would be random, unannounced events, and any student who refused to sign the form would be barred from participating in athletics, even if there was no suspicion of drug use. The program included testing all students at the beginning of the season for both banned and illegal drugs. After the beginning of the season, school district representatives would test an additional, randomly selected 10 percent of athletes each week. Observation of urination was required for the male students; female students were supervised by a same-sex monitor standing outside the bathroom stall door during urination. The urine was then to be tested for temperature and tampering prior to being transferred to a vial.

If the test results were positive, the principal would then arrange a meeting with the athlete and parents at which the student could choose to:

a. participate in a six-week program including weekly drug testing, or
b. be suspended from athletics for the remainder of the season and the next season.

Pat, a high school student athlete who had no connection to drug use, believed that being forced to sign the permission form violated rights guaranteed under the 4th, 5th, and 14th amendments of the Constitution and so, with parental approval, refused to sign the form as a matter of principle. The school district responded by barring Pat from athletic participation for failing to sign the form. Pat sued the school district, claiming that the school district's drug-testing policy was unconstitutional. [Although this scenario is fictitious, the issues are similar to those raised in *Vernonia School District 47 J v. Acton et us.* 515 U.S. 646, 115 S. Ct. 238, 1995]

LEARNING OBJECTIVES

Upon completion of this chapter, the student will be able to:

1. differentiate the rights found in the 4th, 5th, and 14th amendments,
2. discuss the balancing of privacy rights versus the need of a school district to provide safe learning conditions,
3. provide illustrative scenarios of constitutional and unconstitutional locker searches,
4. describe the difference between substantive and procedural due process, and
5. discuss the changing nature of the doctrine of *in loco parentis* and provide opinions about the impact of the doctrine in today's high school and college athletics programs.

4TH AMENDMENT

The right of the people to be secure in their persons, houses, papers, and effects, against unreasonable searches and seizures, shall not be violated, and no Warrants shall issue, but upon probable cause , supported by Oath or affirmation, and particularly describing the place to be searched, and the persons or things to be seized.

—[4th Amendment, U.S. Constitution]

The **4th amendment** is often cited as the part of the Bill of Rights, which guarantees privacy, although you can't find the word "privacy" anywhere in the amendment. Even though "privacy," as a word, is not included, the 4th amendment provides broad protections against governmental intrusion into our possessions and persons. Those protections have historically, but not universally, been considered to be fundamental rights. [The 4th amendment of the U.S. Constitution was ratified in 1791 along with the remainder of the Bill of Rights (first 10 amendments to the Constitution.] Rights that belong to the fundamental right category may only be constitutionally "violated" when the violator can meet the strict scrutiny test of being necessary to accomplish a compelling state interest.

In sport settings, the 4th amendment's protections come into the spotlight whenever drug testing and locker searches are considered. Drug testing involves an invasion of the person; urinalysis involves the testing of bodily fluids and is certainly an invasion of the "security" of the person, even if it's not as great an invasion as a blood test. Searches of lockers bring into play the potential for violating the 4th amendment's promise of security of "papers and effects."

Let's take a look first at searches of lockers. We'll select searches first simply because the legal issues at play in searches are somewhat more straightforward than those involved in drug testing.

LOCKER SEARCHES

Even though the word "privacy" is not explicitly included in the 4th amendment, most people have an expectation of privacy when they lock the door to their car or their home. Although there are exceptions to the 4th amendment prohibition against **state actors** (see Chapter 4) searching homes and cars, generally, such searches of homes or cars may be conducted by state actors only if the **search** is pursuant to a lawful arrest or in the presence of a valid search warrant which was obtained from the court after a showing of "**probable cause**" to support the issuance of the **warrant**. The search of a school locker is another matter, however. When a student locks their locker, the student has a smaller expectation of privacy than when the same student locks the door to the family home. The expectation of privacy is even lower if the lock is owned by the school rather than by the individual student. As the expectation of privacy diminishes, so does the need for legal justification for the search. A school-owned lock reduces the expectation of privacy to a point where a warrant supported by "probable cause" is no longer needed in order for a state actor to constitutionally search the locker.

In the years before the 1985 Supreme Court decision in *New Jersey v. TLO,* [*New Jersey,* 1985] teachers, coaches and school officials relied on the doctrine of *in loco parentis* to free them from constitutional restraints. If they acted as a parent (in place of the parent), the school officials did not have the mantel of "state actor" and therefore could treat students the same way as parents could treat their children. A parent has no need to observe a child's constitutional rights before searching the child's room or closet. Similarly, before 1985's *New Jersey v. TLO,* a teacher, under the doctrine of *in loco parentis* had no significant obligation to provide for the constitutional rights of a child in many, although not all, aspects of the interchange between student and school.

The doctrine of *in loco parentis,* pre-*TLO,* carried with it obligations as well. The school needed to care for the students with much the same diligence as a parent. By 1985, society had decided, via case law, that students needed to bear a bit more self-responsibility. In addition, personal rights were strengthening.

The 1985 *TLO* decision involved a search of a student's bag. The U.S. Supreme Court's decision required **individualized suspicion** in order for the invasion by school officials of 4th amendment rights against searches to be constitutional. So, after *New Jersey v. TLO,* a generalized search by a state actor of school lockers and student bags with the hope of finding *something* in *someone's* locker was a violation of 4th amendment rights. Individualized suspicion was required. The doctrine of *in loco parentis* lost much of its impact and became more narrowly construed after *New Jersey v. TLO.*

Both pre-and post-*New Jersey v. TLO,* a warrant supported by probable cause was, and continued to be, generally required for a **law enforcement**-performed search of a student's locker. Pre-*New Jersey v. TLO,* a **school official** had to justify very little in order to search a student's locker or bag, just as a parent might perform similar searches similar things at home. However, after *TLO's* diminishment of the doctrine of *in loco parentis,* school officials had greater restraints placed on them when they wanted to conduct a search. The new restraints did not rise to the level of a warrant (as was, and generally is, the case for searches by police) but did require that three criteria be met:

1. a reasonable suspicion, and
2. an individualized suspicion, and
3. a reasonable scope.

The third item, reasonable scope, means that if it was reasonably suspected (not rising to the level of probable cause, though), that the individual (let's use the name Lee) possessed drug paraphernalia, a search of Lee's school locker would be more easily justified as to the reasonability of scope than a strip search would be. A locker search involves less invasion of the expectation of personal privacy than a strip search.

DRUG TESTING

Drug testing of athletes is common both on the high school and collegiate levels. The issues differ between the two levels, however. Let's compare the NCAA and the local public high school. The high school is a state actor and therefore must be mindful of its students' constitutional rights. The NCAA has been declared a state actor for some actions and a non state actor for others. A definitive decision concerning the NCAA's status as a state actor when it imposes drug-testing programs has not yet found a place in federal case law [The *Brentwood* case discusses the issue of whether a high school athletic association is a state actor]. While we're unsure of the designation of the NCAA as a state actor for drug-testing purposes, we know that if it were to be designated a state actor, it would have to function without the "parental immunity" that was attached to the doctrine of *in loco parentis* in bygone years. In addition to the contraction of the doctrine of *in loco parentis,* the doctrine's application to older students has always been reduced when compared to younger students.

Although collegiate/NCAA drug-testing issues remain without terminal judicial direction, we do know more about the constitutionality of high school drug-testing programs. In the 1970s, searches by school officials were allowed without significant restraint under the doctrine of *in loco parentis.* After 1985's *TLO* decision, students' constitutional rights were valued more, and restraints on searches by school officials were increased, if only slightly. A decade later, the pendulum moved back toward fewer restraints on searches which are conducted by school officials. Indeed, the 1995 U.S. Supreme Court decision in *Vernonia* [*Vernonia,* 1995) (a high school drug-testing case) pushed the pendulum hard in the direction of decreasing the strength of 4th-amendment rights in general .

5TH AND 14TH AMENDMENTS

Drug testing of athletes brings up not just 4th amendment issues regarding searches but also **5th-amendment** protections against self-incrimination and **14th amendment** equal protection issues. The potpourri of potential constitutional protections that are likely to be violated by school drug-testing programs has not deterred the imposition of such programs either by the NCAA or the local high school.

Reread the chapter-opening scenario and you will have an idea of the issues involved in the *Vernonia case* [*Vernonia,* 1995]. If you were Pat, what amendments would you claim were being violated by the school district's drug-testing program? Let's work our way through the facts:

1. A public high school and school district instituted the drug-testing program. Thus, the violator is a state actor.
2. Only athletes, not the entire student body, were involved in the drug-testing program. Thus, the athletes are being treated differently, thus triggering 14th amendment, equal-protection issues.
3. The drug tests were random, which means no individualized suspicion exists. Thus, 4th amendment and New Jersey v. TLO "individualized suspicion" issues arise.
4. The test included a review of the urine sample for banned as well as illegal drugs. Thus, self-incrimination protections found in the 5th amendment are of concern.

The U.S. Supreme Court's majority opinion in *Vernonia* found the school's drug-testing program constitutional. The opinion noted, yet ignored, the 14th amendment equal protection issues. However, had the 14th amendment issues been discussed in the majority's decision, the issues would have been reviewed using only mild scrutiny: Is the disparate treatment of athletes rationally related to a legitimate state interest? This is because being an athlete does not place the individual in a "suspect class." (See Chapter 4 for a discussion of suspect class membership.)

The U.S. Supreme Court's majority opinion also noted, then ignored, the presence of 5th amendment self-incrimination issues. Urine and blood tests, breathalyzer analyses, and the like are testimony just as is verbal testimony. In this case, however, the court gave very little consideration to 5th amendment issues based in part on the fact that the results of urine tests that were positive for illegal drugs were not being forwarded to law-enforcement agencies for prosecution.

The majority opinion focused on 4th amendment issues. Historically, federal case law has deemed 4th amendment protections against unwarranted searches to be fundamental, thereby triggering strict scrutiny (necessary to accomplish a compelling state interest). With very little supporting explanation, the majority opinion in *Vernonia* cast doubt on the fundamental nature of 4th amendment rights, thus swinging the *New Jersey v. TLO* (1985) pendulum and the vast majority of other 4th amendment federal case law wildly in the opposite direction. It appears, post-*Vernonia,* that no individualized suspicion is needed for school officials to conduct a search—and not just the search of a locker, about which a smaller expectation of privacy exists, but an intrusive, bodily fluid search, where many would believe a large expectation of privacy exists. The majority opinion dismissed the expectation of privacy over an athlete's bodily fluids by noting that athletes are accustomed to dressing together and to undergoing medical screening preparatory to participation. Do you agree with the majority opinion?

DUE PROCESS

The *Vernonia* drug test case (and the scenario at the beginning of the chapter) involved retests of positive tests and incremental punishments. These procedures are used to provide a sense of fairness or, in legal terms, due process.

FIGURE 7.1

Mary, I ve warned you twice about coming late to practice and I ve told you what would happen if you did it again. Unless you can give me a very good reason why I shouldn t, I m going to bench you for the next game. (At the minimum, due process requires a statement of the violation, notice of the intended punishment, and an opportunity to respond.)

The right to due process is promised in two amendments: the 5th and 14th. Originally, the 5th amendment's protections were only guaranteed by federal entities. The 14th amendment, in effect, added state and local "state actors" to those who must protect our 5th amendment due process rights as well as other constitutional rights.

PROCEDURAL VS. SUBSTANTIVE DUE PROCESS

Due process has two personalities: One is **substantive** due process and the other is **procedural** due process. Substantive due process is similar to our understanding of equal protection, and its analysis is parallel. If a fundamental right is being deprived, or a suspect class is being discriminated against, strict scrutiny applies. If a nonfundamental right is being deprived or a non suspect class is being discriminated against, only mild scrutiny applies. Substantive due process considers the fairness of who is selected for a given restriction and whether that restriction is fair. (See Chapter 4 for a discussion of scrutiny.)

Procedural due process relates less to what is being done than to how it is being done. Thus, when the 5th and 14th amendments talk about not depriving persons of "life, liberty, or property without due process of law," they are guaranteeing a fair set of rules for the deprivation, not that the deprivations are fair. In the context of *Vernonia* and the scenario at the beginning of the chapter, substantive due process would be concerned with the fairness of singling out athletes for the drug tests, whereas procedural due process would be concerned with the fairness of the testing process (right of a confirmatory test, incremental punishment, and so forth).

The degree of procedural due process owed to someone depends on the grip the person has on a life, liberty, or property interest. For instance, if a coach employed by a state actor is dismissed at the end of a one-year contract, the coach has no "grip" or expectation of continued employment beyond perhaps a mere hope of being rehired. Therefore the coach would not be owed any procedural due process. However, if the coach were to be dismissed at the end of the first year of a three-year contract, the coach would be owed significant procedural due process because the coach would have had a strong "grip" or expectation of a continued possession of the property interest found in the remaining two years of the contract. The procedural due process owed might require the employer, if a state actor, to provide cogent reasons for the dismissal, an appeal process within which the coach could rebut the reasons, and so forth.

The substantive due process owed increases as the value of the right increases (from non fundamental to fundamental) and as the classification scheme behind discrimination becomes more appalling (non suspect class to suspect class).

The procedural due process owed increases as the person's hold or expectation of a continued interest in life, liberty, or property increases.

A fair, non discriminatory program requires homage to both substantive and procedural due process. The constitution requires that homage of state actors.

MANAGEMENT GUIDELINES

1. Develop, discuss, and follow policies and procedures for searches that include an understanding of the differences between a search led by a police officer and one led by a school official.

2. Understand the differing expectations of privacy between your students/clients and your staff. Consider the use of school locks on lockers and notice.

3. Develop a balance between privacy issues and safety issues that are appropriate for your circumstances.

4. Develop drug policies that rely on behavioral and social alterations more than search and seizure issues.

5. Living by good policies that include both substantive and procedural due process in generous amounts when you have to fire or choose to not reappoint staff is a good idea. Decreasing animosity and defusing frustration by being open, helpful, honest, and fair both in the collegial sense and legal sense, tends to reduce the likelihood of lawsuits based on due process concerns.

6. Develop policies that acknowledge that at a minimum, when due process is required, the minimum that is required includes:

a. notice of the violation or wrongdoing, and

b. the concomitant punishment or resulting action to be taken, and

c. an opportunity for the accused to reply.

7. Develop policies that acknowledge that sometimes the level of due process required can extend to a *quasi*trial format including witnesses, attorneys, and appeals and the like.

CHAPTER SUMMARY

The rights guaranteed by the 4th, 5th, and 14th amendments take many forms. Equal protection, self-incrimination, due process, and privacy concerns are all overlapping in the practice of most sport programs. Due process requirements found in the 4th, 5th, and 14th amendments have an impact on how a drug-testing program is administered as well as how an employee is fired. A successful balancing of expectations of employer/teacher control over employee/student requires both empathy and an understanding of the constitutional issues involved. Scholarships are property interests, and so are jobs. Lockers and bodies involve expectations of privacy. Arbitrary control over students or staff is often a violation of the students' or staff members' constitutional rights where a state actor is concerned.

CASE STUDIES

CASE 7.1

Lee, a talented high school athlete, was expecting college scouts to be at the last game of the season. Lee, feeling more than a bit cocky and self-assured, believed that the behavior code for all team members only applied only to the other athletes. Two days before the last game, Pat, probably the "weakest link" on the team, approached the coach and told of seeing Lee coming out of the town bar at 2 a.m. the night before. Team rules included both a 9:30 p.m. curfew and a ban on drinking. The coach, who was tired of Lee's arrogance, decided this would be a good way of teaching Lee a lesson about authority and so decided to keep Lee on the bench for the last game. Lee was very upset by the decision because it would meant the scouts at the game would not be able to watch Lee play. Discuss the scenario's procedural and substantive due process issues.

CASE 7.2

One of a set of twins, Chris, coaches basketball at the college and the other twin, Pat, teaches at the elementary school. Last Tuesday, both schools received notices from an anonymous caller that illegal drugs were located on campus. Pat's principal decided to call in the police to search the lockers of everyone in the fifth and sixth grades on the theory that they were older and more likely to be involved in drugs than the other students. Chris knew that the sibling of one of the team members had once smoked an illegal substance. Because Chris had a master key for all the school's lockers, Chris decided to search that team member's locker. Consider the constitutional issues and legal doctrines related to both searches.

KEY TERMS

4th amendment of the United States Constitution
5th amendment of the United States Constitution
14th amendment of the United States Constitution
Drug Testing
Individualized Suspicion
In Loco Parentis
Probable Cause
Procedural Due Process
Search
State Actor
Substantive Due Process
Unconstitutional
Warrant

QUESTIONS FOR DISCUSSION

1. Reread *Vernonia*. Discuss the arguments made in the dissenting opinion.
    Do you agree with the dissenting opinion, or would you have been supportive of the majority opinion? Why?
2. If you had to decide which type of due process, substantive or procedural, was the most valuable to an employee being fired, which would it be and why?
3. A coach often has athletes who are better liked or easier to get along with than others. Assume one of the less well-liked athletes was accused by another athlete of breaking a team rule. Because the accused athlete has been testing your authority, questioning your methods, and generally being more difficult to work with than the other team members, you're tempted to "throw the book" at the athlete and remove the athlete from the team.
    What are the constitutional issues related to this chapter that might be of concern to you or the athlete if you barred the athlete from participation? Would the issues be any different if the athlete was a scholarship athlete who was looking forward to a professional contract upon leaving school?
4. The case law has been on a swinging pendulum where the doctrine of *in loco parentis* is concerned. What do you think about the doctrine? Should it be stronger or weaker and why?

REFERENCES

4th amendment of the United States Constitution
5th amendment of the United States Constitution
14th amendment of the United States Constitution

Brentwood Academy v. Tennessee Secondary School Athletic Association et al. 2001 U.S. Lexis 964, 69 U.S. L.W. 4085, (2001)

Carpenter, Linda J. "The Supreme Court's View of Drug Testing High School Ath letes." *Strategies,* February, 1996, pp. 13-16.

New Jersey v. T.L.O. 469 U.S. 325, 105 S. Ct. 733 (1985)

Vernonia School District 47J v. Wayne Acton, et ux., etc. 515 U.S. 646, 115 S. Ct. 2386 (1995).

CHAPTER 8

EQUITY ISSUES: BEYOND JURISDICTION AND ENFORCEMENT OF TITLE IX

The budget of the Big Time Football College (BTFC)'s Division I athletic department was particularly tight. The athletic director and male alumni pressured the university's president to safeguard 100 percent of the football team's budget from the impending cuts.

The president, a football fan and graduate of BTFC, was a bit fearful of the alumni's power and so agreed, although he knew that BTFC's football team took in money from ticket sales but spent much more money than it took in (as is the case with most Division I schools). Thus, the team was going deeper and deeper into deficit territory each year. Indeed, just last year the BTFC football team brought in receipts of one million dollars but had expenditures (not counting stadium maintenance, lighting, athletic training, and so forth) of over two million. The president agreed to the protection of the football budget but was unable to find additional money to help protect other teams from budget cuts.

The athletic director had to find somewhere to cut. He knew that there were at BTFC, as on many campuses, many skilled women who wanted to play on varsity teams, but there were not enough teams to meet their needs. Cutting a women's team would only make Title IX matters worse. So the athletic director selected the men's wrestling and gymnastics teams to cut. He rationalized that although the athletes on the two teams were dedicated and skilled, they enjoyed little fan or alumni support. Thus the potential uproar from the cuts would not be overwhelming.

The president announced the cuts, by stating disingenuously that they were forced by the need to meet Title IX's gender equity requirements. The wrestling and gymnastics athletes were shocked and outraged. They filed a Title IX lawsuit claiming sex discrimination because no women's team had been canceled. The male athletes lost.

LEARNING OBJECTIVES

Upon completion of this chapter, the student will be able to:

1. enumerate the 13 program areas that guide an evaluation of Title IX compliance within an athletics program,
2. differentiate and discuss the three-pronged test for meeting Title IX's requirement concerning access to athletic participation opportunities,
3. discuss the difference between the notions of proportionality and quotas,
4. identify four "contact sports" and explain the significance of such a designation under Title IX,
5. explain why Title IX generally is of no impact when used as a means for male athletes to fight team cancellation,
6. identify where Title IX compliance is measured in dollars and where Title IX compliance is measured by comparing benefit,
7. explain the impact of Title IX when determining how much needs to be spent on uniforms for football versus track,
8. enumerate the significance of at least four landmark Title IX cases and explain their importance,
9. discuss the issues involved and identify at least one case dealing with the question of whether athletic associations such as local conferences or the NCAA might fall within Title IX's jurisdiction,
10. define *quid pro quo* sexual harassment and provide two examples related to sport, and
11. clearly explain the required Title IX treatment of goods or money received from boosters.

TITLE IX

Title IX states,

"No person in the United States shall, on the basis of sex, be excluded from participation in, be denied the benefits of, or be subjected to discrimination under any education program or activity receiving federal financial assistance."

—[Title X, 1972]

Although Title IX applies to all education programs that receive federal money, most of the debate in the decades since its enactment focuses on its application to athletics. (Chapter 5 gives a filler discussion of Title IX's history, jurisdictions and enforcement.)

The one-sentence law augmented by the detailed Regulations that have the force of law lacked significant details about Title IX's requirements in sport, athletics, and physical education programs. Following extensive debate and lengthy discussions, the **Office for Civil Rights** (OCR), the federal agency charged with Title IX administrative enforcement, issued its Policy Interpretations/Guidelines. The Policy Interpretations focus on

Title IX's requirements in intercollegiate and interscholastic athletics as well as intramurals. The Policy Interpretations don't have the force of law but are given great deference. Additional major requirements found within the Policy Interpretations have, however, been tested in the courts and have been found to be appropriate. Thus taken together the law, Regulations, and Policy Interpretations provide clear and supportable mandates for compliance.

THIRTEEN PROGRAM AREAS

Let's take a look at what Title IX requires. Title IX requires that when programs as a whole are reviewed (not on a sport-versus-sport basis), equity exists. To aid in the review, 13 **program areas** are used. The areas are:

- Athletic financial assistance
- Accommodation of interests and abilities
- Equipment and supplies
- Scheduling games and practices
- Travel and per diem allowances
- Tutors
- Coaching quality and availability
- Locker rooms, gyms, fields
- Medical and training services
- Housing and dining
- Publicity
- Support services
- Recruitment

BENEFIT VERSUS DOLLARS

Equitable treatment is judged on the basis of **benefit** received rather than dollars spent on all but two of the 13 program areas. An example of "benefit" might be the quality, quantity, and replacement frequency of uniforms. It costs a great deal more money to outfit a football player with one set of a medium quality uniform, shoes, and pads than it would cost to outfit a sprinter with a medium-quality uniform and shoes. Equity and Title IX require that the male football player and the female track team member each receive an equal benefit regarding uniforms but do not require that an equal amount of money be spent to provide this benefit. Thus, benefit received is the yardstick, not dollars spent.

The only place where equity involves a discussion of dollars, not benefit, is financial assistance.

The number of dollars spent for financial assistance for the total women's program must be substantially the same as the percentage of females in the program. The same is not true for recruitment. Some would argue that financial assistance expenditures are effective enticements for athletes to participate in the program and that using the mandated ratio formula serves to maintain inequity rather than to increase equity of opportunity. In any case, Title IX's current requirements on this topic are firm: the participant ratio is the rule for determining the allocation of dollars for financial assistance between women's and men's programs.

PARTICIPATION OPPORTUNITIES

Another of the 13 program areas that has involved heated debate and produced significant case law is the requirement to provide equal access to opportunity through "accommodating the **interests and abilities**" of the historically underrepresented sex.

The Policy Interpretations provide a **three-pronged test** to determine compliance. An institution only needs to meet one of the three prongs in order to comply with the interest and abilities requirement. The other program areas don't offer a "one of three" option. These are the three prongs:

1. the intercollegiate or interscholastic level of participation opportunities for male and female students is provided in numbers *substantially proportionate to their r e - spective enrollments,* or
2. the institution can show a *history and continuing practice of program expansion* that is demonstrably responsive to the developing interests and abilities of the underrepresented sex (almost always females in this context), or
3. the institution can show that the *interests and abilities* of the members of the his- torically underrepresented sex have been fully and *effectively accommodated* by the present program.

Cohen v. Brown University (Cohen, 1997) was a hard-fought case involving the first prong, which is sometimes referred to as "proportionality". Brown University was an energetic opponent of the proportionality prong. Most institutions that moved toward Title IX compliance in a timely fashion have been able to demonstrate their compliance through either prong two or three. The OCR has reiterated its commitment to allow an institution an unfettered choice of which prong to meet. Indeed, an institution that se- lects the proportionality prong is given the bonus of a "safe harbor" By "safe harbor," OCR means that if an institution meets the proportionality prong, OCR will not look any further to see if the institution is actually providing fully for equal access to opportu- nity by meeting the interests and abilities of the historically under represented sex.

The *Cohen v. Brown University* (Cohen was victorious) case was denied *certiorari* by the U.S. Supreme Court. Because the case's facts would have been a perfect foil on which to discard the proportionality prong had the Court wished to do so, the denial of *certio- rari* is significant. The Court did not choose to hear the case nor did it grant certiorari when faced with a large number of similar cases with which it was presented [Among the similar cases dealing with the '**proportionality** prong' are found, *Favia v. Indiana Univer- sity of Pennsylvania.* 7 F 3d 332 (1993); *Boucher v. Syracuse University.* 164 F 3d 113 (1999); *Pederson v. Louisiana State University.* 213 F3d 858 (2000); *Horner v. Kentucky High School Athletic Association.* 43 F3d 265 (1994); and *Roberts v. Colorado State Board of Agriculture.* 998 F2d 824 (1993]. Thus, following the *Cohen v. Brown University* case, the legal argument against the use of the proportionality prong by those schools choosing to do so seems dead.

Some who want to continue to try to breathe life into the dead issue of trying to block the inclusion of the proportionality prong do so using the term "quota." Quotas are not involved in Title IX in any way, shape, or form. If a school feels the need to reach out to otherwise disinterested females and force them to play in their athletics programs (this scenario is often cited as a possibility by anti-Title IX voices), that same school would have already met the third prong and would have no need to meet any other additional prong. So, allegations that Title IX requires quotas are erroneous and reflect a lack of understanding of the three-prong test.

Assume that your school has not yet met any of the three prongs. A group of female students approach you, as their athletic director, and ask that the women's lacrosse club be made a varsity team. The members of the group are well-skilled lacrosse players and represent a cadre of other female athletes who are interested and who have the ability to be potential varsity lacrosse players. Sufficient competition is available at other schools within your school's normal competitive geographic boundaries.

Is a club-level lacrosse program sufficient in these circumstances to meet the Title IX requirement of meeting the interests and abilities of your female athletes? No. The level of competition (club versus varsity) also needs to meet the interests *and* abilities of the potential athletes.

If someone on your staff volunteers to start a women's volleyball team, thus saving the expense of hiring a lacrosse coach, can you satisfy the need to provide participation opportunities by creating a varsity volleyball team rather than a varsity lacrosse team? No. The students' interest is in lacrosse. Even if the female athletes were skilled in volleyball as well as lacrosse, their interest lies in lacrosse. You must meet their interests AND abilities unless you satisfy one of the other two participation prongs.

If you add a varsity women's lacrosse team, do you need to change the status of the men's lacrosse club to a varsity? No. The circumstances of this scenario identify the women as the historically underrepresented sex, and Title IX's protections flow to them rather than to the men. In any case, the men on your campus (since you don't meet the "proportionality" prong) are already participating at levels out of balance with their representation in the general student body.

If you hire a highly qualified male lacrosse coach for your new women's varsity team, are you violating Title IX because you didn't hire a female? No. Although your athletes may have missed an opportunity to have a female role model, Title IX does not mandate any specific gender for hiring coaches. If you discriminated in the hiring process, however, in order to hire a male, there would be Title IX, Title VII, and 14th amendment issues arising.

If you hire a highly qualified female lacrosse coach for your new women's varsity team but decide to pay her less because she is a female, could the student athletes file a Title IX lawsuit (not an administrative complaint)? No. The students would have no legal standing. In the court's eyes, the issue would have had to be whether the female athletes in your program had access to a coach with the same skill, experience, and competence as students in your men's program, not who is paid more. However, the coach *would* have legal standing to file a Title IX lawsuit because *her* salary is discriminatorily determined. The female coach would also be able to pursue Title VII and 14th amendment action against you.

HISTORICALLY UNDERREPRESENTED SEX DESIGNATION

The chapter-opening scenario that involves males trying unsuccessfully to use Title IX to block the cutting of their teams demonstrates the target of Title IX protections. Title IX was enacted to protect the historically underrepresented sex. In nursing programs, that designation might likely fall to males, but in athletics, the designation is generally the domain of females. Therefore, the males in the opening scenario were not the protected class. In most cases where men's teams are cut, even after the cut, the proportionality prong has not been met, adding to the realization that inequity still exists resulting in the diminished representation of females in athletics programs.

Managing roster size as a way of moving toward the proportionality prong on campuses where neither of the other two prongs is available has also been frustrating for male athletes who can no longer find a place on the newly downsized team roster. An interesting case to read concerning this issue is *Neal et al. v. The Board of Trustees of California State Universities* [Neal, 1999]. The *Neal* case, heard in the Ninth Circuit U.S. Court of Appeals, which vacated an injunction previously granted by the District Court, indicates that although not a *recommended* method, roster management is a *legal* method of moving toward compliance and those males affected by that management are not designated as the "historically under represented sex" and thus are not the focus of Title IX's protections.

Title IX and the NCAA

Renee Smith had only used three years of eligibility before she graduated [*Smith, 1999*]. Her undergraduate school lacked a graduate program in her field, so she changed schools as she entered the graduate level. She hoped to use her fourth year of eligibility at her new school as a graduate student. The NCAA allows graduate students to use their remaining eligibility but requires a waiver when used at a school different from the athlete's undergraduate school. The NCAA repeatedly denied Smith a waiver. Smith brought suit claiming that the NCAA was within Title IX's jurisdiction because it received federal money via the dues from its member institutions that themselves undeniably received federal money. If the NCAA was within Title IX's jurisdiction, then it violated Title IX's provisions when, Smith argued, it more frequently granted waivers to male athletes than to female athletes.

The U.S. Supreme Court did not rule on whether the NCAA's denial of a waiver was a discriminatory act; it limited its decision solely to the very narrow issue of whether dues placed the NCAA within Title IX's jurisdiction. The Court ruled that dues to the NCAA do not trigger jurisdiction, but the Court left open whether other federal money closely associated with the NCAA, such as federal NCAA Youth Sport Grants, would. Case law has not yet included an answer to the open question, however, the NCAA moved quickly to build corporate "fire walls" between federal money and the NCAA. Only time and future lawsuits will tell if the fire walls successfully keep the NCAA out of Title IX's reach.

Revenue/Non-revenue Sports

Are some sports more important than others? Sometimes athletics departments rank the importance of sports by tiers, by major and minor sport designations, or by revenue versus non-revenue sports. Title IX does not rank the importance of sports. A designation as a "revenue" sport by a department of athletics does not remove that sport from inclusion in the evaluation of compliance with Title IX's requirements. Therefore, a school cannot explain a gender-based imbalance in number of coaches, locker-room facilities, uniforms, and other items on the 13 program areas list by simply saying that the imbalance is due to "revenue" sports receiving better treatment than "non-revenue" sports. In reality, very few teams actually produce a profit, and so the term "'revenue'" is quite misleading. However, regardless of the reality, the designation as a "revenue" sport is irrelevant in relation to Title IX.

BOOSTERS AND TITLE IX

Boosters and corporations often give earmarked money and goods to specified teams within an athletic program. What are the equity issues of giving that exclude other teams from the benefit of the gifts? The answer is well settled. The source of money or benefit is irrelevant. The institution cannot evade its legal obligation to provide equal benefit to its male and female athletes.

Thus, if the men's program accepts a spring trip from **boosters'** fund-raising efforts, or team bags from a sporting goods manufacturer's generosity, the athletic department must find a way to provide an equal benefit for the women's program. An athletic director who has no means to provide the required equal benefit needs to either (1) reeducate the donor about the need to support the whole program rather than a subunit of it or (2) refuse the gift.

At first glance, the Title IX treatment of boosters' money and corporate gifts seems ungrateful and arbitrary. However, the treatment reflects the realization that those who are not supporters of equity would otherwise use the booster pathway to funnel funds and benefits in a manner that circumvents Title IX's purpose of ensuring gender equity.

COED PARTICIPATION, THE RIGHT TO TRY OUT, AND CONTACT SPORTS

Participation on athletics teams is most often determined by a competitive format. The Regulations acknowledge the involvement of competitiveness and physiology when they permit single-sex competitive teams, noting that equality requires more than simply the right to try out for a team. "Where selection for . . . teams is based upon competitive skill or the activity involved is a contact sport," single-sex teams may be formed [34 CFR, section 106.41 (b) (1999)]. The need to effectively accommodate the interests and abilities of the historically underrepresented sex would be thwarted if all that was promised was a right to try out.

Physical education classes are also under Title IX jurisdiction, and the requirement for coed physical education classes is perhaps the most high-profile issue. Developing good pedagogy and adaptation of old single-sex facilities are the two main stumbling blocks to creating coed physical education programs that serve both females and males well. A clear understanding of what is and is not required helps limit the scope of the challenge.

According to Title IX, all physical education classes must be coeducational except those that are defined as "contact sports" (wrestling, boxing, rugby, ice hockey, football, and basketball) or which have bodily contact as their major objective. Does this mean that contact sports need to be single sex? No. They *may* be conducted as single-sex units/classes but do not have to be.

SCHEDULING OF PHYSICAL EDUCATION CLASSES

Some schools that prefer not to comply with Title IX's requirement for coed physical education classes use creative scheduling techniques to produce *de facto* sex segregated classes. For instance, football is sometimes offered opposite aerobics, or baseball is offered opposite modern dance, hoping that the students will segregate themselves by sex. When such elective offerings exist, most often the result is single-sex classes. This form of sham scheduling is against the law.

SEXUAL HARASSMENT

Title IX is not the only federal legislation that includes protection from sexual harassment. Title VII, which perhaps, is a more effective tool than Title IX for combating sexual harassment, is the second of a triad that also includes the 14th Amendment of the U.S. Constitution. Harassment based on sex is a form of sex discrimination and is thereby actionable by any of the triad. However, Title VII covers only the workplace, and the 14th amendment covers only people affected by a state actor.

The definition of sexual harassment is not universal within the triad of Title VII, Title IX, and the 14th amendment. Only Title VII has a formal, explicit definition of what is sexual harassment, but Title IX borrows at least half of Title VII's definition and often all of it.

Title VII defines two types of sexual harassment: *quid pro quo* and hostile environment. Title IX case law almost universally covers at least the *quid pro quo* definition. *Quid pro quo* sexual harassment is the more overt, easy to recognize, less subjective of the two definitions. When someone offers a promotion to a worker in return for sexual favors, there is *quid pro quo* harassment. When a coach offers a place on the team to a student in return for sexual favors, there is *quid pro quo* sexual harassment. Both the worker and the student could use Title IX to combat the *quid pro quo* sexual harassment.

The second type of sexual harassment defined by Title VII and generally, but not always, acceptable in Title IX's case law, is known as hostile environment sexual harassment. When a worker is repeatedly fondled by a supervisor, or a coworker's behavior in the workplace includes a daily litany of demeaning and crude sex-based jokes, the worker may be the victim of hostile environment sexual harassment. The harassment needs to become so severe or pervasive that the environment is made hostile. Sexual harassment is discussed in greater detail in Chapter 9, but it is important to know here that sexual harassment is a form of sex discrimination and is, thus, actionable under Title IX as well as often Title VII and the 14th amendment.

Under Title IX, the issue of sexual harassment perpetrated by a peer carries special requirements. Liability for peer harassment does not fall on the institution under Title IX unless the institutional official with authority to intervene actually knew of the situation and reacted to that knowledge with deliberate indifference, thereby failing to stop the harassment [*Davis*, 1999]. Each campus is required to have a designated Title IX officer on campus, but that person might not also be the "official with authority to intervene."

MANAGEMENT GUIDELINES

The costs associated with Title IX compliance can be daunting if an institution has failed to move toward compliance previously. Moving expeditiously toward compliance while engaging both students and staff in the process may help postpone complaints and lawsuits.

Correct the disparities that cost little or no money immediately. Rearranging a trophy case, equitable sharing of the best facilities and the best hours for practice and competition, scheduling support of pep squads for both the male and female programs equitably don't require financial resources but do bring a number of obvious areas on campus into Title IX compliance.

In-service training and professional development in the area of Title IX helps avoid discrimination. Hire good managers, supervise staff, create clear lines for receiving complaints and deal evenhandedly with complaints and concerns. Avoid appearing defensive or being a foot dragger.

The identity of the specific official at the institution who has been designated as the individual with the authority to intervene in cases of sexual harassment should be widely publicized. Allegations of sexual harassment within a program are a manager's greatest nightmare. The manager needs to take the allegations seriously while also protecting the rights of the accused during the investigative process. The existence of good policies makes a difficult process easier.

CHAPTER SUMMARY

Title IX is decades old. Its requirements are clear, although some people enjoy a continuing debate about well-settled issues. Therefore, if you manage a program at an institution that receives even indirect federal money, don't ignore Title IX's requirements [*Grove City's* second issue, indirect funding, was not affected by the Civil Rights Restoration Act of 1987]. If you do ignore them, you are risking both your program's federal money as well as compensatory and punitive damages.

Title IX protects the historically underrepresented sex. Title IX compliance is based on benefits received rather than dollars spent, except in the areas of financial assistance and recruitment.

The presence of the "proportionality" prong as one of the three prongs used to evaluate compliance with the requirement for providing equal access to participation opportunities is well-settled law. Title IX does *not* encourage nor does it require that male teams should be cut in order to find money for complying with Title IX's requirements.

Sexual harassment and retribution are covered by Title IX. *Quid pro quo* sexual harassment is covered by Title IX and, in some cases, hostile environment sexual harassment is also covered.

Recent case law has informed us that when a peer is the sexual harasser, the specific institutional official with authority to intervene must actually know of the situation and react to that knowledge with deliberate indifference, thereby failing to stop the harassment in order to impose liability on the institution under Title IX.

CASE STUDIES

CASE 8.1

Pat, a high school girl, is also a talented volleyball player. She wants to play on the boys' varsity volleyball team because there is only a club team for the girls. The state high school athletic league, as well as Title IX, allows girls to participate on boys' teams in these circumstances. However, the state high school athletic association requires both a fitness test and a medical examination in order to participate on a team of the opposite sex. The fitness test and medical examination are not required for the rest of the team members.

Among the medical examination's components is a sexual maturation test that requires a physician to review breast development and the presence or absence of pubic hair. Although such sexual maturation tests are unsupportable as indications of the female athlete's ability to physically or emotionally participate safely in volleyball, they are required by the state high school athletic association. Because the agency employing the tests did not receive direct federal money even though it served as the gatekeeper for participation in sport programs of public schools that definitely did receive federal money, Title IX complaints and lawsuits have as yet not been filed against the use of the test. While in use, the tests serve as a discouragement for females thinking of participating on a male's team. Discuss the legal issues that should be considered if a Title IX lawsuit were to be brought against the state high school athletic association by a female who wants to participate on a male team.

CASE 8.2

Heather Sue Mercer was a successful high school football player [*Mercer*, 2001]. She wanted to continue her football participation in college while at Duke University, and after working with the team as a manager she was chosen for an intrasquad game where she kicked the winning field goal. Following her success in the intrasquad game, the coach announced to the press that Mercer was now a member of the Duke football team. In the following months, the coach changed his mind. With rather sexist comments, such as suggesting that Mercer consider entering beauty pageants instead of playing football, the coach created an "inactive player" category and refused to give Mercer equipment given to other team members. The evidence presented at trial made it clear that Mercer sought to resolve the issue, but officials at Duke were less than forthcoming as they refused to speak with her.

Mercer filed a Title IX lawsuit against Duke and was awarded $1 in compensatory damages and $2,000,000 in punitive damages. $2,000,001 represents only one percent of the federal funds annually received by Duke. In addition, the Court awarded Mercer attorney's fees.

What is the significance of the $1 compensatory damages award? Do you think that Duke's unwillingness to work to resolve the issue and its demeaning remarks about Mercer were appropriate risk-management techniques?

KEY TERMS

Benefit
Booster
Interests and abilities
Office for Civil Rights
Program areas
Proportionality
Three pronged test
Title IX

QUESTIONS FOR DISCUSSION

1. When NCAA's roster size limits make compliance with Title IX difficult, whose rules should you follow? Why?
2. Title IX counts the number of participants not the number of teams when it reviews compliance. Why would counting teams be likely to produce more discrimination within the opportunity to participate category than counting participants?
3. Identify four changes at your institution which would involve minimal cost but which would increase your institution's compliance with Title IX. Discuss possible reasons why these four low cost changes have not been made previously. Determine how a student or a coach might best cause these changes to be made. Defend your choice of methods.
4. Select five of the 13 program areas. Conduct a mini-compliance review in those five areas on your campus. Develop a compliance plan if you determine that any of the five areas is out of compliance.
5. The Office for Civil Rights has determined that cheerleading is not considered a sport for the purposes of counting participation opportunities. This determination is not intended to be a statement about the athleticism or commitment involved in cheerleading. What do you think were among the policy issues involved in reaching this decision?
6. Identify your institution's official with authority to intervene in Title IX sexual harassment cases. Is the person the same person as the Title IX designated employee? Make an appointment and discuss the Title IX informational outreach programs regarding Title IX's rights and responsibilities which are conducted on campus by that person or designee. Consider whether those outreach programs are effective.

REFERENCES

A Policy Interpretation: Title IX and Intercollegiate Athletics. 44 Fed Reg. 71 (Dec. 11, 1979).

Boucher v. Syracuse University. 164 F3d 1113 (1999).

Cohen v. Brown University. 991 Fd2d 888 (1st circ 1993), remanded to 879 F Supp 185 DRI (1995), aff'd in part and rev'd in part 101 F3d155 (1st Circ 1996), cert. denied 520 US 1186 (1997).

Davis v. Monroe County Board of Education. 526 U.S. 629, 119 S. Ct. 1661 (1999).

Favia v. Indiana University of Pennsylvania, 7 F 3d 332 (1993).

Grove City v. Bell. 465 U.S. 555 (1984).

Horner v. Kentucky High School Athletic Association. 43 F 3d 265 (1994).

Mercer v. Duke University et al., No. 97-CV-959 (MDNC, Mar. 12, 2001).

Neal et al v. The Board of Trustees of California State Universities. 198 F3d 763 (1999).

NCAA v. Smith. 525 U.SD. 459, 119 S. Ct. 924 (1999).

Pederson v. Louisiana State University. 213 F 3d 853 (2000).

Roberts v. Colorado Board of Agriculture. 998 F2d 824 (1993).

Title IX. 20 USC sections 1681-87 (1988) as amended by the Civil Rights Restoration Act of 1987, Pub. L. No. 100-259, 102 Stat. 28 (1988) (codified USC section 1687).

CHAPTER 9

EQUITY ISSUES:
BEYOND JURISDICTION AND
ENFORCEMENT
ADA, 14TH AMENDMENT, EPA, AND TITLE VII

Chris works as an assistant athletic director at State University. Pat, Chris' sibling, works across town at Private University, also as an assistant athletic director. Their schools are in separate conferences and seldom compete, but the siblings share several things in common. For instance, both Chris and Pat are hearing impaired.

Chris and Pat became hearing impaired due to a recent explosion in the family garage while they were visiting their parents for Thanksgiving. Fortunately, Chris and Pat were not injured in any other way, and doctors hope that both may regain their hearing but, for now, both must count on either the written word, sign language, or reading lips for their communications from other people. Both Chris and Pat are adept at sign language, because a childhood friend was hearing impaired, and so as children Chris and Pat had both learned to sign.

Chris and Pat informed their respective employers of their hearing impairment and asked for reasonable accommodation in the form of a signing interpreter. Both employers refused. Chris and Pat sued their respective employers for money damages under Title I of the ADA. Only one of the siblings won.

LEARNING OBJECTIVES

Upon completion of this chapter, the student will be able to:

1. differentiate between Title VII's legal theories of disparate impact and disparate treatment, and provide an example of each within a sport context,
2. identify the administrative agency which is charged with enforcing each of the following: Title VII, Title IX, ADA, and the EPA,
3. discuss the impact of the 11th amendment on individuals seeking protection under the ADA,

4.   compare and contrast Title VII and the Equal Pay Act,

5.   discuss the "religious school" exception to Title VII's coverage,

6.   define two types of sexual harassment and provide a sport-related example of each,

7.   understand the variation in the applicability of Title VII, EPA, the 14th amendment, and the ADA in the context of sport,

8.   explain the significance of a "comparator employee,"

9.   design a learning activity for understanding the difference between sexual harassment and the "normal-by-some-definitions," if also crude, give and take within the workplace, and

10. explain the balance between accommodating a disability and creating an "uneven playing field."

Federal statutes such as Title VII, the Equal Pay Act, the Americans with Disabilities Act, and Title IX, serve as legislatively imposed tools for protecting against discrimination. Chapter 5 provides a fuller discussion of the jurisdictional requirements and enforcement provisions for these statutes, and others. Here we will discuss the impact of three of these four statutes in the realm of sport and physical activity. A similar discussion of the impact of the fourth, Title IX, is found in Chapter 8.

The 14th amendment of the United States Constitution (see Chapter 4) provides constitutional protections against the discriminatory behavior on the part of state actors. Although the 14th amendment may protect a different subset of individuals, it joins the EPA, ADA, Title VII, and Title IX in the work against discrimination.

TITLE VII

Let's take a look at **Title VII** first. Title VII applies only in the workplace; it does not apply to students. Its protections are broader than any of the other three statutes (Title IX, the EPA, and the ADA), because it prohibits discrimination based on more than gender (EPA and Title IX) and more than one basis, such as disability (ADA). Title VII protects against discrimination based on race, color, religion, national origin, and/or sex. The EEOC is charged with Title VII's administrative enforcement. (see Chapter 5 for more details).

Title VII's coverage in the workplace extends both to employees and would-be employees. In addition to the broad protections it offers, Title VII is a particularly useful tool in combating sexual harassment. This is so because of Title VII's clear definitions of sexual harassment and its considerable case law on the topic.

SEXUAL HARASSMENT

For instance, from *Oncala* we have learned that **sexual harassment** does *not* require that the harasser and the victim be of opposite sexes (*Oncala*, 1998). This major step in case law reflects experiential realities both about harassment and discrimination. Also reinforced in *Oncala* is the fact that Title VII's definition of sexual harassment applies to harassment based on sex, gender, *and* sexual orientation realities and perceptions. In short, if the harassment is based on sexual topics, including sexual orientation, and otherwise fits into either the *quid pro quo* or hostile environment definitions of sexual harassment, it is actionable under Title VII.

A paraphrase of the 1984 Policy Statement on Sexual Harassment issued by the Equal Employment Opportunity Commission (EEOC) tells us more about what sexual harassment is: unwelcome sexual overtures or requests or contact or verbal harassment constitute sexual harassment when:

1. the recipient's term or condition of employment hinges on submission to the harassing conduct,
2. submission is used as a basis for employment decisions, or
3. the conduct's purpose or effect is to unreasonably interfere with the recipient's work performance or creates an intimidating, hostile, or offensive work environment. (Equal Employment Opportunity Commission, *Policy on Sexual Harassment,* 1984).

Let's review Title VII's two definitions for sexual harassment. The first category, *quid pro quo,* is the most obvious form. This category involves threats or promises that in return for sexual favors, the victim will be given promotions, higher grades, better working conditions, tenure, or similar rewards.

Hostile environment sexual harassment is more difficult to see. The third part of the EEOC's definition above begins to describe hostile environment sexual harassment. In short, "hostile environment" means that sexual harassment via jokes, unwanted contact, pictures, and so forth, may create an environment in which the victim finds it unreasonably difficult to work or attend school or participate.

Located in the facts of the 1998 U.S. Supreme Court decision in *Faragher v. City of Boca Raton* is the picture of a lifeguard who found the behavior of her immediate supervisors to be sexually harassing (*Faragher,* 1998). After Faragher quit, she filed a Title VII suit against her employer claiming that the sexual harassment had altered the terms and conditions of her employment. In addition to illustrating hostile environment sexual harassment, the *Faragher* decision tells us that liability can be vicariously laid at the door of the employer when the harasser is an employee's immediate supervisor, who has authority over the employee, even when no tangible employment action is taken against the victim.

The *Faragher* decision also tells us that the employer has available an affirmative defense to that vicarious liability. This defense is only available however, if no employment action was taken against the employee. The defense has two required elements:

(a) "the employer exercised reasonable care to prevent and correct promptly any sexually harassing behavior and,
(b) the employee unreasonably failed to take advantage of any preventive or corrective opportunities provided by the employer or to avoid harm otherwise." (*Faragher,* 1998)

The impact of no notice was of importance in the U.S. Supreme Court's 1998 decision in *Gebser v. Lago Vista Independent School District* (*Gebser,* 1998). No notice is required for Title VII vicarious liability to be placed upon an employer whose employee harasses a subordinate. Title VII requires the employer to provide a workplace free of harassment, and lack of knowledge about existing harassment does not deflect the employer's liability. However, is notice required under Title IX in order to place vicarious liability upon the employer when an employee harasses a student? The *Gebser* decision, handed down only four days before the *Faragher* decision, tells us that in Title IX cases, unlike Title VII cases, the employer must have notice of the harassment in order to receive vicarious liability. Notice of the harassment must be given to a school official who has authority to institute corrective measures on the school's or district's behalf *and* then the official must have been deliberately indifferent to the misconduct.

A year later, the Court revisited the issue of notice, but this time with regard to harassment between peers rather than teacher to student. In *Davis*, the Court made it even clearer that notice to a school official with authority to intervene must be present in order to place vicarious liability on the school (*Davis*, 1999). Elementary school student Davis was being harassed by a youngster in her class. The harassment was overt, pervasive, persistent, sexual, gross and disturbing. The teacher, to whom complaints were made, finally moved the students' seats. The harassment continued. A series of complaints were made. The harassment continued. Davis' grades plummeted, and Davis even tried to commit suicide as a result of the unrelenting sexual harassment.

The facts in *Davis* are so appalling that it would seem to have provided sufficient notice to any school official actually carrying out a modicum of official duties that harassment was taking place; however, the Court found that the official *with power to intervene* did not have notice and thus no Title IX liability resulted.

Remember that while no notice of harassment is required in order to impose vicarious Title VII liability, the contrary is true for Title IX. Following the *Davis* decision, publicizing the identity of the correct campus official to receive Title IX complaints became even more important.

THEORIES OF DISCRIMINATION UNDER TITLE VII

Some employment policies and actions are neutral on their face. Perhaps a useful example might be found in a job announcement for an athletic director that requires a successful applicant to have "at least three years of Division I football playing experience." The job announcement appears to be free of gender bias. However, because there is no pool of females who have or are likely to have the required experience and because it would be difficult to demonstrate that the required playing experience was a necessary and related prerequisite to being an athletic director ("a bona fide occupational qualification reasonably necessary to the normal operation of that particular business or enterprise"), the *impact* of the gender-neutral announcement would be disparately harsh on women even though the announcement, on its face, appears to *treat* all applicants alike (Title VII, 1964). Disparate *treatment* would be present if the job announcement boldly said, "Women need not apply."

There are four main theories of liability under Title VII. Those categories are:

- systemic disparate treatment
- individual disparate treatment
- disparate impact
- retaliation

We've already looked at an example of the first, systemic disparate treatment, in our "No women need apply" example. Systemic **disparate treatment** exists when an employer's policies or application of those policies produce treatment that disfavors one group. Disparate treatment means that policies are overtly discriminatory and may be so either on a systemic basis or on an individual basis.

Individual disparate treatment occurs when the employer's policies or their application produces treatment that disfavors a particular individual based on the individual's membership in a protected class. The fact that another member of the same protected class has been treated fairly doesn't dispel the fact that the plaintiff is being treated disparately based on membership in the disfavored class.

When disparate treatment is alleged, the plaintiff can either provide evidence—such as a policy that says, "No women wanted"— or provide inferential evidence concerning the treatment of class members sufficient to meet the weight of establishing a *prima facia* case. Let's use our football-experience-requirement-for-the-athletic-director's-job scenario described above to outline the process. The female plaintiff/applicant for the athletic director's job can prove her case by showing:

1. her membership in a protected class—in this case, sex (alleged discrimination was based on race, sex, religion, etc.), and
2. she applied for the position of athletic director, and
3. she was qualified for the job (understood football in addition to having other qualifications), and
4. she was not hired, and
5. the athletic director's job was either filled by a non-class member (in this case a male) or the position was left open.

If our example involved some sort of discrimination against an *employee* rather than an *applicant,* the plaintiff's list of proofs would be:

a. class member
b. performing satisfactorily
c. discharged or adversely affected by a change in working conditions
d. work assigned to a non-class member

Once the plaintiff has demonstrated discrimination exists, the burden shifts to the employer to show a nondiscriminatory reason for the apparent discrimination. In our athletic director scenario above, the employer might try to do this by presenting evidence that an understanding of football is necessary for a successful athletic director. If the employer's reason is compelling, the plaintiff still has one last opportunity to demonstrate that the reason offered by the employer is merely pretext rather than the true reason for the apparent discrimination. The plaintiff might argue that while a knowledge of football may indeed be a valuable and necessary asset for a successful athletic director over a program that includes football, that knowledge could be acquired in a variety of ways. The plaintiff might continue by showing that the requirement of three years of playing experience is one that doesn't seek a knowledge of football but rather is a requirement that seeks to exclude female applicants.

Much of the same evidentiary effort is required of the plaintiff in a disparate impact case. The only significant difference is that the plaintiff is trying to show that an employer's policies, which appear neutral, produce, when applied, a situation which that improperly disfavors a particular individual or group. Statistical evidence is frequently offered to show the discriminatory impact. For instance, in our scenario, the plaintiff might try to show that there are no females, otherwise qualified, who would possess football Division I experience.

In sum, there are only two defenses to either a disparate treatment or disparate impact Title VII case. They are:

1. The group or individual is not actually disfavored by the disparate impact or disparate treatment or,
2. There is a *bona fide* occupational qualification that requires the disparate treatment or impact.

A *bona fide* occupational qualification is a defense under Title VII, but it is not a universal defense. It cannot be used for disparate treatment or disparate impact based on race or color. A *bona fide* occupational qualification can only be used as a defense for disparate treatment or disparate impact concerning the other areas covered by Title VII: religion, gender, and national origin. It is the burden of the employer to prove a *bona fide* occupational qualification. The employer cannot use client preference: "our students prefer to have male coaches," or "our clients feel more comfortable with Christian camp leaders" as a basis for proving a *bona fide* occupational qualification.

Retaliation, the fourth theory of liability under Title VII, is reasonably self-explanatory. If the employee who complains about either disparate treatment or disparate impact via Title VII is the subject of retaliation for that complaint, a separate theory of liability exists: retaliation.

RELIGION AND TITLE VII

Discrimination based on religion, is allowed under Title VII if, and only if, membership in a particular religion is "a *bona fide* occupational qualification reasonably necessary to the normal operation of that particular business or enterprise *and* if the institution is, in whole or in substantial part, owned, supported, controlled, or managed by a particular religion or by a particular religious corporation, association, or society or if the curriculum of such a school . . . is directed toward the propagation of a particular religion (Title VII, 1964). So, if Oral Roberts University was searching for a new professor to teach religion classes, the search could lawfully exclude applicants based on their religious preferences.

EQUAL PAY ACT

Unlike Title VII, which covers race, color, and other forms of discrimination, the **Equal Pay Act** (EPA) limits its concerns to gender discrimination and, more specifically, gender discrimination in the solitary employment issue of compensation. The EPA prohibits employers from paying a member of one sex differently from a member of the other sex for "equal work on jobs the performance of which requires equal skill, effort, and responsibility, and which are performed under similar working conditions" (Equal Pay Act, 1993). Sport offers an excellent forum in which to see disparity in salaries based on the sex of the employee because of the gender segregation upon which most programs are designed.

Unlike Title VII, the **EPA** requires the identification of a "comparator employee." The comparator employee needs to be someone of the opposite sex who has a higher level of compensation even though the person's work as described above is substantially the same as the plaintiff's work. The comparator employee needs to be a real person employed by the same employer. It doesn't matter if other employees of the opposite sex are treated as badly as the plaintiff; only one comparator employee needs to be identified. Once identified, the plaintiff has the burden of showing that the comparator employee is doing substantially the same work in similar working conditions.

SIMILAR SKILLS

"Similar skills" relate only to those skills actually required by the job. Additional talents, skills, or experiences are irrelevant. Thus, if a male coaches the high school boys' basketball team and a female coaches the girls' basketball team, the fact that the male has the additional skill of being a world-respected opera signer is of no consequence when evaluating whether the two individuals bring equal skills to the job.

JOB TITLES

The EEOC is the administrative enforcement agency for both Title VII and the EPA. The EEOC understands the employment world sufficiently to know that the actual requirements of the job are what needs to be compared rather than titles or unenforced job descriptions.

REVENUE PRODUCTION

Revenue and fund-raising produce interesting issues when evaluating job similarities. If a male coach raises more money than his female counterpart, does it necessarily follow that the male works harder and should be paid more? The EEOC will look beyond the obvious to determine if the male coach's fund-raising efforts are more fully supported by the institution than the female's efforts. It would not be fair if an institution were allowed to create a situation, by supporting the male's efforts, that was then used to rationalize a discriminatory disparity in pay.

RATIONALES FOR DISPARATE SALARIES

The EEOC views the area of athletics as an area in which complex EPA questions arise. To that end, the EEOC has published its *Enforcement Guidance on Sex Discrimination in Compensation of Sports Coaches in Educational Institutions*. The *Guidance* discusses many of the defenses/explanations for disparate pay used in sport situations and their relative validity. Among the defenses/explanations frequently used are the following:

1 a. "You have to pay a male more—everyone does." Reliance on the employee's prior salary as a non-gender-based factor for disparate pay is often offered as a defense.

However, prior salaries are often higher because of prior discriminatory acts at other institutions and/or in society in general and should not be the basis for supporting currently disparate pay scales. Therefore, the employer who wants to use prior salary as a nondiscriminatory basis for paying the male a higher salary needs to show that the prior salary was, in fact, determined by consulting the prior employer, and that the prior salary was nondiscriminatory, and based on the employee's skills, education, and experience, and that the current employer did not rely totally on the prior salary in setting the current one.

2 b. "He demanded more money in the negotiations, and we were afraid we would lose him to the school across town." Negotiation of salaries is not always carried out with members of both sexes. If the employer negotiated the salary with the male candidate but offered a set, take-it-or-leave-it, salary to the female, it would be unlikely that the employer could support a claim that the male candidate had to be paid more just to obtain him as an employee.

3 c. "Our male basketball coach also has the title of Associate Athletic Director." Additional duties, if they are actual duties and not just titles, are a defense to pay disparity only if the extra pay is in fact directly related to and appropriate for the extra duties. In addition, the extra duties cannot have been offered only to the male.

4 d. "Our male basketball coach has three years experience as an assistant volleyball coach and five years as a head coach. Our women's basketball coach has five years' experience as a head coach but only two years' experience as an assistant basketball coach." Experience may be used as a defense to pay disparity but only if the experience is related directly to the specific job and if its presence makes the employee more valuable within that job. Thus it would be difficult to show that a greater number of years of experience as an assistant coach for a different sport was of more value than a slightly shorter experience as an assistant coach within the sport in question.

Title VII and the EPA both work as tools to combat pay discrimination based on sex. Because Title VII does not require the identification of a comparator employee, Title VII is often the easier road for a plaintiff to take. Title IX can also be used to address pay inequities based on sex, but its effectiveness in doing so is not high.

THE ADA AND THE ELEVENTH AMENDMENT

The **11th amendment** of the United States Constitution says, "The Judicial power of the United States shall not be construed to extend to any suit in law or equity, commenced or prosecuted against one of the United States by Citizens of another State, or by Citizens or Subjects of any Foreign State."

Although the text of the 11th amendment may be confusing, its meaning, in the context of our discussion here, can be outlined as follows: States are generally immune from being sued for money damages for violating federal laws. Case law has ignored the details "of another State."

Case law has also limited the immunity granted to the states by the 11th amendment to only *states* and excludes extending the immunity to local, city, or county governments and their agencies.

Let's consider the impact of applying the 11th amendment. Would employees of a state university be covered by the **Americans With Disabilities Act**? The answer is, "No." Would employees of a private school be covered by the Americans With Disabilities Act? The answer is, "Yes," even though their peers across town at the state university are not covered.

It seems unfair for employees and students of a state university to be excluded from the coverage of such important federal legislation as the ADA, but the 11th amendment does exclude them by providing the state with immunity from suit for money damages. The reality is not quite as dim as might be assumed, because all states have enacted *state* statutes that carry at least some of the protections afforded by the ADA (although some of the statutes are quite minimal in their coverage).

Did Congress know that states and state entities would be excluded, via 11th amendment immunity, when it enacted the ADA in 1990? No. Could Congress have done something to bring states within the jurisdiction of the ADA? Probably yes. The legal discussion that surrounds defense claims by states that they are immune from being sued in federal court for money damages due to the impact of the 11th amendment is important to understand as well as being difficult to comprehend. Let's give it a try.

The legal discussion involves an interplay of three parts of the Constitution to determine whether various federal statutes such as the ADA, EPA, Title VII, and Title IX may be successfully used to sue states and state agencies in federal courts. The three parts of the Constitution are:

1.   the 11th amendment,
2.   Section 1 of the 14th amendment, and,
3.   Section 5 of the 14th amendment.

Section 1 of the 14th amendment says, "All persons born or naturalized in the United States, and subject of the jurisdiction thereof, are citizens of the United States and of the State wherein they reside. No State shall make or enforce any law which shall abridge the privileges or immunities of citizens of the United States; *nor shall any State deprive any person of life, liberty, or property without due process of law; nor deny to any person within its jurisdiction the equal protection of the laws."*

Section 5 of the 14th amendment gives Congress the power to enforce Section 1 when it says, "The Congress shall have power to enforce, by appropriate legislation, the provisions of this article."

We seem to have a conflict. Section 5 of the 14th amendment tells Congress it has power to enforce the Equal Protection Clause by making federal laws, but the 11th amendment gives the states immunity from such enforcement. Does this mean that every anti-discrimination law enacted by Congress has no applicability to the states? No, the immunity granted to the states is not absolute, but the federal legislation must meet a two-pronged test in order to bypass the 11th amendment. If the specific law can meet both parts of the two-pronged test, the successful plaintiff can use the law to obtain money damages from the state. The two prongs that must be met to bypass the state's 11th amendment immunity are these:

1.   When Congress passed the law, Congress unequivocally intended to abrogate (bypass) the states' 11th amendment immunity, and
2.   Congress based its authority to pass the law on Section 5 of the 14th amendment's power to enforce Section 1 of the 14th amendment and the use of money damages was "congruent and proportional to the wrong being remedied" (*Board v. Garrett,* 2001).

When a state claims 11th amendment immunity, the two-pronged test is applied to see if, when the federal law in question was enacted, both prongs were met. The court doesn't ask Congress today what it intended yesterday. Instead, it examines the legislative history created at the time of the enactment. The *Federal Register,* which includes much of the debate, transcripts of committee hearings, and supporting documents offered with the bill itself form the main corpus of the legislative history.

Sometimes, because the majority of Congress is supportive of the bill early in its progress through the legislative history, the record of intent or perceived authority is slim. It's logical that there may be less debate or even supporting rhetoric when there is no significant group within Congress whose votes need to be sought. However, the absence of such a record sometimes comes back to haunt Congress when one of its laws is challenged by a state claiming 11th amendment immunity.

When enacting the ADA, Congress supported its action by finding, "historically, society has tended to isolate and segregate individuals with disabilities, and despite some improvements, such forms of discrimination . . . continue to be a serious and pervasive social problem" (Americans With Disabilities Act, 1990 at 12101 (a) (2)). Congress went on to give considerable examples of past discriminatory acts against disabled individuals, some perpetrated by the states and others by private employers. The ADA covers both.

It was reasonably clear from the legislative history that Congress was using Section 5 to enforce Section 1 of the 14th amendment. Thus, the first prong was apparently met. Were the statements and examples of discrimination sufficient to meet the second prong? That was the question addressed by the 2001 U.S. Supreme Court's 5–4 decision in *Board of Trustees of the University of Alabama v. Patricia Garrett (University of Alabama v. Garrett,* 2001).

Patricia Garret, Director of Nursing, needed to take substantial time off work as she successfully fought breast cancer with surgery, radiation and chemotherapy. When she returned to work she was demoted to a lower paying position. The ADA requires 'reasonable accommodation' in a variety of forms including, "(A) making existing facilities used by employees readily accessible to and usable by individuals with disabilities; and (B) job restructuring, part-time or **modified work schedules,** (emphasis added) reassignment to a vacant position, acquisition or modification of equipment or devices, appropriate adjustment or modifications of examinations, training materials or policies, the provision of qualified readers or interpreters, and other similar accommodations for individuals with disabilities" (Americans With Disabilities Act, 1990 at 12111 (9)).

It would seem that Garrett's breast cancer fit into the ADA's definition of a disability:

"(a) a physical or mental impairment that substantially limits one or more of the major life activities of such individual; (b) a record of such an impairment; or (c) being regarded as having such an impairment" (Americans With Disabilities Act, 1990 at 12111 (8)).

Garrett filed an ADA lawsuit seeking money damages against her employer, the University of Alabama, a state entity. The University of Alabama claimed 11th amendment immunity from Garrett's ADA claims. The U.S. Supreme Court decided that although Congress may have met the first prong of the test, it failed to meet the second. Congress had failed to include sufficient specific examples of state entity acts of discrimination as well as failing to demonstrate the irrationality of the state's behavior in trying to preserve scarce state funds by assigning employees who, unlike Garrett, had no need for reasonable accommodation. The rationality test rather than the strict scrutiny test was used by the Court because discrimination on the basis of disability does not rise to the level of 'suspect class' (See Chapter 4 for a discussion of 'suspect class') and thus does not require strict scrutiny.

As a review, reread the opening scenario for this chapter. Which sibling do you think was victorious? Why was the other sibling's case unsuccessful?

Because Congress's actions in passing the ADA only met the first prong in the eyes of the Court, the ADA was found to not abrogate a state's 11th amendment immunity to be free of suit for money damages in federal court. The U.S. Supreme Court has not yet heard a case in which the 11th amendment was used as a defense against Title VII, the Equal Pay Act or Title IX. Each of these three federal antidiscrimination statutes carries with it its own legislative history and source of Congressional power for its enactment. Thus, applying the result in the *University of Alabama v. Garrett* ADA case to these other federal statutes would be foolhardy until such time as the U.S. Supreme Court actually renders a specific decision.

THE ADA AND PROFESSIONAL SPORT

Three months after the Garrett decision, in *PGA v. Casey Martin*, the United States Supreme Court answered two narrow but interesting questions about the applicability of the ADA within the context of professional sport (*PGA*, 2001). The two questions, unlike the very broad question in the *Garrett* case, are narrowly applicable in a legal sense, but perhaps in a philosophical sense provide for a potentially insightful and heated debate about the meaning and place of sport and competition in society.

The Garrett case involved the applicability of the ADA's Title I (employment). Title II of the ADA covers public services such as access to subways, public school libraries, and city government offices. Title III of the ADA applies to public accommodations and services operated by private entities such as Little League Baseball and, as we learned in the *PGA Tour v. Casey Martin* case, the Professional Golf Association. ADA's Title III requires that "no individual shall be discriminated against on the basis of disability in the full and equal enjoyment of the goods, services, facilities, privileges, advantages or accommodations of any place of public accommodation by any person who owns, leases, or operates a place of public accommodation" (Americans With Disabilities Act, 1990 at 12182 (b) (2) (A) (ii)). To what degree does a private entity have to go to avoid discrimination? The ADA requires that *"reasonable"* modifications' are required unless the private entity "can demonstrate that making such modifications would fundamentally alter the nature of such . . accommodations.

The two questions to be answered by the *PGA v. Martin* case are:

1. Is the PGA Tour a provider of public accommodation, thus bringing it within   the jurisdiction of the ADA, and
2. Does allowing Martin, who suffers from a circulatory problem in his leg, the use of a golf cart to travel the course fundamentally alter the nature of the game/competition?

There is no 11th amendment problem in the *PGA Tour v. Martin* case because the PGA Tour is not a state entity, but legislative history is still important to the case. The legislative history surrounding the ADA indicates that Congress intended Title III to apply to a broad definition of "public accommodations" and that Congress intended the list to be liberally construed.

The second question, that of whether access to a golf cart fundamentally altered the game was one of heated debate, at least outside the halls of the Supreme Court. Certainly, altering the diameter of the hole, the Court stated, would fundamentally alter the game, but not the tangential issue of riding in a golf cart. The issue of creating an uneven playing field by having some players fatigued by walking the course while Martin rode the course was dispatched by the Court's acceptance of the uncontested District Court's finding that Casey's physical disability creates more fatigue through riding than the fatigue generated by his competitors through walking. Thus the Court determined that providing Martin with a cart was a required and reasonable accommodation under the ADA.

DISABILITIES AND THE HIRING PROCESS

Title I of the ADA applies to employment situations. It provides that "no covered entity shall discriminate against a qualified individual with a disability because of the disabilities of such individual in regard to job application procedures, the hiring, advancement, or discharge of employees, employee compensation, job training, and other terms, conditions, and privileges of employment" (Americans With Disabilities Act, 1990 at 12112). Pat Garrett, the plaintiff in the *University of Alabama v. Garrett* case discussed above, was demoted and her salary decreased when she returned to work from her battle with breast cancer. If the University of Alabama had been a private or city university rather than a state university, evidence relating to whether the demotion and pay cut were prohibited by the Title I statutory language would have been considered. There would be little doubt that the demotion and pay cut would have fallen into the prohibitions outlined in Title I above.

The ADA covers job applicants as well as employees. It is for this reason that the selection of interview questions needs to exclude any which have to do with the applicant's disabilities. If the applicant is otherwise 'qualified' (meets the stated minimum requirements), but would need reasonable accommodation in order to carry out the duties of the job, the presence of the disability may not be negatively taken into account in the hiring' process. Therefore, questions during the interview process about an applicant's disabilities provide the not hired, disabled candidate with a logical belief that the hiring decision was based on the disability, whether it was or not. It is difficult for the hiring entity to justify why questions about the disability were asked during the interview if the answers were of no significance in the hiring decision. Thus it is best not to ask the questions in the first place.

Once the job is offered to the disabled candidate, the employer may lawfully inquire about the need for reasonable accommodation. This post offer inquiry is allowed because it no longer can have an impact on whether an offer is to be made.

MANAGEMENT GUIDELINES

The reasonable accommodation required by the ADA may, when viewed by tradition-bound eyes, not appear "reasonable." However, managers who work for non-state entities, need to take a nontraditional view and meet the needs of disabled clients, students and employees with creative, inclusive solutions to difficulties of access and participation. Often, the creative, inclusive solutions are more easily found if a positive dialogue is developed between the disabled person and the manager.

Sexual harassment complaints are one of the most difficult issues with which to deal. However, clear definitions of prohibited behavior, well disseminated policies concerning sexual harassment, procedures for investigating and reaching conclusions about claims of sexual harassment are all factors which make the issue easier to deal with fairly. A good manager will hire good supervisors, take complaints seriously and protect both "sides" judiciously. A good manager will tolerate no borderline behavior and will set good examples both publicly and behind closed doors.

Salary scales which are created with detail, disseminated, and adhered to, help keep even the fair minded employer on track. A review of all salaries within the department will help spot inequities. Dealing with inequities by raising the salaries of those which are inexplicably out of line without cutting the higher salaries helps avoid ill feelings within a department. Raising everyone's salary by the same percentage is not necessarily equitable. By definition, doing so will cause the higher salaries to increase more than the lower salaries. The disparity between the haves and have-nots will increase as will frustrations within a department. EPA, Title VII and ADA complaints are generally born of frustration.

If someone has a title, they should be expected to perform the duties associated with the title. Using fancy administrative titles to mask inequitable pay scales is a generally ineffective undertaking. If duties, with or without a new title, are added to an employee's portfolio, compensation relating to those duties also needs to be added.

When recruiting a new employee, carefully ponder whether you use the same intensity and creativity in the recruitment and negotiation process for your male and female candidates. If you don't, do.

When interviewing candidates for a new position, discuss with the interviewing committee members what types of questions will be asked and why others should not be asked.

Consider also the format of a question; the same information can be obtained through a "legal" question as through an illegal one in most instances. Focus on the job related information you are seeking.

CHAPTER SUMMARY

Title VII, the EPA, the ADA and Title IX all play a role in increasing equity. The statutes are useful tools, positive guides and yet also strong weapons when their provisions have been ignored. They have an impact on various populations including in the aggregate, race, religion, color, disability, gender and national origin. They have significant differences in their applicability to specific circumstances. For instance, the ADA does not apply to those suing a state/state entity in federal court for money damages.

CASE STUDIES

CASE 9.1

After three years of coaching on the field from a wheelchair, Coach Smith was distressed when the Little League Baseball administration adopted a new policy banning wheelchair bound coaches from on-field coaching. Although the Little League did not offer any evidence of the presence of an on-field wheelchair bound coach creating a danger to players, the Little League made that argument. Although the ADA does not require a public accommodation (Title III) such as the Little League to permit a disabled person to participate when their participation 'poses a direct threat to the health or safety of others,' the Court rejected the Little League's unsupported argument about the danger. Do you agree with the court's decision? Why? Create an more compelling argument on the side of the Little League and then create a compelling argument on the side of the coach.

[Adapted from *Anderson v. Little League Baseball, Inc.* 794 F. Supp. 342 (1992)]

CASE 9.2

Jan was an exceptional basketball player. Several Division I colleges offered Jan "full ride" scholarships, including Best Big Time Sport Public University (BBTSPU). Jan accepted BBTSPU's offer and moved to campus. Just before the season started all of BBTSPU's varsity athletes underwent an annual physical examination. Because there was a medical school on campus, the examination was quite rigorous. Jan's examination discovered a serious heart defect which did not affect Jan's day-to-day life but which might be a life threatening problem during strenuous exertion such as might occur in a Division I basketball program.

The director of athletics, fearful that Jan's health might be compromised, refused to allow Jan to join the basketball team and instead proposed that Jan serve as the official scorekeeper for the team. After reading *Knapp v. Northwestern University*, 101 F 3d 473 (7th Cir. 1996), which dealt with a similar case but which was based on the Rehabilitation Act rather than the ADA, Jan sued under Title II of the ADA. Title II of the ADA is based on section 504 of the Rehabilitation Act. In order to be successful, Jan would need to show the elements required for an ADA Title II claim which are:

1. Jan was a qualified individual with a disability,
2. Jan was "otherwise qualified" (qualified except for the disability) for the activity of Division I basketball,
3. Jan was denied participation on the team solely because of the heart defect (disability), and
4. that the athletic program at BBTSPU is a public entity.

   Which of the four elements would be most difficult for Jan to prove? (Hint: Is Jan actually disabled?) Consider whether playing basketball is a major life function compared with walking, breathing, eating, etc. See Chapter 5 for more details.

KEY TERMS

11th amendment
14th amendment, sections 1 and 5
Americans with Disabilities Act-ADA
Comparator employee
Compensatory damages
Disparate treatment
Disparate impact
Equal Pay Act (EPA)
Hostile environment
Money damages
Punitive damages
Quid pro quo
Sexual harassment
Title VII
Title IX

QUESTIONS FOR DISCUSSION

1. How should the hostility of a hostile environment sexual harassment situation be measured? Should it be viewed through the eyes of the harasser's intent or through the eyes of the recipient or by some objective standard?
2. If you were wrongly accused of sexually harassing a coworker, how would you hope that the issue would be handled by your supervisor?
3. Find a classmate to create a debate on both sides of the *Casey Martin* case. Then switch sides and debate again.
4. Identify a worker at your place of employment. Then identify a comparator employee for that person. Is there a disparity in pay between the two?

5.   Read the *Stanley* cases and discuss the issues involved in determining comparability of work load in athletics.

REFERENCES

Americans with Disabilities Act, 42 U.S.C. section 12101-12213, 1990.

Anderson v. Little League Baseball, Inc., 794 F Supp. 342 (1992).

Board of Trustees of the University of Alabama v. Patricia Garrett, 2001 U. S. Lexis 1700.

Davis v. Monroe County Board of Education, 526 U.S. 629 (1999)

Enforcement Guidance on Sex Discrimination in Compensation of Sports Coaches in Educational Institutions. EEOC, Number 915.002, October 29, 1997

Equal Pay Act, 29 USC section 206 (d)(1), 1963.

Faragher v. City of Boca Raton, 534 U.S. 775, 118 S. Ct. 2275 (1998)

Gebser v. Lago Vista Independent School District, 524 U.S. 274, 118 S. Ct. 1989 (1998)

Knapp v. Northwestern University, 101 F 3d 473 (7th Cir. 1996).

Oncala v. Sundowner Offshore Services, 523 U.S. 75 (1998).

PGA Tour, Inc. v. Casey Martin, 121 S. Ct. 1879, 149 L. Ed. 2d 904 (2001).

Stanley v. University of California, 13 F3rd 1313 (9th Cir. 1994)

Stanley v. University of California, 178 F3d 1069 (9th Cir. 1999)

Title VII, Section 2000e-2(e), 1994.

PART IV

PROGRAM MANAGEMENT AND CONTROL

CHAPTER 10

CONTRACTS IN SPORT AND PHYSICAL ACTIVITY

Private Ivy University is about to open another intercollegiate basketball season, hosting a team from a distant state. The field house is packed to the rafters. Season ticket holders are awash in the luxury of their private boxes. The Private Ivy boosters have a special cheering section. The strobe lights are in place. Several hundred maintenance workers, security guards, police officers, food servers, building engineers, ticket takers, concession operators, parking attendants, site supervisors, and systems technicians are at hand, as well as the cadre of coaches, trainers, media representatives, volunteers, conference supervisory personnel, and game officials—all poised for action.

How did everybody get there? Many are university employees or volunteers. Scores of others, or their employers, are *parties to a contract*. In other words, persons, nonprofit institutions, and businesses, have entered into formalized agreements or contracts to provide goods and services for the respective advantage of all parties. Even the opposing team's institution signed a contract to come to Private Ivy and play basketball. Contracts are, in a significant sense, the oil that make the gears of enterprise go around.

Thus, legal relationships between people and organizations are often the product of and defined by agreements that they make with one another. Obligations created when two or more persons promise each other to do "x" in return for "y" are recognized in the law as *contracts*. In the above scenario, we can readily see that contracts are widely used in the areas of sport and physical activity: contracts to play an opponent; contracts to perform services; contracts for the sale of goods; contracts of employment, to name a few.

LEARNING OBJECTIVES

Upon completion of this chapter, the student will be able to:

1. identify and explain the elements of a contract,
2. explain and give practical illustrations of the nature and relative enforceability of oral and written contracts, oral modifications to written contracts, and situations involving the parol evidence rule, and
3. enumerate practical guidelines for the use of contracts in the management of sport.

CONTRACT APPLICATIONS IN SPORT AND PHYSICAL ACTIVITY

For most of us, it's virtually impossible to go through our lives without being in some way affected by contracts. We recognize the importance of a contract when we purchase a car, rent an apartment, or accept a new job, but we tend to overlook most of the indirect interactions that, nevertheless, affect our activities.

A typical event such as an intercollegiate basketball game, for example, requires the coordination of an array of independent activities. To list but a few: licenses and permits may need to be obtained, tickets must be printed, special equipment may need to be purchased or rented, security must be provided, food and beverages will be sold, game officials and other event management personnel must be in place, parking facilities need to be managed, traffic will need to be controlled before and after the event, and HVAC and electrical systems need to be maintained. The college or university typically engages independent contractors to conduct, manage, or supervise some portion of these activities. These service providers and vendors enter into written agreements with the institution that specify the responsibilities of each of the involved parties. Indeed, even those functions provided by employees of the institution will probably be subject to a union employment contract.

WHAT IS A CONTRACT?

Reduced to simple terms, a contract is an agreement between two or more parties that imposes some kind of obligation or responsibility on each. Contracts may exist in oral or written form and must be considered in light of their **effectiveness** as well as their **legal enforceability.** The effectiveness of any given contract is a simple matter of whether it results in the actions required of each of the parties. For example, if Pat promises to pay Chris a sum of money in return for Chris' support of a new venture that Pat is undertaking, the effectiveness of the contract will be a simple matter of whether Chris provides the required support and Pat pays the appropriate sum of money. If either Pat or Chris feels that the other has breached the contract, the question of whether the court would take action to enforce it depends on the presence of a number of specific elements.

First there would have to be evidence of a **meeting of the minds.** In other words, the parties to the contract must have a mutual understanding of the context and content of their agreement. If, for example, Chris thought that "support" meant providing a verbal endorsement, and Pat thought that it included actively sharing in the planning and development of the marketing strategy, there was no meeting of the minds. If, on the other hand, both viewed "support" as meaning the provision of a specific number of written and verbal endorsements, each party would have the same understanding of the other's promise, and the requirement for a meeting of the minds would have been met.

Contracts are created when one or more parties make an **offer,** which is, in return, **accepted** as stated by another party or parties. Once Chris accepts Pat's offer, each party has made a promise. If, on the other hand, Chris accepts but under different terms or accepts part, but not all, of the offer, that communication is known as a **counteroffer.** A counteroffer is, in essence, a rejection of Pat's offer. Therefore, Pat would need to accept Chris's counteroffer if a contract is to be created. To have a legally enforceable contract, there must be some form of **consideration.** Something of value must be exchanged. In our example, Pat receives Chris' support while Chris, in turn, receives the agreed-upon compensation. Thus, something of value has been promised for exchange between the parties, and the requirement for consideration has been met. The enforceability of the contract also depends on the **specificity of the terms** used. Ambiguous language in a contract can lead to complications should the contract be litigated. The contract must be sufficiently specific about material items such as dates of performance, amount of compensation, identification of persons who will act, and so forth so that the parties share an understanding of what's required under their respective promises. If, in our contract example, Pat believes that Chris will personally deliver 10 testimonials endorsing Pat's new product, while Chris believes that a single personal appearance would suffice followed by nine public references to Chris's endorsement, the wording of the agreement lacks sufficient specificity to guarantee that both parties share an understanding of the requirements.

All parties to a contract must possess sufficient **legal capacity** for the contract to be held binding and enforceable. Under the law, minors and persons who suffer from mental incapacity cannot be held to binding contractual agreements. Contracts signed by such persons are generally considered **voidable.** Minors, for instance, may enforce agreements they make, but they can also revoke them at will and remain free from contractual enforcement. Assume, for the sake of our continuing example, that Pat is a 16-year-old child prodigy. Under the previously described contract conditions, Chris provided the first three of 10 scheduled endorsements, at which point Pat decided that verbal endorsements were not having the desired impact and, unilaterally, pulled out of the agreement. Because of Pat's age, the contract was voidable from the very beginning. It's extremely unlikely that Chris will be able to require Pat to complete the contract. The court may, however, be willing to award Pat compensation for the three completed endorsements since Pat has received the **tangible benefits** of Chris' efforts in this regard. The reverse, however, would not be true. If Chris decided after three endorsements that the product was not of sufficient quality to justify the claims and chose to forego the last seven testimonials, Pat, as a minor, could probably hold Chris to the remainder of the contract. The contract can only be enforced against Chris, the party who has legal capacity. For this reason, contracts involving minors are commonly made with their parents or legal representatives upon whom the requirements can be enforced.

Finally, the courts will rarely enforce a contract that has, at its core, an **illegal subject.** For example, a contract between two people to divide proceeds of illegal gambling earnings or to purchase a large quantity of anabolic steroids for their own use would likely be held by the courts to be in violation of public policy and thus unenforceable. Neither Chris nor Pat would ever do such a thing and, even if they did, they would have more sense than to expect the courts to help them enforce the contract, so we won't try to stretch this issue into our example.

Certain types of contracts are governed by a nationally promulgated series of laws based on a "uniform" statute known as the Uniform Commercial Code. Although specific provisions of the Uniform Commercial Code have been modified from state to state, some form of the Code is the law of the land in every state. Typically, the type of contracts covered are, as the name implies, **commercial transactions.** These would include contracts for the sale of goods, such as uniforms, basketballs, and equipment. Also included is the law governing **negotiable instruments**—checks, bills of lading, letters of credit, and other documents used to facilitate the payment of monies for the sale of goods. A third category of goods covered under the Uniform Commercial Code as enacted in the various states is that of **secured transactions.** These are contracts in which one party pledges or gives an interest in goods as security for the transaction. Examples of a secured transaction would be the purchaser of athletic equipment giving a security interest or a right of a seller to take back equipment should the bill not be paid.

WHAT IF YOU DON'T CALL IT A CONTRACT?

It's not necessary to label an agreement as a contract in order for the courts to view it as such. The following written materials have been viewed, in some contexts, as the substantive equivalent of contracts, and thus have been enforced by the courts:

Personnel manuals
By-laws of an association
Company employee bulletins
Procedures manuals
College catalogs
Published rules and regulations
Operations manuals
Disciplinary rules
Waivers, permissions, releases, and other exculpatory documents

CONTRACTS AND THE COURTS

WRITTEN VERSUS ORAL CONTRACTS

Contrary to popular belief, a contract need not always be in written form. There are many examples of valid, enforceable and binding oral contracts in the field of sport and physical activity. Still, a party seeking to enforce a contract in court faces a much more daunting task when it has not been reduced to written form. The problems of proving what, in fact, constituted the specific elements of an oral "meeting of the minds" can be insurmountable. Conversely, in the case of a written contract, under the law, the written terms generally are said to "speak for themselves."

While all contracts do not have to be in writing to be enforceable, certain types of contracts will not be enforced unless they have been reduced to written form and signed by the party against whom enforcement is sought. This concept is referred to in law as the **statute of frauds.** Examples of contracts that must be in writing are contracts that convey an interest in real property, contracts for the sale of goods valued at more than $500, contracts to answer for the debt of another; and contracts that will not be performed within one year of their creation.

A bigger problem with regard to the enforceability of oral agreements occurs when an oral modification is made to a previously existing written contract. Such modifications are extremely difficult to prove. Thus, the same principles that led you to commit the original contract to written form should dictate that any subsequent changes be similarly formalized.

PAROL EVIDENCE RULE

If a written contract is complete and unambiguous on its face, the parol evidence rule dictates that the court will not consider items outside of the contract such as prior oral understandings, interpretations, or other written material. Thus, a contract providing for the purchase of athletic equipment, which has complete terms and details of the transaction and is intended as the final expression of the parties, cannot be altered by such things as evidence of negotiations or the oral understandings of any of the parties prior to the signing of the final written agreement. A relatively common exception to the parol evidence rule is seen in the case of written documents that are ambiguous, or where it is alleged that the party was defrauded prior to entering into the contract. Here, the court will normally consider parol evidence.

BREACH OF CONTRACT

A breach of contract occurs when one of the parties fails to fulfill promises made in the contract. An **immaterial** or **partial breach** of contract is relatively minor or insignificant and generally will not cause the remainder of the contract to be ruled invalid. A **material** or **total breach,** on the other hand, usually excuses the injured party from fulfilling their promises and affords them the opportunity to sue for breach of contract.

JUDICIAL REMEDIES FOR BREACH OF CONTRACT

A party who sues for breach of contract must request the particular form of relief desired. This is known in the law as **election of remedies.** In most cases, a party seeks to recover **damages** by way of a remedy for a breach of contract. The obvious efficiency of the remedy of money damages is that they ideally allow the nonbreaching parties to be restored to the condition they would have been in had the contract not been breached. There are, however, instances where court-ordered payment of damages may not provide adequate relief to the injured party.

Sometimes a party will ask the court to enforce the contract—that is, to require the breaching party to honor the terms of the contract, either by completing the promised transaction or by fulfilling the promised act. This remedy is known as **specific perfor-mance.** The remedy of specific performance is often sought where the asset that consti-tutes the subject matter of the contract is particularly unique (e.g., a parcel of real estate). Additionally, a court may issue an **injunction.** This is a special form of court order that directs a party to perform a particular act or prohibits them from doing so. If, for ex-ample, a regional athletic association contracted with a local college for the use of their stadium for regional soccer championships, and two weeks before the event the college decided to pull out of the agreement, the courts might issue an injunction requiring that the stadium be made available for the event, as stated in the contract. Also, while the courts do not normally impose the remedy of specific performance on contracts for per-sonal services, some courts have granted relief to professional teams whose athletes or coaches have induced breaches of contract.

Finally, a court can issue an order of **rescission,** which has the effect of canceling the contract and restoring all parties to their original positions, or an order of **reformation** that reforms or rewrites the contract to conform to what the court determines to have been the original intent and agreement of the parties.

Some laws prevent a party from enforcing a contract with a government agency unless certain prerequisites, such as prior notice of a claim, are met. For example, a New Jersey law, the New Jersey Contractual Liability Act, requires any person who enters into a contract with the State of New Jersey to notify the state in writing of any situation or occurrence that could result in a claim that the state has breached a contract. There are time limits for the notice to be given, and a party who enters into a contract with the state may not start a lawsuit until the expiration of 90 days from the date the claim is filed (New Jersey Statutes, Title 59).

In addition, certain contracts with the federal government or an agency of the Fed-eral government are subject to federal laws that govern the enforcement of such contracts. For example, the Tucker Act (28 USC) generally requires that claims against the federal government in excess of $10,000 must be brought in a particular court—the Court of Federal Claims. The Contracts Dispute Act (41 USC) mandates that certain contract disputes with the federal government are subject to administrative adjudication, after which appeals can be made to the federal courts.

MANAGEMENT GUIDELINES

1.   Remember that, as a general rule, the best and most binding contracts are created with the advice and assistance of an attorney. The greater the value of the goods or services involved, the more consideration you should give to using legal counsel.

2.   If you're making an agreement with another person or organization, and if you really care whether they live up to their end of the bargain, be sure you have a written contract that clearly and specifically identifies all relevant items and issues.

3.   Be certain the contract clearly and specifically identifies all relevant items and is-sues.

4.   Be sure that all parties have the legal capacity to enter into a legal contract. If minors are involved, be sure to secure the signatures of their legal representatives.

5.   Before you enter into a contract on behalf of your employer, be sure that you have

the legal authority to do so. Employers should develop clear policies with regard to the question of which, if any, employees may execute contracts on their behalf, and the limits of the commitments or expenditures they can make. This information should be shared with commonly used vendors and contractors. If a party to a contract reasonably believes that an employee has the authority to contract on the employer's behalf, the employer may be obligated to perform even though the employee actually had no such authority.

6.   If you cared enough to commit the contract to writing in the first place, don't accept verbal modifications afterward.

7.   Pay careful attention to such things as college catalogs, personnel manuals, organizational by-laws, and the like. Often these are recognized as the legal equivalent of a contract. If, for instance, you enrolled at Laybak and Reid College in order to pursue a program outlined in their current catalog, and that program was discontinued in your second year without provision for the completion of currently enrolled students, you might be able to successfully pursue an action for breach of contract.

8.   In general, consider the following when electing remedies. If you believe that the other party acted fraudulently, and you have not suffered significant monetary damage, seek rescission. Your best bet is to be restored to precontract conditions and be free from the fraudulent contractor. If you believe that the problem is the result of an honest mistake on the part of one or more of the parties, seek reformation. In essence, the courts can put things right and say "Go and sin no more." Seek specific performance only when the issue involves some very unique product object or service that cannot be obtained or accomplished in any other reasonable manner. A contractor who has been forced to perform as a result of a breach of contract action is unlikely to be particularly enthusiastic or to provide much beyond the minimal legal requirements. For most other situations, monetary damages will probably be the most reasonable option.

CASE STUDIES

CASE 10.1   THE TERMS OF A CONTRACT

On December 18, 1979, Franklin "Pepper" Rodgers was removed from his position of Head Football Coach at Georgia Institute of Technology with just over two years remaining on his contract. His employer, the Georgia Tech Athletic Association (a nonprofit organization managed by the Athletic Director of the University), continued to pay his salary through the end of his contract. However, the contract of employment stated that Coach Rodgers was entitled to a number of "perquisites." These perquisites were approximately 29 in number and included automobile expenses, secretarial services, country club memberships, housing, insurance, tickets to sporting events, and profits from television and radio shows and football camps.

Although the court found the term "perquisites," as used in Rodgers' employment contract, ambiguous, the employer argued that, since the contract specified that Rodgers was entitled to the perquisites "as an employee of the Association," he would be entitled to only those perquisites that all Association employees receive. Coach Rodgers, on the other hand, argued that all 29 items were part of his compensation and thus the consideration for his agreement to serve as Head Football Coach. The court took an analytical approach to Pepper Rodgers' 29 perquisites. Three such perquisites, secretarial and administrative assistant services and reimbursement for attendance at conventions and clinics, were directly related to his responsibilities as Football Coach and thus, upon his being relieved of those responsibilities, the underlying support services were no longer necessary.

Certain other perquisites had, in fact, been discontinued by the university long before Coach Rodgers' services were terminated. Other perquisites were, in fact, gifts from parties outside the university made with no promise that they would continue. In fact, Coach Rodgers admitted that he did not receive all of the gifts mentioned in the list of perquisites every year of his contract.

In total, eight of the 29 perquisites were excluded as an element of damages. The remaining 21 items were permitted by the court to be proved by Coach Rodgers. The Georgia Tech Athletic Association and Coach Rodgers subsequently settled the lawsuit. Nevertheless, the lesson is clear. Employment contracts need to be professionally drafted so as to avoid ambiguities that can lead to litigation. [*Rodgers v. Georgia Tech Athletic Association, 303 SE 2nd, 467*]

CASE 10.2 SCHOLARSHIPS AS CONTRACTS

Gregg Taylor was a heavily recruited high school football player who attended Wake Forest University on a football scholarship. To obtain the scholarship, Gregg and his father signed a document drafted by the university. Gregg agreed that his grant-in-aid would be for four years if Gregg conducted himself "in accordance with the rules of the [Atlantic Coast] Conference, the NCAA, and the Institution [Wake Forest University]." Gregg also agreed to maintain his athletic eligibility under the rules of the Atlantic Coast Conference and the university, including the university's training rules for intercollegiate athletics.

Gregg played football in 1967. At the end of his first semester, his grade average was 1.0—well below the 1.35 grade average required of a Wake Forest freshman. After the start of the spring semester, Gregg notified the football coach that he would not appear at spring practice until his grades improved. In the spring semester of 1968, Gregg's average improved, but Gregg did not play football in 1968. As a result, in the spring of 1969, Wake Forest held a hearing at which time the faculty athletic committee of the University indicated to Gregg that they would recommend that his scholarship be terminated.

Gregg sued for breach of contract, claiming as damages the $5,500 he would have received as his scholarship funds during the school years that he did not play football. The court ruled that the scholarship was predicated on both athletic and academic achievement, and it was Gregg's responsibility under the contract to maintain a grade point average sufficient to make him eligible. He was also required to attend practice with other players, but he failed to do so. Thus, the university complied with its end of the bargain, but Gregg did not. Gregg Taylor lost his case for breach of contract against Wake Forest University. [*Taylor v. Wake Forest University, 191 SE 2nd, 379*]

CASE 10.3 "TICKETS, PLEASE"

In 1981, Max Rayle paid Bowling Green State University $2,000 for the right to obtain two "chair seats" in the Bowling Green "Stadium Club." The Stadium Club provided enclosed seating for Bowling Green home football games. The payment of $1,000 per seat gave Rayle the right to purchase season tickets and pay a service charge each year in exchange for reserved seating in the Stadium Club for each home game and complimentary refreshments. Each year from 1981 through 1997, Rayle purchased his season tickets at prices ranging from $32 to $75 and paid the required service charge of $50 to $75 per seat.

In 1997, in anticipation of planned renovations to the Stadium Club, the university notified Rayle and all other Stadium Club season ticket holders that the total cost per seat would be $1,000 per year for the next five years. Rayle was advised to notify the university by a certain date if he was interested in keeping his seats or, in the alternative, the university would "buy back" the seats for $2,000 and offer seating at a different price elsewhere in the stadium.

In response to this letter, Rayle wrote the university complaining about the increased prices. Thereafter, the university sent Rayle a check for $2,000 as a refund for his seats. Rayle wrote back stating that he did not consent to a new assessment and he would not accept the offer of $2,000. In fact, Rayle did not cash the $2,000 check.

The university wrote back stating that his seats were reassigned. Rayle sued the university for breach of contract. The court ruled that the contract gave Rayle the right to keep his two seats only if he paid the annual price of two season tickets and the service fees. The original contract did not contain a "cap" of the service fees, so Rayle was bound to accept or reject an increase that the university was permitted to charge, under the terms of the contract. This case illustrates the concept of *offer* and *counteroffer*. Each year, when Rayle paid the price charged by the university, he accepted the offer for Stadium Club privileges. When Rayle rejected the university's offer in 1997, there was no contract for the ensuing season. [*Rayle v. Bowling Green State University, 739 NE 2nd, 1260*]

CHAPTER SUMMARY

Contracts are important because they define the legal relationships among organizations and individuals employed by or supplying goods and services to programs of sport and physical activity. Written contracts are preferable, in all cases, to oral agreements. Some agreements, in fact, are required to be in writing for them to be enforceable. While there are several judicial remedies available for violations of contracts, it's best to avoid such problems by using the services of an attorney in the development of all significant contracts. Finally, attention should be given to the written materials promulgated by organizations, as these will often be construed and enforced by the legal system as contracts.

KEY TERMS

Acceptance
Consideration
Counteroffer
Damages
Effectiveness
Election of remedies
Enforceability
Immaterial or partial breach of contract
Injunction
Legal capacity
Material or total breach of contract
Meeting of the minds
Negotiable instruments
Offer
Parol evidence rule
Reformation
Rescission
Specific performance
Specificity of terms
Statute of frauds
Uniform Commercial Code
Voidable contracts

QUESTIONS FOR DISCUSSION

The Hardrock High School athletic director is currently negotiating with the Flab Fighters Fitness Club, a well-respected commercial facility, for a program whereby the school pays the club to provide individualized year-round fitness programming for all athletes from the high school. The purpose of the program is to provide targeted fitness training for athletes while avoiding the need for expensive facility development and staff expansion at the school.

Discuss the pros and cons of a written contract for this program.

What issues or items should be covered in the contract?

Suggest possible ways in which this contract might be breached, and suggest remedies for each.

ADDITIONAL READINGS

Carpenter, L.J. (2000). *Legal concepts in sport: A primer.* Champaign, IL: Sagamore Publishing.

Wong, G.M. (1994). *Essentials of amateur sports law.* Westport, CT: Praeger Publishers.

CHAPTER 11

EMPLOYMENT

Susie was a full-time employee at Suburban University, where she served as the women's basketball coach and assistant athletic director. SU's men's basketball coach, Bud, had the additional title of associate athletic director but had no significant duties relating to the administrative title.

SU paid Bud $60,000 per year, and his full-time assistant coach, Fred, was paid $35,000. Susie received a total of $25,000 for her responsibilities as women's basketball coach and assistant athletic director. Susie had two part-time assistant coaches who were paid $1,000 each by Susie, not SU.

SU lacked any written policies concerning salary scales for either coaches or athletic administrative personnel. Both Bud and Susie had similar coaching backgrounds, degrees, and years of experience, with the exception that Susie had an increasingly winning record and was more active in professional associations. Both Bud and Susie arrived at SU in the same year.

SU's athletic director, Frank has been heard berating Susie's physical appearance and discussing her bra size at staff meetings (where Susie was the only female present), and he has told the other coaches in the conference that Susie's sexual preference is "questionable."

Susie repeatedly requested salary increases, to no avail. She repeatedly requested Frank to stop his harassing and demeaning behavior toward her, also to no avail.

After receiving a Right to Sue letter from the Equal Employment Opportunity Commission (EEOC), Susie filed suit in federal court against SU alleging violations of **Title VII, Title IX,** and the **Equal Pay Act (EPA).**

SU argued that Bud's higher salary was due to his having received a "bonus" for having won a championship eight years earlier and because his duties as head men's basketball coach involved greater responsibility than Susie's, including supervising two full-time assistant coaches. On the witness stand, Frank, much to the chagrin of SU, testified that Bud's and Susie's duties were the same except that Susie had more responsibility because of her assistant athletic director duties. The answer to the next question put to Frank was particularly disconcerting to SU's attorney:

"Q: If their duties were similar, why were Bud and Susie paid dissimilar amounts?"

"A: I'd never pay a girl as much as a man."

After a few hours of deliberation, the jury awarded Susie $800,000. [Some, but not all of the facts in this scenario are similar to *Perdue v. City University of New York et al.,* 13 F. Supp 2d 326, (1998).]

LEARNING OBJECTIVES

Upon completion of this chapter, the student will be able to

1. draft interview questions that elicit proper and useful information from a prospective employee but which avoid providing a basis for complaint,
2. create and understand the value of useful employment practice policies,
3. list and provide examples of the general categories of employee behaviors that may be successfully used as reasons to terminate an employee,
4. discuss the differences, advantages, and disadvantages of independent contractors and employees,
5. provide a brief and accurate description of the topic of workers' compensation and its application or lack of application to employees, independent contractors, and scholarship athletes,
6. identify the governmental agencies in charge of processing administrative complaints under the Equal Pay Act, Title VII, and Title IX,
7. state the minimum requirements for the Equal Pay Act, Title VII, and Title IX to apply in the workplace as well as discuss their relative applications,
8. accurately describe the difference between quotas and affirmative action,
9. understand the risk-management significance to the employer of hiring skilled employees with the appropriate credentials versus skilled employees lacking appropriate credentials,
10. discuss the significance of creating appropriate "paper trails,"
11. differentiate the level of due process owed to a terminated employee versus a non-reappointed employee, and
12. design a termination plan that enhances risk-management goals.

Relationships between employees and employers are in many ways similar to familial relationships in that respect, clear expectations, fair play, and hard work help the relationships flourish. When any of these items is missing, the continuation of a happy and productive relationship is in jeopardy. The legal guidelines for providing positive and productive employee/employer relationships are documented in, among other statutes, Title VII, Title IX, the ADA, and the EPA. See Chapters 5, 8, and 9 or details.

HIRING

Clarity and exactness in the hiring process is particularly valuable from a risk-management point of view.

DEVELOPMENT OF JOB ANNOUNCEMENT

The creation of a complete and considered **job announcement** is central to a good employee/employer relationship as well as to prudent risk-management techniques.

Suppose your school is searching for a new volleyball coach. Your department wants to send a subtle message to the rest of the school that physical education and athletics are full partners in the academic endeavor of the school. Thus, your job announcement includes these words: "Applications for a Division III college level volleyball coach are invited. The successful candidate will have the following attributes: *Ph.D. in a related field,* at least 10 years of coaching experience on the college level, thorough knowledge of NCAA rules, demonstrated recruitment skills, experience in successfully supervising assistant coaching staff, ability to work well with peers and students of diverse backgrounds, current Red Cross CPR or equivalent."

The job announcement has significant legal ramifications for the search. In reality, the job announcement sets forth the minimum requirements for the job. If one or two applications have all the criteria listed, yet your department believes that, after the interview, another applicant who lacks the Ph.D. would make a better coach, legal issues arise.

For instance, potential applicants who did not submit an application because they took you at your word that a Ph.D. is required, and they lacked the Ph.D., will have good reason to feel unfairly treated when you hire someone without a Ph.D. If the would-be applicants are members of a protected class lawsuits might be lodged against your institution. (See Chapters 4 and 5 for details about protected classes.)

Job announcements asking for all the minimum job requirements but not asking for, "would-be-nice-but . . ." extras, help the prospective employer find the greatest pool of qualified applicants from which to select a new employee.

AFFIRMATIVE ACTION AND THE JOB ANNOUNCEMENT

Successfully hiring a new employee also requires an understanding of the value of diversity. Some people equate **affirmative action** with quotas. They are wrong to do so. Some people equate affirmative action to having to hire someone who is less or unqualified simply because the applicant is a member of a protected class. They are also wrong.

Affirmative action as a principle applied in sport and education settings means that once a *qualified* (meets minimum requirements set out in the job announcement) candidate pool is determined, then and only then is any preference given to a member of a protected class. There is no requirement to meet a quota of employees belonging to any particular protected class. However, the absence of members of protected classes creates a rebuttable presumption that something other than honest and fair hiring practices is taking place.

Most educational institutions realize that a broad and diverse applicant pool is valuable to the institution and thus try to find ways to disseminate the job announcement to often-overlooked, yet qualified, applicant audiences. All applicants who meet the specific minimum requirements as outlined in the job announcement are qualified. Thus when any affirmative action preference is given to a member of a protected class from within the pool of qualified candidates, that preference is, by definition, being given to a qualified candidate.

Take great care in the development of the job announcement, because its contents ultimately define who is a qualified candidate. Its contents, if stringent beyond what the job actually requires, can artificially narrow your search and deprive you of applicants who would do a good job.

INTERVIEWING APPLICANTS

After the job announcement is broadly disseminated and qualified applicants have been culled from the general pool, an **interview** usually takes place. Interviewing a job candidate provides an opportunity to get to know an applicant in ways beyond the paper record. A good interview experience lets those present see how the candidate's mind works, animates the candidate's personality, and allows in-depth questioning to take place. The questions asked of each candidate need not be identical but the interview experience and general content should be substantially similar in order to meet the requirements of fairness.

The law does not arbitrarily prohibit telephone interviews of some candidates if others are interviewed in person. However, such disparate interview experiences may add fodder to the Title VII complaints of a rejected applicant who claims discrimination in the interview process based on membership in a protected class.

If face-to-face interviews are too costly, consider using the telephone to interview all candidates you have decided to talk to. After you have narrowed down your pool to two or three, re-interview these candidates face-to-face.

Although format of an interview is not prescribed by law, some questions within the interview may be proscribed. Some questions (Are you religious? How many children do you have? How old are you?) may have the purpose of eliciting valuable and permissible information, but the format of the questions is not permissible. For instance, the question, "Are you religious?" may be seeking information about the availability of the applicant to work on weekends. The sought information is appropriate, but the question seeking that information should be worded directly to the relevant job requirements: "Are there any reasons you would not be able to work on weekends?"

"How many children do you have?" might be a question seeking information on the applicant's ability to work nights or perhaps the potential need for the applicant's duties to be covered if child care plans collapse. The question as worded, however, is seeking information tangential to the applicant's marital status or, perhaps, sexual preference. Again, the question should be worded in a way that directly applies to the job requirements: "Do you have any personal obligations that might cause you to be absent from work without prior scheduling and, if so, how might you meet the need to cover your duties during such an absence?"

Asking a candidate's age during a job interview carries with it considerable legal risk if the candidate believes age was the basis of not being hired. Remember, Title VII covers age discrimination and applies not only to employees but also to applicants for jobs. The only legitimate reason for wanting to know the age of an applicant is that the interviewer is concerned that the older applicant may not have the strength or other physical attributes necessary to meet specific job requirements or the young applicant may not be an adult. Thus, the question seeking such information should be reframed to relate directly to the job requirements: "The position as gymnastics coach requires you to spot college-aged students; do you have any doubts you'll be able to do so effectively?"

Interviewing candidates is not small talk. Obviously the interviewer wants to glean as much information as possible with which to evaluate the candidate's likelihood of success if employed, but great care needs to be spent framing the questions to be used for that purpose.

INDEPENDENT CONTRACTOR VERSUS EMPLOYEE

The nature of the worker's relationship to the agency also needs to be carefully thought through. Is the worker going to be an employee or an independent contractor? The designation, employee or **independent contractor**, makes a difference to the boss, the worker, and the IRS.

An **employer/employee relationship** obligates the boss to pay half of the employee's Social Security obligation (total obligation is a bit over 15 percent of the employee's salary) as well as, in many cases, taking care of unemployment insurance premiums, workers' compensation premiums, and the paperwork associated with IRS income tax withholding. An independent contractor relationship places the entire burden on the worker. The worker in an employer/employee relationship takes home less money per paycheck but ultimately is ahead more than 7.5 percent. This is the case because if the worker was an independent contractor rather than an employee, the worker, not the boss, would be obligated to pay not only the worker's share of Social Security but also the share paid by an employer. On the other hand, some workers prefer more money now and will worry about saving for the IRS and paying not just 7.5+ percent now but the full 15+ percent of their pay for Social Security later. If the worker is self-disciplined, the money is set aside for the time when it's needed, but if not, independent contractors may find themselves in a situation in which they owe more money than they have.

The IRS cares whether the worker is an employee or an independent contractor and has a specific yet subjective list of indicia it uses to define membership in the proper category. A few of those that point toward a designation as an independent contractor are:

- workers bringing their own tools,
- workers setting their own work hours,
- workers determining their work plan.

Other than determining who pays Social Security obligations, does it really matter if a worker is designated as an employee or an independent contractor? Yes, it matters, and particularly for the worker. Many protections from the full brunt of liability for acts of negligence don't apply to independent contractors. For instance, most employees working at public institutions are protected from the financial liability and defense costs for acts of ordinary negligence occurring in the furtherance of their duties by way of being sheltered by Hold Harmless Laws. A worker classified as an independent contractor at the same institution remains outside the protective shelter of Hold Harmless laws. Similarly, liability for claims of negligence against an independent contractor is unlikely to be able to be shared with superiors at the institution, unlike employees. In other words, while an employer is liable for the negligence of its employees, an institution is generally *not* liable for the negligence of an independent contractor.

CERTIFICATION VERSUS LICENSURE

In addition to the decision on the worker's status as an employee or independent contractor, successful job applicants often may need specific documentation of their qualifications such as degrees, **certifications and licenses**. The difference between certifications and licenses is blurred somewhat. However, normally, licenses are issued by the state and are required by the state for participation in certain professions. For instance, a physician needs a state-issued license in order to comply with laws allowing someone to work as a physician.

Certifications are generally not issued by the state but by an educational institution or professional association upon the candidate's completion of a set of minimum education or training requirements. For instance, not all states license athletic trainers. However, a university within a state that doesn't license athletic trainers might still grant a certification indicating completion of a specific course of study in athletic training as approved by the university. Additionally, the National Athletic Trainers Association may also grant a certification to the student when the NATA's minimum education and training requirements have been met. Such certification may then be one of the requirements the student will need to show when seeking a license from a state which issues licenses for athletic training. Whatever the requirements for certification or licensure in your state, when you hire an employee you will need to consider what documentation you or your state requires for the position.

When you're hiring a worker, you may require the worker to possess certain degrees, certifications, and licenses. The usefulness of such requirements to the employer is threefold.

First, if the employer is required by state or local law to hire only people possessing specific documentation, by following through, the employer is in compliance with the law. For example, if a state or local law requires an athletic trainer to be present at all football games, hiring a documented athletic trainer allows the employer to comply.

Second, requiring potential employees to possess specific relevant documentation allows the employer to screen out applicants who are more likely to lack the knowledge and skills required by the job. However, sometimes applicants actually have the knowledge and skills yet lack the documentation, and in these instances, requiring documentation precludes the employer from hiring this particular group of knowledgeable and skilled applicants.

Third, when employees possess appropriately required documentation, a rebuttable presumption is formed that the employer has hired staff prudently. For instance, when in court following a swimming pool accident, it's much easier for an employer to point to a lifeguard's current Red Cross certification as evidence that the employer prudently hired competent staff than to try to prove that a knowledgeable and skilled, yet undocumented, employee was in fact an appropriate person to hire as a lifeguard.

If you require degrees, licenses, or certifications, make sure your employees have them and that they remain current. An employee hired three years ago with a current certification may no longer possess a current certification. It's for the employer to explain in court why the certification or license was critical when the employee was hired but not critical three years later. Keep track of the expiration dates and view and maintain copies of all certifications and licenses you require your employees to have.

NEGLIGENT HIRING

No one sets out to hire incompetent employees, yet every now and then incompetents are hired. The employer has a duty to act as a reasonable, prudent, up-to-date employer would act in the hiring process. Thus the employer searching for a new employee is obligated to carefully delineate minimum qualifications and to extend a job offer only to someone who meets those minimums.

Making sure the new employee meets the minimum job requirements is only part of the employer's duty. In addition to being qualified, the new employee must be fit for the job. In this context, fitness relates to the absence of criminal propensities that foreseeably place students, program participants, athletes, or peers at risk. The employer thus has a duty to hire qualified employees and fit employees. Harm caused by the employer's breach of either prong of this duty may subject the employer to claims of negligence.

Although some writers refer to this particular type of employer negligence as **negligent hiring**, it differs from negligence in no way other than existing in a specific context: the care exerted to hire qualified and fit employees. The elements of *duty, breach, cause,* and *harm* must still exist for negligence to be found. The standard of care is judged by the same yardstick: what would a reasonable, prudent, up-to-date employer have done in similar circumstances to protect participants from the foreseeable risk of unreasonable harm? Although there might be room for varying points of view on the details of prudent, reasonable, up-to-date behavior, there is general agreement that it includes at least:

- *Hiring competent, qualified employees.*
    1. Hire only those possessing the stated minimum qualifications.
    2. Verify required licenses and certifications.
    3. Check references.
- *Hiring fit employees.*
    1. Complete criminal background checks. The level of the check needs to be commensurate with the duties and populations involved. For instance, hiring an employee who will be working in an unsupervised environment with young girls may require a fuller background check than would hiring an employee who will only be working in the heating plant under close supervision. When an employee will be working with the disabled, the elderly, or children, the importance of completing criminal background checks is even more important.

As the employee's duties or population to be serviced change, prudent, reasonable, up-to-date employer behavior requires updated checks on the competence and fitness of the employee.

NEGLIGENT SUPERVISION

Negligent supervision is similar to negligent hiring: it is simply negligence in a particular context. The context is that of an employer failing to monitor an employee's inappropriate behavior, abuse, sex-based language or activity, or criminal actions that place program participants at risk. An employer who fails to monitor these things may be breaching the duty to supervise employee fitness. Harm caused by that breach is all that remains to establish the four required elements of negligence.

CREATING AN EMPLOYMENT CONTRACT

Chapter 10 provides more complete information on the nature and requirements of a personal service **contract**, but a brief word here may be helpful. After the interview and the selection process, the creation of a clear and complete contract is extremely important. Many coaches, as well as other sport staff, can only look to the most minimal, informal documentation about the terms of their employment. Many have only a "letter of agreement" stating that in return for coaching the field hockey or tennis team they will be paid $XXX. No mention is made of start and end dates, whether they are expected to recruit, if they must fund raise, attend postseason competitions or conduct preseason camps. Many coaching contracts are silent about whether the coach will be supplied with assistants, what will form the basis of evaluation for continued employment, or even the date by which the employee will be informed about contract renewal. There are often no liquidated damages clauses specifying in advance what happens if the contract is breached or prematurely terminated by one party or the other.

These items don't matter in the halcyon days of hiring, but when something goes awry in the employer/employee relationship, it's too late to go back and make unsaid expectations and obligations clear or binding. Whether you're an employee or employer, think through the details and possible future problems during the hiring process. Negotiate and reduce those negotiations to a clear and forthright writing in the form of a contract. When you have access to legal counsel, use it; have the attorney review the written contract.

WORKERS' COMPENSATION

When hiring an employee or determining if a worker will serve most appropriately as an employee versus an independent contractor, an understanding of **workers' compensation** is useful. Workers' compensation is a form of insurance for which premiums are paid by the employer. Workers' compensation provides compensation to the employee who is injured on the job in the furtherance of the employer's interests. The advantage to the employee is that the worker does not need to go to court and try to prove negligence. The employee, under workers' compensation, can be compensated for all covered workplace injuries regardless of whether negligence was involved. The advantage to the employer is that the employer knows in advance the extent of liability and is protected from negligence lawsuits brought by an employee. The risk is shifted from the employer to the insurance provider, and thus the employer's liability is limited to the premiums paid.

An employee is required to maintain workers' compensation insurance when the following two elements exist:

1. an employee/employer relationship, and
2. the worker was injured in the furtherance of the employer's interest.

If the employee's injuries occur when the employee is washing the employee's personal car at the workplace after work hours, no workers' compensation is owed because element #2 above is absent. Similarly, if the worker is serving as an independent contractor rather than an employee, element #1 above is absent.

Element #1 offers the basis of potentially interesting discussion concerning the nature of big-time athletics. Consider a football player at a Division IA college where the coaches, trainers, officials, telecasters, security, maintenance, ticket takers, and so on are all paid, but the football player receives only financial aid. Is the football player an employee? What if the same scenario included the factor that the college was one of the very few in the United States that actually makes a profit from its football team? The discussion is informative and interesting. The legal reality is that most states have not addressed the issue and of those that have, most have excluded football players from workers' compensation either through case law or by statute. The fact is that in most states where any legal action has evolved on the topic, football players have been excluded from workers' compensation. This exclusion doesn't diminish the vividness of a debate on the topic. An interesting review of the issue of workers' compensation and scholarship athletes is found in "Comment: College Athletes Should Be Entitled to Workers' Compensation for Sports-Related Injuries." 28 *Akron Law Review* 611 (1995) and in "Workers' Compensation and the Scholarship Athlete" *Journal of Higher Education,* Volume 23, #4, August, 1982. A couple of interesting cases on the topic, some parts of which have been overturned either by later case law or by legislative action but which still provide cogent arguments are: *Van Horn v. Industrial Accident Commission,* 219 Cal. App.2d 457, 33 Cal. Rptr. 169 (1963) and *Rensing v. Indiana State University,* 437 N.E. 2d 78 (Ind. App.1982) rev'd 444 N.E. 2d 1170 (Ind. 1983).]

AT WILL OR FOR TERM CONTRACT?

Many coaching contracts are silent about the length of the employment, so in many jurisdictions an "**at will**" relationship is created. The at will relationship results in no expectation of continued employment, and thus no right to due process exists when the employee is told, "Pack up, you're fired." From the employer's point of view, there is no expectation that the employee is obligated to work through the end of the season.

EMPLOYMENT

As our discussion progresses from hiring to firing, let's pause for a few words about employment and hope that outside the pages of this book, careful hiring practices coupled with positive employment practices will produce an employer/employee relationship that never progresses to firing. A good place to start is with a current, complete, appropriately disseminated, and updated set of policies that is honored by adherence. Adherence to good policies is the best risk-management activity in the realm of employment. Let's take a look at a few issues that would be wisely included in a set of good policies.

CRITERIA FOR RETENTION

Friendship is a valuable commodity and collegiality in the workplace is important. However, in order for employers to avoid unconsciously discriminating for one reason (i.e., personality) or another (membership in a protected class which the employer fails to value equally with other employees) clearly stated criteria must form the core of the employee evaluation processes. The criteria must be job related, non-discriminatory on their face, not disparate in their impact and evenhandedly applied. See Chapter 9.

PAPER TRAIL

Collegiality carries with it a desire to help and support one another, and this is good. However, when **evaluation**, observations, and reviews are conducted, they need to be carried out honestly.

If an employee is not working out, it's only fair that the employee's verbal and written evaluations reflect the problems. This gives the employee a chance to do better. If change is successfully achieved, the employer saves the cost, time, and disruption of conducting a search for a replacement. If the problems do not get better, the **paper trail** of honest and frank evaluations serves as evidence of warnings and also serves as the first steps toward due process. Honest evaluations also provide evidence of nondiscriminatory reasons for the termination of the employee. Such evidence is useful in defending discrimination claims.

Unfortunately, many employers take the easier road of creating glowing or, at least, satisfactory evaluations, when in reality the worker's performance needs considerable improvement. Later, when the employer decides to terminate the employee, no paper record exists that demonstrates the negative reality. Early honesty helps both the employee and the employer.

HARASSMENT IN THE WORKPLACE

In addition to providing a workplace safe from the foreseeable risk of unreasonable physical harm, the employer must also provide a workplace free from sexual harassment. The policy manual should include a specific section on harassment. Title VII and Title IX both apply to the workplace; Title IX also applies to students (see Chapters 5 and 8). Both Title VII and Title IX include in their protections the freedom from sexual harassment (see Chapters 5 and 9).

Employer liability for sexual harassment (either between peers or between supervisors and subordinates) under Title VII applies whether the employer had notice of the harassment or not. On the other hand, employer liability for sexual harassment under Title IX protections is only triggered when the employer or an agent of the employer with the authority to intervene actually knew of the situation and reacted to that knowledge with deliberate indifference, thereby failing to stop the harassment.(*Davis*, 1999)

FIRING AND NONREAPPOINTMENT

Our discussion relating to firing or not reappointing an employee hinges on the calendar. The legal requirements differ greatly if the employee is fired during the contract term versus non-reappointed for another contract term. In the first instance, firing, due process is owed to the employee; in the second instance, non-reappointment, no due process is owed. Due process is owed only when someone has a valid expectation of continued employment. The person who has a job that terminates at the end of a set time period, such as in a one-year contract from 9/1 to 8/31, has no legal property right or expectation of employment after 8/31.

When due process is owed, the amount of due process is determined by the level of expectation of continued employment. For instance, a tenured professor logically has a strong expectation of continued employment (property interest) and is thus owed a lot of due process, such as a formal appeal process, hearings with the employee's lawyer present, and so on. In contrast, when an employee with only a one-year contract is fired before the end of the year, the employee is owed much less due process. An employee with an "at will" relationship is owed no significant level of due process.

In much the same way that due process is owed to the fired employee but not to a **non-reappointed** employee, reasons for the personnel action are also owed only in cases of firing, and not in cases of non-reappointment. Will just any reason do? No. Reasons for firing need to fall within at least one of three general "I" categories:

- **Incompetence**
- **Insubordination**
- **Immorality**

The first two categories are self-explanatory, but the third, immorality, may need a bit of elaboration. Immorality in an employment context does *not* have anything to do with sexual activity or preferences unconnected with the job. In an employment context, immorality includes such situations as these:

1. An employee fraudulently submits reimbursement requests not earned.
2. An employee plagiarizes the work of another.
3. An employee makes up data or alters data so that research outcomes change.
4. An employee violates **sexual harassment** prohibitions.

All valid reasons for firing someone fit into one or more of the three general "I" categories. Personality conflicts, lack of collegiality, or other similar reasons for preferring that an employee would either change or leave seldom fit into one of the three general "I" categories and are thus not legally valid reasons for firing an employee in midterm of the contract. Remember, no reasons are needed for non-reappointments at the end of a contract term.

Firing someone is seldom a happy occasion for anyone involved. It is, however, an occasion that occurs more smoothly when the process is thought out ahead of time and where collegiality is high and emotional involvement is low. If an employer suspects that an employee has serious workplace deficiencies and that a possible non-reappointment or firing looms in the future, the employer needs to plan ahead. First, the deficiencies should be discussed openly and clearly with the employee so that the employee has a chance to improve. A paper trail of the discussions, observations, and problems needs to be developed carefully, with the employee aware of each item and its contents.

When the decision is made to fire an employee, the employer should provide the reasons in a forthright manner. The fired employee has a legal right to the reasons, and to make the employee's access to reasons torturous serves only to alienate the fired employee more, which encourages consideration of legal action. Heavy-handed firing behaviors such as having a security guard show up to watch as the employee cleans out the desk is seldom a good idea. There are very few instances where the cause of the employee being fired produces a basis to suspect the employee of retaliation or sabotage by stealing the stapler. The smart employer stays friendly and supportive throughout the process.

FEDERAL LEGISLATION AFFECTING THE WORKPLACE

So far, much of this chapter has used well-settled legal principles to frame a discussion of employment issues. Let's look at the sources of some of those legal principles.

Federal legislation adds layers of protections to those constitutional protections that are guaranteed (at least to those who work for state actors: see Chapter 4). Federal legislation such as Title VII, Title IX, the Americans With Disabilities Act, and the Equal Pay Act all contribute to our understanding of what is fair and legal treatment of employees, and in some cases, even applicants for jobs.

Title VII is administratively enforced by the EEOC (Equal Employment Opportunity Commission) and applies only to the workplace. Title VII applies only to workplaces having an impact on interstate commerce and having 15 or more employees working at least 20 calendar weeks. The requirement for having an impact on interstate commerce is easily met. (The requirement for a connection to interstate commerce is present because the Interstate Commerce Clause of the U.S. Constitution is the source of Congress' authority for the enactment of Title VII.) Title VII's coverage is extended to applicants as well as to job holders. Title VII does *not* require the presence of federal funds, nor does it require that the employer be a state actor for jurisdiction to apply.

Title VII extends to issues of "compensation, terms, conditions, or privileges of employment." Sexual harassment is an activity, based on membership in a Title VII protected class (discrimination based on sex), that affects the terms and conditions of employment. Thus, claims of sexual harassment are among the issues actionable under the protections of Title VII. Under Title VII, the employer is obligated to provide a workplace free of discrimination, and the employer need not have notice of the discrimination in order to be held liable. Thus, if a co-worker or superior is sexually harassing an employee, the employee may seek money damages under Title VII even if the employer had no knowledge of the behavior. For a fuller discussion of sexual harassment, see Chapter 9.

Title IX, administratively enforced by the Office for Civil Rights of the U.S. Department of Education, applies both to students and employees and protects them from discrimination based on sex. It does *not* protect from discrimination based on other factors such as race or religion. Title IX's jurisdiction applies, unlike Title VII, only to education programs that receive federal money. Similar to Title VII, however, no requirement exists that the perpetrator be a state actor. Title IX has not had great strength as a protector of the employee's rights generally. Its greatest strength where employees are concerned has been in the area of sexual harassment and retaliation. Title IX's definition of sexual harassment has, by *de facto* means, tracked that of Title VII. Using the *quid pro quo* definition of sexual harassment for Title IX cases is easier than trying to employ the hostile environment definition. Because Title IX, unlike Title VII, doesn't include a specific definition of sexual harassment, Title IX is more comfortable borrowing the more concrete definition of *quid pro quo,* and less comfortable borrowing the more subjective definition of hostile environment. Both Title VII and Title IX provide for money damages, but Title VII has some specific limitations as to the maximum amount available.

The ADA, administratively enforced by the EEOC does not require the presence of a state actor, nor does it apply only to education programs. Its reach is much greater than either Title VII or Title IX, but access to money damages under its provisions has become more constrained than either Title IX or Title VII. A 2001 U.S. Supreme Court case denied access to money damages for employees of state institutions [*Board of Trustees of the University of Alabama,* 2001]. Thus, if you work for a state university, the ADA will not provide you with the enforcement strategy of seeking money damages. The Court's decision is a complex one but, stated briefly, the legal foundation for it is that a plaintiff cannot sue a state entity (different from a "state actor") such as a state university for money damages based on the federal legislation known as the ADA because of the **11th Amendment.** The ADA is not the first federal antidiscrimination legislation to be restricted in this way. Just over a year earlier, the Supreme Court in *Kimel v. Florida Board of Regents* [*Kimel,* 2000] took the same action with age-discrimination legislation known a the ADEA, and other federal antidiscrimination legislation may follow the footsteps of these cases. See Chapter 5 for more information about the ADA's jurisdictional requirements.

The Equal Pay Act (EPA) has fewer jurisdictional requirements than Title IX, Title VII, or the ADA but does require the designation of a **comparator employee.** A comparator employee is an employee in the same workplace who is carrying out comparable duties. This is often a large hurdle for the plaintiff to overcome. Thus Title VII is often the preferred method of seeking redress for illegally unequal salaries, because the requirement of a comparator employee is not found in Title VII. The EEOC is responsible for the administrative enforcement of the EPA and to that end has issued a very helpful *Guidance on Application of Anti-Discrimination Laws to Coaches' Pay at Education Institutions* [*Guidelines,* 1997]. See Chapter 5 for more information about the jurisdiction of the EPA; see Chapter 9 for its application to sport environments.

MANAGEMENT GUIDELINES

Policy manuals, paper trails, and positive personnel practices are the key to avoiding unhappy employee/employer relationships. Title VII, the EPA, Title IX, and similar legislation such as the ADA help define the proper contents of policy manuals and the proper format for paper trails. Personnel practices directed by a deeply held sense of fairness cannot often lead you astray in your risk-management plan.

Here is a list of risk-management guidelines to consider:

1. Develop, adopt, and promulgate policies.
2. Review the adopted policies periodically for their compliance with changing law.
3. Periodically redistribute policies so that employees and supervisory staff are reminded of their contents.
4. Expect all to adhere to the policies, including yourself.
5. When a policy is routinely ignored or broken, review and alter it if necessary.
6. Conduct training programs for all employees and focus particularly on positive personnel practices for supervisors.
7. Practice what you preach.
8. Develop risk-free reporting mechanisms for sexual harassment as well as all other policy or personnel problems.
9. Respond to problems and complaints promptly and consistently.
10. Hire good supervisors.
11. Monitor complaints and the effectiveness of solutions.
12. Put it in writing; review contract contents.
13. Be honest, not generous, in evaluations.
14. When termination occurs, take the high road and try to maintain an environment free of accusation and emotion.
15. Don't be afraid to terminate an employee if termination is needed; just be sure to do it right.
16. Set and disseminate salary scales and their criteria. Where secrecy exists, lying begins.

CHAPTER SUMMARY

The workplace needs to be free of discrimination and harassment. In addition to those constitutional guarantees for the employees of state actors, significant legislation such as Title VII, Title IX, the ADA, and the EPA provide additional protections. Depending on the legislation involved, considerable risk of liability exists for the employer who discriminates, as was noted in the scenario involving Susie and Suburban University in the opening paragraphs of this chapter.

The nature of the worker's relationship to the boss is of legal importance. Independent contractors have both positive and negative aspects compared to employees.

The completeness of the contract at the beginning of employment often determines the positive nature of the relationship at the end of employment.

Policies can and should direct employment practices. Thus, complete policies need to be developed, updated, disseminated, and adhered to.

CASE STUDIES

CASE 11.1

Pat, an Asian-American, Catholic female, is paid considerably less for serving as head coach of the 12-person water polo team than is Chris, an African-American, Buddhist male, for serving as head coach for the 24-person rowing team. Both have the same level of experience, workload, and fund-raising responsibilities, and neither has an assistant coach. Consider, and argue pro and con, the applicability of Title IX, Title VII, and EPA protections for Pat.

CASE 11.2

You are hiring a new sports information director. Design a job announcement and justify each item you are asking the qualified candidate to bring to the job. Then design at least 10 interview questions that will elicit useful information but that are also appropriate questions within the constraints of the Constitution and federal legislation. Then develop a list of the items that should be included in the written contract with your new sports information director.

KEY TERMS

Affirmative action
Americans With Disabilities Act
At will personal service relationship
Certification and licensure
Comparator employee
Contract
Eleventh Amendment
Employer/employee relationship
Equal Pay Act
Evaluation
Immorality
Incompetence
Independent contractor
Insubordination
Interview questions
Job announcements
Liquidated damages
Negligent hiring
Negligent supervision
Non reappointment
Paper trail
Policy manuals
Sexual harassment
Title VII
Title IX
Workers' compensation

QUESTIONS FOR DISCUSSION

1. Read the *Van Horn* and *Rensing* workers' compensation cases. Discuss the issue of workers' compensation and the scholarship athlete.
2. Read the *University of Alabama v. Garrett and Kimel v. Florida Board of Regents* cases. Discuss the disparity of protection offered students and employees at a state university versus a private university based on your reading of the two cases.
3. Reread the opening scenario at the beginning of this chapter and create a set of salary and harassment policies. Discuss how, if implemented, they might have produced a more amicable resolution to the issues than a lawsuit.

REFERENCES

Board of Trustees of the University of Alabama, et al., v. Patricia Garrett. 531 U.S. 356, 121 S. Ct. 955 (2001).

Carpenter, Linda. Workers' Compensation and the Scholarship Athlete" *Journal of Higher Education,* Volume 23, #4, August, 1982.

Davis v. Monroe County Board of Education 526 U.S. 629, 119 S. Ct. 1661, 1999.

Guidance on Application of Anti-Discrimination Laws to Coaches' Pay at Education Institutions. Issued October 31, 1997 and available via the internet at www.eeoc.gov/press/10-31-97.html or by writing EEOC's Office of Communications and Legislative Affairs, 1801 L Street, N.W., Washington, D.C. 20507.

Kimel, et al. v. Florida Board of Regents, et al. 528 U.S. 62, 120 S. Ct. 631 (2000).

Perdue v. City University of New York, 13 F. Supp 2d 326 (1998).

Rensing v. Indiana State University, 437 N.E. 2d 78 (Ind. App. 1982) rev'd 444 N.E. 2d 1170 (Ind. 1983).

University of Alabama v. Garrett, 531 U.S. 356, 121 S.Ct. 955 (2001).

Van Horn v. Industrial Accident Commission, 219 Cal. App.2d 457, 33 Cal. Rptr. 169 (1963).

Woodburn, David. Comment: "College Athletes Should Be Entitled to Workers' Compensation for Sports-Related Injuries." 28 *Akron Law Review* 611 (1995).

CHAPTER 12

THE ROLE OF
GOVERNING BODIES

Professor Jerry Tarkanian became tenured in 1977—four years after being hired as head men's basketball coach at the University of Nevada, Las Vegas (UNLV). UNLV is a publicly funded institution and a member of the National Collegiate Athletic Association (NCAA). Several years earlier, the NCAA Committee on Infractions had notified UNLV's president of an "inquiry" into charges that the university had committed violations of NCAA rules regarding recruitment. Following the direction of the NCAA, UNLV launched its own investigation, enlisting the aid of its attorneys and the Attorney General of Nevada. In the fall of 1976, UNLV concluded its investigation. Tarkanian and the university were exonerated.

Following its procedures for dealing with such allegations, the NCAA Committee on Infractions conducted four days of hearings that resulted in a finding of 38 violations of NCAA rules, 10 of which were attributed to Coach Tarkanian. Under NCAA rules, the Committee on Infractions, after conducting its investigation and hearings, made a recommendation to the NCAA Council, which was empowered to accept or reject the recommendations. Almost five years after UNLV was first apprised of the investigation, the NCAA Council adopted the recommendations of the Committee on Infractions. A two-year period of probation as well as a two-year exclusion from postseason play and television appearances was imposed. Coach Tarkanian expected to be suspended during the probation period because the NCAA Council had threatened more severe sanctions for the university if the suspension was not carried out.

As a result, UNLV did impose the suspension. Tarkanian sued the university in state court in Nevada, claiming that he had been deprived of property and liberty without due process. The trial judge agreed with Tarkanian and issued an injunction that prevented UNLV from taking the action against Tarkanian.

The NCAA, which was not sued, filed papers in court, appearing as *amicus curiae*—a "friend of the court"—that is, a party "with strong interest in or views of the subject matter of an action, but not a party to the action [who] may petition the court for permission to file a brief, ostensibly on behalf of a party, but actually to suggest a rationale consistent with its own views" *(Black's Law Dictionary,* 1990). The NCAA took the position that its disciplinary proceeding was being undermined by the court's action and that as a result the NCAA should be permitted to appear in the action. The NCAA argued that, in any event, Mr. Tarkanian was neither denied due process nor treated in any way inconsistent with UNLV's obligation to him. The Supreme Court of Nevada agreed with the NCAA that the NCAA was indeed a necessary party to the lawsuit and reversed the decision of the trial court. Subsequently, the coach brought another lawsuit, this time against both his employer and the NCAA.

Mr. Tarkanian won his trial four years later in the Nevada courts. Deciding that the NCAA was engaged in state action and had denied the coach due process of law, the trial court once again ordered that no suspension could be imposed on Jerry Tarkanian. In addition, the court ordered that there were to be no further proceedings against or penalties imposed on UNLV.

The NCAA appealed to the Supreme Court of Nevada. The Court found that the NCAA was indeed a *state actor* (acting, albeit indirectly, in the place of the government) and that Mr. Tarkanian had not been afforded due process of law in the proceedings that culminated in the recommendation of a two-year suspension.

On December 12, 1988, in a decision that sent substantial shock waves through the sports law community, the U.S. Supreme Court, in *National Collegiate Athletic Association v. Tarkanian* (1988), reversed the judgment of the Nevada Supreme Court, declining to rule the NCAA's role in the penalty meted out to Mr. Tarkanian as *state action.* Justice Stevens wrote for the court:

"Neither UNLV's decision to adopt the NCAA's standards nor its minor role in their formulation is a sufficient reason for concluding that the NCAA was acting under color of Nevada law when it promulgated standards governing athlete recruitment, eligibility, and academic performance. UNLV delegated no power to the NCAA to take specific action against any University employee. The commitment by UNLV to adhere to NCAA enforcement procedures was enforceable only by sanctions that the NCAA might impose on UNLV itself" *(NCAA v. Tarkanian,* 1988).

LEARNING OBJECTIVES

Upon completion of this chapter, the student will be able to:

1. distinguish between voluntary associations and governing bodies mandated by law,
2. define the limits of legal authority granted to governing bodies imposed by statute administrative and case law,
3. determine if and when governing bodies and other associations will be held to constitutional standards of due process of law,
4. articulate the legal significance of a governing body's internal rules and regulations,
5. trace the steps necessary to mount a successful legal challenge to a disciplinary action taken by a governing body, and
6. identify the actions of governing bodies most likely to inspire legislative reform.

WHO GOVERNS SPORT?

Amateur sport in the United States is regulated and controlled by a broad spectrum of organizations that include the following:

- Associations
- Committees
- Voluntary, government-sponsored, and legislatively authorized national governing bodies
- Groups advocating the advancement of a particular sport
- Groups associated with regulating participation in sport for particular institutions such as schools, colleges, and international competitive sport recreational facilities

These organizations range from the local Little League to the mammoth NCAA, whose $325.6 million budget and far-reaching tentacles envelop the major colleges and universities throughout the United States. The NCAA was once described by the Supreme Court of Kansas as a "plump fowl with tempting luxurious plumage" *(NCAA v. Kansas Department of Revenue,* 1989).

How do these groups derive their authority, and how do they affect practitioners? What role does the legal system play in defining the limits of their power? Finally, what do today's practitioners need to know about their rights and responsibilities in dealing with governing bodies?

THE GOVERNING BODIES AND THEIR AUTHORITY

Amateur sport for school and college athletes is subject to the pervasive influence of two national organizations: the NCAA and the National Federation of State High School Associations. These are the "plump fowl" that, together with their related subgroups, chapters, conferences, and affiliated state organizations affect the majority of amateur athletes and would-be athletes in the United States. These two institutions and a dozen or so smaller, unrelated organizations such as the National Association of Intercollegiate Athletics, National Little College Athletic Association, National Christian College Athletic Association, and National Junior College Athletic Association are, legally speaking, "voluntary associations" created by and made up of constituent members that are, for the most part, educational and academic institutions.

Still other organizations exercise their authority along geographical or participant classification lines. Among many others, these include, Special Olympics International, Pony League, Pop Warner Football, Little League Baseball, Inc., Disabled Sports USA, and the American Amateur Racquetball Association.

Finally, federal and other legislation have recognized the existence of so-called "national governing bodies" whose focus is sport-specific and whose authority takes up where the academic institutions and lower-level competition groups leave off. Examples are The Athletic Congress of the U.S.A., the U.S. Gymnastics Federation, the Amateur Basketball Association of the USA, and the Amateur Athletic Association.

A seemingly infinite number of college and high school conferences and leagues are superimposed across the national structure of the various governing bodies that embrace and regulate competition among high schools and colleges. Some of these conferences and leagues govern a broad spectrum of sport activity, whereas memberships in others is optional.

HOW THE GOVERNING BODIES AFFECT PRACTITIONERS

Legally speaking, these conferences and leagues are another layer of voluntary associations that academic institutions may choose to affiliate with for any number of reasons, not the least of which is the prestige associated with being a member of a certain conference or league. Other membership privileges may include access to a specially selected officiating staff, the certainty and predictability of scheduling competition, and the ability to exert greater control over the conditions of competition than mere membership in one of the national associations permits. This control most often takes the form of academic requirements for eligibility, playing rule modifications, and, particularly at the college level, financial requirements.

LIMITS OF POWER

In practice, each of these conferences and leagues constitutes its own form of governing body that regulates the athletes enrolled in the institution and is itself subject to be sued and can sue where legal rights are being asserted.

Nevertheless, the nature of the dominion exercised by the national associations requires that the rules of the local and regional conferences and leagues be no less restrictive than their own. Otherwise member institutions would be in violation of the by-laws or regulations of the national bodies to which they belong and have agreed to subscribe.

RIGHTS AND RESPONSIBILITIES OF PRACTITIONERS

What this means in practical terms for the student athlete and the member institution is that the most restrictive rule of any organization to which the institution belongs will be applied. Athletic administrators, coaches, and athletes must therefore be aware not only of the rules, regulations, and by-laws of the groups to which their schools belong, but also of the procedures by which rules are enforced. For it is often in the enforcement that the denial of procedural due process or violation of the contract rights of the athlete or institution will invalidate what would otherwise be an enforceable rule, regulation, or by-law. Thus, it's as important for you to be familiar with the by-laws and related regulations of all conferences and associations to which your institution belongs as it is for coaches to be well versed in the playing rules of their sports.

"State action" is by no means an absolute prerequisite for aggrieved parties to vindicate their rights in court when associations fail to abide by their own rules in imposing sanctions or penalties. Similarly, when an association's rules run afoul of the concept of conscionability, enforcement may be denied by the courts.

But the power to regulate sports depends on the sport and the level. By law, organizations that are **state actors**—that is to say, that take action akin to government action—must afford due process and equal protection safeguards as expressed in the 5th and 14th Amendments to the U.S. Constitution. Thus, even voluntary, private associations of schools and colleges are often state actors and so are bound by the due process and equal protection amendments to the Constitution (see Cases 12.3 and 12.4).

Both administrators and officials of governing bodies should thus encourage adherence to both procedural and substantive due process in their administrative proceedings as an added safeguard against costly and unproductive litigation. Conversely, practitioners able to make justified claims that organizations did not afford due process will be able to assert their rights effectively.

Keep in mind, however, that constitutional rights are only one area in which the courts can and will intervene when a governing body becomes involved in a serious dispute with a member or nonmember school or athlete or with another governing body or organization. In addition, where membership in a particular organization is a virtual prerequisite for economic reasons, courts are more likely to intervene in the internal affairs of such an association to prevent one from being wrongly excluded or penalized. For example, for a football referee, membership in the State Football Officials' Association might be required if the official is to receive any engagements to officiate. Thus, membership is not voluntary but mandatory in the context of that particular member's rights to participate and earn income. In such cases, courts will intervene to prevent or remedy an injustice when the internal rules of such a governing body are disregarded by that body.

This example shows the importance of knowing the legal relationship between participants and governing bodies. When a question arises concerning legal rights and liabilities, look first to the rules or by-laws of the governing body. Finally, recognize that constitutional, legislative, and case-made precedent may all limit the authority that governing bodies and would-be governing bodies are able to exercise in all areas of amateur sports and physical activity. Theories of recovery available to an aggrieved party may include remedies based on violations of an organization's by-laws, the U.S. Constitution, federal, state, and local legislation, and contract theories.

In some cases, major sports governing bodies take the legal form of a corporation governed by a set of internal rules known as **by-laws.** These rules delineate the rights and responsibilities of the members of the body and frequently provide the mechanism for dealing with violations. Unincorporated associations have similar sets of rules, by-laws, or constitutions by which they and their members are bound. Those who become part of an association through membership, whether they are individual persons or other constituent associations, are said under the law to have entered into a **contract** with the association of which they are members. By the terms of this contract, all parties—both the members and their association—agree to abide by the association's rules. For this reason, even in cases where state action is not present because the association is a private organization that is not sufficiently involved with state governmental institutions or functions, courts have enforced rights of both members and associations when by-laws have been violated (see Case 12.1).

Twelve years after the U.S. Supreme Court ruled, in *NCAA v. Tarkanian,* that the NCAA was not a **state actor,** the question of whether most if not all state high school athletic associations are state actors has, at long last, been answered by the United States Supreme Court in *Brentwood Academy v. Tennessee Secondary School Athletic Association* (2001). The Supreme Court considered a decision of the United States Court of Appeals for the Sixth Circuit, which reversed a Tennessee trial court's finding that the Association was in fact a state actor and enjoined the Association from enforcing a rule prohibiting "undue influence" in recruiting practices. The plaintiff, Brentwood Academy, was a parochial high school and a member of the defendant Association. Brentwood was penalized under the "undue influence" rule for writing the parents of incoming students and the students about Spring football practice. The school was placed on four years' probation, fined $3,000, and declared ineligible to participate in boys' basketball and football playoffs for two years. The school claimed the enforcement of the rule was a violation of the 1st and 14th Amendments to the United States Constitution.

Finding that the Tennessee Secondary School Athletic Association had as members 85 percent of the public schools in the state and provided the standards, rules, and regulations for interscholastic athletics in the public schools of Tennessee, the Supreme Court concluded that 290 public schools in the State of Tennessee, by joining the State Association were, in fact, exercising their own authority to meet their responsibility to coordinate in orderly fashion interscholastic athletics within the state. The Court noted that the Association was largely financed by dues from public schools, council or board meetings of the Association were held during school hours and, in total, the organization was utilized by public school officials "to provide an integral element of secondary public schooling." In fact, the Court recognized that public school officials ". . . do not merely control but overwhelmingly perform all but the purely ministerial acts by which the Association exists and functions in practical terms."

The authority of state high school athletic associations to "provide an integral element of public schooling" by governing interscholastic athletics was dealt a brief although temporary blow early in 1996 in Wichita, Kansas. Eligibility rules promulgated by the Kansas State High School Activities Association, Inc., were challenged in *Robinson v. Kansas State Interscholastic Athletic Association, Inc.* The plaintiffs were fathers of student athletes who challenged rules prohibiting high school basketball players from participating in competitive team camps during the summer months or practice sessions at school during the spring or summer months. In addition, the Kansas Association's rule restricted basketball coaches from contact with their players in spring or summer except for a one-week team camp that was specifically authorized. Another rule prohibited a high school basketball player from participating on another team during the basketball season. Yet another rule prohibited more than a single player on a team from receiving private instruction from nonschool employees during the basketball season.

The trial court granted an injunction prohibiting the Kansas Association from enforcing these rules on the grounds that the rules were void because the Kansas State Legislature unconstitutionally delegated its power to a private association.

However, on May 31, 1996, the Supreme Court of Kansas reversed and remanded the case, holding there was no unconstitutional delegation of legislative power and the trial court should have considered the fathers' claims on the merits. The Kansas Supreme Court noted that the plaintiffs did not claim that the rules in question violated the students' constitutional rights but rather challenged the Association's very authority to make rules.

Noting that the Kansas Association had been in existence since 1910 and had issued sanctions for violation of its rules since the 1920s, the Court concluded that no rule-making authority had ever been expressly delegated by any Kansas statute to the Association, but rather that the Association's rules were in essence by agreement between members of a voluntary association. Thus, the Supreme Court of Kansas returned the matter to the trial court with the instruction to determine whether the rules were arbitrary, capricious, or unreasonable and also whether the rules were an invalid attempt to control activities outside of the school setting.

Student athletes, coaches, athletic directors, and member schools that seek to use the legal system to challenge the action of a state actor often include a violation of the U.S. Constitution in their complaints. If the plaintiff alleges that his or her activities are protected under some part of the Constitution, the court must determine whether the activity is a **fundamental right** under constitutional law—that is, a right guaranteed by the U.S. Constitution (*Prince v. Cohen, 1983; Sidle v. Majors,* 1976). To be enforceable, the denial of one of these fundamental rights by a state actor must be able to withstand the test of **strict scrutiny**. The strict scrutiny test requires that the association prove to the court that the step taken to prohibit or limit the activity (1) was necessary to carry out a **compelling state interest** and (2) was the minimum step necessary to carry out the compelling interest of the state.

Conversely, the strict scrutiny test does not apply if a student athlete, coach, administrator, or member school claims that the action of a state actor caused the denial of a right that is not protected by the Constitution and is therefore not a fundamental right. In such cases, the association need only show there was a **rational basis** for the association's action that affected the right, interest, or status of the plaintiff *(Kite v. Marshall,* 1981; *NAACP v. Button,* 1963).

Fundamental rights undoubtedly extend to freedom of speech, freedom of religion, and freedom of assembly. Fundamental rights also include the right to be free of sanctions predicated on **suspect classifications**. Examples of suspect classifications are race, religion, and national origin.

Practitioners who work in the area of high school sports should note that, for all the arguments advanced by disgruntled athletes who have run afoul of state high school athletic association rules regarding eligibility; freedom of association, travel, transfer, and residency; nonschool activities, courts generally do not characterize participation in interscholastic athletics as a fundamental right protected by the Constitution (see Case 12.2). In fact, the U.S. Supreme Court has specifically rejected even the concept of education as a fundamental right *(Goss v. Lopez,* 1975).

Regardless of whether and to what extent the action of a governing body such as a state high school athletic association impinges on a fundamental right, courts will generally not support an association that does not follow its own rules and regulations in taking action against an athlete or member institution. In general, the obligations of member schools or organizations and of the participating athletes are grounded in the fact that all parties made legally binding agreements to abide by the rules of the governing body at the time they joined it. Therefore, a practitioner's best hope of defeating a governing body in court is to prove that the body failed to follow the rules contained in its own constitution, by-laws, or other materials.

Although courts are generally reluctant to interfere in the internal affairs of associations, they will take action if a right is lost because an association has disregarded its own rules. Although such lapses may not be grounded in constitutional law, they nevertheless can spell the difference between a governing body that is able to enforce its actions and one that weakens itself by making rules and breaking them.

Courts generally require that an aggrieved party exhaust an association's procedures for redressing a wrong or appealing an unfavorable decision before bringing suit. Even so, you should seek the advice of counsel even before beginning to appeal an association's decision through its appeals and review process, particularly if its rules are extensive or complex. The constitution, by-laws, and rules and regulations of the New Jersey State Interscholastic Athletic Association, for example, span about 160 pages and encompass regulations running the gamut of activities from all-star games through the use of artificial limbs in athletic competition.

Hearings for violations of rules and regulations are typically conducted by the association's attorney, and various court-like formalities, such as the stenographic recording of the proceedings by an official court reporter, are commonplace. In these hearings, anything you say can and will be used against you. Thus, you should know when to seek professional help in exercising or defending your rights.

Like their college counterparts, high schools also participate in local and regional conferences, leagues, and alliances that may legally enforce stricter rules for competition, eligibility, and restrictions on athletes than national organizations. All of these local and regional organizations must be considered a part of the governing process.

MAJOR GOVERNING BODIES

The governing bodies described in this chapter have many forms. Some governing bodies exert a profound influence over an almost innumerable number of participants that transcends geographical, sport-specific, and even demographic boundaries. Three such organizations—the National Federation of State High School Associations, the NCAA, and the United States Olympic Committee— are explored in the sections that follow.

NATIONAL FEDERATION OF STATE HIGH SCHOOL ASSOCIATIONS

Interscholastic sports in North America are principally governed by the 65-member National Federation of State High School Associations, headquartered in Indianapolis, Indiana. The Federation began in 1920 as the Midwest Federation of State High School Athletic Associations, composed of the Illinois, Indiana, Iowa, Michigan, and Wisconsin state association representatives. It has grown to an organization that serves about 17,000 high schools and 10 million students.

The day-to-day governing of interscholastic athletic competition resides with the 51 state (including the District of Columbia) Federation associations, and 16 affiliated U.S. and Canadian institutional members, which serve as governing bodies for high school athletics and in some cases other activities, in their respective jurisdictions, promulgating rules for competition, eligibility, equal opportunity for male and female athletes, coaching and officiating standards and qualifications, conference and postseason championship arrangements, academic standards that affect eligibility, and many related items. The associations range in size from the District of Columbia Interscholastic Athletic Association with 16-member schools to the giant Texas University Interscholastic League, which serves 1,178 schools and has 47 full-time employees.

In addition to promulgating rules and training vehicles in 17 sports, the Federation embraces other high school activities such as speech and debate, music, programs dealing with drug abuse, and school spirit workshops.

Historically, associations such as these have been legally termed **voluntary associations** because they are, for the most part, private and not public entities and because the decision to join them resides with individual school boards. In addition, it's not uncommon for association membership to be open to private and parochial schools as well as public schools.

State high school athletic associations typically have purposes such as those set forth in the constitution of the New Jersey State Interscholastic Athletic Association (NJSIAA), which are as follows:

Section 1.   To foster and develop amateur athletics among the secondary schools of the state.

Section 2.   To equalize athletic opportunities by standardizing rules of eligibility for individuals, and classifying for competitive purposes the institutions that are members of the Association.

Section 3.   To supplement the physical education program of the secondary schools of New Jersey by making a practical application of the theories of physical activity.

Section 4.   To promote uniformity in the arrangement and control of contests.

Section 5.   To protect the mutual interests of the members of the Association through the cultivation of ideals of clean sports in their relation to the development of character and good citizenship. (*NJSIAA By-laws,* 1991)

Given both the purposes for which most state high school athletic associations are formed and the composition of their membership, it's no surprise that, even before the United States Supreme Court decided the issue in *Brentwood Academy v. Tennessee Secondary School Athletic Association,* American courts repeatedly ruled such associations to be state actors for purposes of constitutional law. In some states, legislatures have enacted laws specifically granting authority to school boards to join such an association and making the association answerable to a state official, such as the commissioner of education. For example, a New Jersey statute provides that:

> "A Board of Education may join one or more voluntary associations that regulate the conduct of student activities between and among their members, whose membership may include private and public schools. Any such membership shall be by resolution of the Board of Education, adopted annually. No such voluntary association shall be operative without approval of its charter, constitution, by-laws, and rules and regulations by the Commissioner of Education. Upon the adoption of said resolution the Board, its facility, and students shall be governed by the rules and regulations of that association. (New Jersey Statutes Annotated, 1979)."

In New Jersey, if the Commissioner of Education disapproves a rule passed by the NJSIAA, the rule cannot take effect.

State public agencies also govern interscholastic athletics in other states. In some cases regions, counties, or other geographical areas maintain their own associations, which oversee the athletic competition of high schools within their exclusive jurisdiction.

Especially since *Brentwood*, the high school athletic director, coach, or administrator should recognize that associations that oversee scholastic athletics are by and large state actors in the Constitutional sense, regardless of whether they are public or private. As such, they must comply with the 5th and 14th Amendments to the Constitution when these associations flex their disciplinary muscles.

As has been discussed, courts generally decline to interfere in the internal dealings of these associations unless an association takes action in conflict with its by-laws or violates the due process and equal protection clauses embodied in the Constitution. In other words, courts are most likely to interfere with a state interscholastic athletic association's decisions if the association either violates its own rules or takes action or maintains rules that have the effect of denying a participant either due process of law or equal treatment with fellow participants under the law.

The legal remedies for perceived abuses by state interscholastic athletic associations depend somewhat on the legal authority under which the association derives its existence. In New Jersey, for example, the state legislature has enacted a law specifically permitting a board of education to join a voluntary private association whose purpose is to regulate the conduct of student activities. The same law prescribes the following pecking order for enforcing the voluntary association's rules and regulations:

> The said rules and regulations shall be deemed to be the policy of the Board of Education and enforced first by the internal procedures of the association. In matters involving only public school districts and students, faculty, administrators and boards thereof, appeals shall be to the Commissioner and thereafter the Superior Court. In all other matters, appeals shall be made directly to the Superior Court. The Commissioner shall have authority to direct the association to conduct an inquiry by hearing or otherwise on a particular matter or alternatively, direct that particular matter be heard directly by him. The association shall be a party to any proceeding before the Commissioner or in any court. (New Jersey Statutes Annotated, 1979).

This New Jersey law makes a statutory distinction between an alleged deprivation of rights involving only public schools and a similar situation involving a private school as a party. In all cases, the association's procedure for grievances and dispute resolution must be followed. However, if the dispute involves only public school matters and persons associated with public schools, appeals from the decision of the state high school association must be made to the Commissioner of Education, a state government official. Only after the appeal is made to the commissioner may a dissatisfied party go to court to seek relief. In matters involving a private school or persons connected with a private school, an appeal of the decision of the association cannot be made to the commissioner of education but must be made directly to the courts.

Some reported cases in which disciplinary actions taken by a state high school athletic association have been challenged in court do not deal simply with deprivation of constitutional rights. The Oklahoma case of John Mozingo and Mark Neighbors is an example. These two young men were denied "hardship exceptions" to an Oklahoma Secondary Schools Activities Association by-law that required that students, to be eligible for sports, cannot participate at any school other than the public high school of the district where their parents reside. Mozingo and Neighbors claimed that the application of this "transfer rule" to them was arbitrary and capricious, and that because they were not recruited by a school outside their residence district (the evil the rule was meant to eliminate), the rule did not accomplish its intended purpose. Therefore, they reasoned, they qualified for an exemption from the rule. The court, taking no note of any claim that either boy was deprived of his constitutional rights, simply recounted that the high school athletic association was voluntary and that:

> as a general rule, courts should not interfere with the internal affairs of voluntary associations. . . . In the absence of mistake, fraud, collusion, or arbitrariness, the decisions of the governing body of an association should be accepted by the courts as conclusive. . . . The Courts will not substitute their interpretation of the by-laws of a voluntary association for the interpretation placed upon those by-laws by the voluntary association itself so long as that interpretation is fair [and] reasonable. *(Mozingo v. Oklahoma Secondary School Activities Association,* 1978).

Like the history teacher who admonished her students that "the one thing you can learn from history is that you can learn nothing from history," those who study sport law may learn nothing from court decisions involving state high school athletic associations—except that such associations must follow their own rules and that they will be treated by the courts as state actors. As such, they are required to afford equal protection and due process to those who will be directly affected by their rulings.

NATIONAL COLLEGIATE ATHLETIC ASSOCIATION

The premier governing body for collegiate sports in the United States is, of course, the behemoth 1,268-member National Collegiate Athletic Association (NCAA). The NCAA provides its institutional members—colleges and universities—with a comprehensive set of rules, regulations, and standards including the oft-litigated eligibility and recruitment regulations, playing rules, restrictions as to number of participants and coaches and detailed guidelines for the recruiting, care, and feeding of athletes.

The *2000-2001 NCAA Division I Manual,* nearly 500 pages in length, includes the NCAA Constitution Operating By-laws and Administrative By-laws. Each division of the NCAA has its own division-operating manual, which deals with the following topics:

- Ethical conduct
- Conduct and employment personnel
- Amateurism
- Recruiting
- Eligibility: academic and general requirements
- Enforcement
- Financial aid
- Awards, benefits, and expenses for enrolled student-athletes
- Playing and practice seasons

The NCAA constitution consists of the following articles:

- Name, purposes, and policy
- Principles for conduct of athletics
- NCAA membership
- Organization
- Legislative authority and process
- Institutional control

You must also consult each of the three divisions' own operating manuals. These tomes, read together with the master manual, yield a complete, though confusing picture of the operational structure of this giant governing body.

To give an idea of the breadth and depth of such an organization, items covered in the *Division I Operating Manual* range from the definition of an "award" ("an item given in recognition of athletics participation or performance," p. 121) to providing that a member institution may fund housing and transportation expenses for parents or legal guardians and the spouse of a student athlete and a student athlete's teammates to be present where the athlete suffers a life-threatening injury or illness or, in the event of a student athlete's death, to provide these expenses in conjunction with funeral arrangements. (*NCAA Division I Operating Manual*, p. 130)

Whether the governing body is large or small, whether the procedure for dealing with a violation of its by-laws is a simple voice vote hearing or reference to an intricate and complex manual consisting of hundreds of pages of procedure, case examples, and administrative layering, it is clear that a governing body must follow its own rules in taking action that affects its membership, particularly if membership in an association is an economic necessity for the member or if the association is engaged in state action. But if a governing body's rules are so complex and its procedures so convoluted that it takes several hundred pages of text to describe them, implementation is fraught with the danger of litigation. Thus, the NCAA has been the defendant in a significant number of litigated cases, many of which involve challenges to its sanctioning powers.

These powers are exercised by means of a complex framework of procedural steps that could, and have, filled a volume larger than this book. For present purposes, the following is a necessarily brief, simplified overview of NCAA procedures. Should the NCAA receive information as to a rules violation, the enforcement staff may proceed with a "preliminary inquiry" that communicates suspected violations to the member institution. If the charges are more grievous, an "official inquiry" may commence. An official inquiry directs the member college to reply to the charge. If a coach is involved, the coach is supposed to be informed of the charges; whether the association observes this practice is open to question.

NCAA by-laws give the NCAA Committee on Infractions power to grant immunity from discipline under the NCAA system to student athletes who are willing to disclose information in exchange for such immunity. In theory, as an investigation takes shape, both the member institution and the enforcement staff are afforded time to gather information in preparation for prehearing conferences and then formal hearings. After the hearings, the committee (paying heed to a complex structure of procedural and substantive rules) has the option of imposing various penalties ranging from minor sanctions aimed to correct what may be technical violations to the so-called "death penalty," which is reserved for major violations that are repeated within a five-year period. The "death penalty" cancels some or all competition in the sport involved for a one-to two-year period. In addition, the institution may also be penalized by other sanctions, ranging from eliminating grants-in-aid and recruiting activities for two years to suspending committee appointments and voting privileges for four years.

When coaches are found in violation, both the coaches and their member institutions are targeted for corrective action. The NCAA makes penalty decisions and corrective actions for coaches and members public.

All in all, the controversy over the NCAA's disciplinary machinery began long before Congress held hearings in the House of Representatives Subcommittee on Oversight and Investigations in the late 1970s. Lawsuits brought against the NCAA have included charges that it had violated **federal antitrust laws** (laws designed to prevent monopolistic business enterprises from interfering with free competition in the marketplace) by contracting with television networks to control broadcasts of college football to charges that it had deprived coaches of their livelihood.

Indeed, the NCAA appears to have been the first nonprofit association in sport to be held liable in a civil suit for violation of antitrust laws (*NCAA v. Board of Regents* (468 U.S. 85 1984), when an NCAA plan to televise Division I football limited the number of games to be aired. When member institutions were disciplined for their role in participating in a contract to televise certain of their football games negotiated through the College Football Association—a group independent of the NCAA—the schools were threatened with sanctions by the NCAA. Both schools involved, the Universities of Oklahoma and Georgia, sued the NCAA. The case was finally decided by the United States Court of Appeals for the Tenth Circuit, which upheld the decision of the trial court that the NCAA had violated the Sherman Antitrust Act by imposing an unreasonable restraint of trade and price fixing in violation of the Act.

When NCAA rules were challenged in subsequent cases, litigation came from players and agents alike. Nevertheless, the United States Court of Appeals' decision from 1984 regarding the University of Oklahoma and the University of Georgia did not come back to haunt the NCAA until 10 years later, when a group of college basketball coaches brought suit against the NCAA in Federal Court in California claiming that the Association's "restricted earnings coach" rule violated—to their damage —the Sherman Antitrust Act by restraining the "trade" of college coaching. The rule had been instituted by the 305-member NCAA Division I to prohibit institutions from paying their third assistant basketball coaches more than $12,000 per year and also to restrict camp and clinic income to $4,000 per year. In this case, the trial court entered an injunction against the rule limiting the salaries of coaches.

Thereafter, the plaintiff coaches prevailed at trial, recovering a jury verdict for $22.3 million, which was trebled to $66.9 million because antitrust laws provide for treble damages in such cases. Subsequently, the case was settled, with the NCAA agreeing to pay $54.5 million. The settlement funds were to be divided according to a plan approved by the court for class action lawsuits.

Other plaintiffs who have sued the NCAA include persons who challenged academic eligibility requirements, athletes, and others filing claims under disabilities laws, and various other claimants who have challenged NCAA policies and procedures.

Clearly, the concept of holding the NCAA's disciplinary feet to the fire under principles of antitrust law is now a viable theory for aggrieved athletes, individuals, and institutions under the proper circumstances. As the operating budget of organizations such as the NCAA increases, so, apparently, does the likelihood that governing bodies and other sports organizations, although nonprofit in purpose and form, may be held to be business enterprises for the purpose of laws regulating businesses, such as antitrust laws.

In addition to litigation, legislation has, in recent years, attempted to regulate the activities of the NCAA. So dreaded is the specter of NCAA enforcement action, which can deprive a member institution of millions of dollars in emoluments from national television, tournament play, and related income, that several state legislatures have enacted laws regulating NCAA procedures. These laws generally set forth a number of procedural and constitutional safeguards by which the NCAA is required to conduct its investigative and enforcement processes. Not surprisingly, the states that enacted such legislation did so after major educational institutions in their states had been heavily penalized by the association.

The requirements of these laws range from obligating the NCAA to conduct hearings utilizing the state code of evidence to allowing full and detailed pretrial discovery and disclosure. One state goes so far as to accord those accused of violating NCAA bylaws the right to disclosure that is given to criminal defendants under state penal statutes.

The Nebraska College Athletic Association Procedures Act (1990 Neb. Laws 397) simply and flatly requires the NCAA—by name—to apply due process of law guarantees contained in Nebraska state law and the Nebraska constitution to "every stage and facet of all proceedings of a collegiate athletic association, college or university that may result in the imposition of a penalty for violation of such association's rule or legislation" *(Id.)* The Illinois Collegiate Athletic Association Compliance Enforcement Procedures Act (Ill. compiled statutes 25/1 [1991]) contains lists of various procedures that organizations such as the NCAA must follow in conducting investigations and disciplinary proceedings. The law forbids a collegiate athletic association from imposing any penalty, or requiring a college or university to impose any penalty on a student or employee, unless it complies with the act and holds a formal hearing. The law specifically lists various due process safeguards such as the following:

> Any individual employee or student who is charged with misconduct must be notified, in writing, at least two months prior to the hearing of the specific charges against that individual, that a hearing will be held at a specific date and time to determine the truth of the charges, and that a finding that the misconduct occurred may result in penalties imposed on the institution or imposed by the institution on the individual. The institution shall also be notified in writing on the hearing of the charges . . . Any such person or institution has a right to have counsel present, to interrogate and cross-examine witnesses, and present a complete defense.
>
> — (Collegiate Athletic Association Compliance Enforcement Procedures Act,
> Illinois, 1991)

What's more, "clear and convincing evidence" is required for action to be taken by an association. If anyone charged with a violation so requests, the association must supply a transcript of any hearing without charge. Penalties must be reasonable for the violation and reasonable in relation to sanctions applied in the past for similar violations. Time limits are provided for the filing of charges and the conduct of a hearing. There are even rules that specify the procedure an investigator must use to interrogate the possible subject of an investigation.

The four laws restricting NCAA actions share the following characteristics:

1. They either specifically name the NCAA as the subject of the law or define "collegiate athletic association" as an organization of colleges and universities that exists to promote and regulate college athletics, that has at least 200-member institutions in at least 40 states, and further that the member institutions collectively receive at least $2 million annually in revenue from broadcasting rights. The Nevada statute defined such an association as a group of institutions in 40 or more states who are governed by the rules of the association relating to athletic competition." (Nev. Rev. Stat. s. 398. 055, 1991, p. 387)

2. They specifically authorize judicial review of NCAA action—in other words, grant access to the court to overturn an NCAA decision if a party suffers a loss because the NCAA has not complied with the law.

3. They provide for damages amounting to all financial losses suffered (and possibly litigation expenses and attorney's fees if a party wins the case against the NCAA).

4. They make the remedies contained in the laws cumulative, that is, in addition to and not exclusive of, other lawsuits and actions an aggrieved party may pursue.

5. They forbid an association from taking retaliatory action against an individual or institution that seeks redress under the law. For example, the NCAA may not expel an institution for suing it under the law (Illinois and Florida), or impose a penalty against any member college or university because a student or employee of the college or university brings a lawsuit under the law (Illinois and Florida).

One of the most comprehensive statements of the justification in the minds of the legislators for the enactment of such laws is in the preamble of the Illinois act, a virtual laundry list of the reasons why NCAA procedures should be subject to the controls of government:

> The State has a duty to protect citizens, institutions of higher learning, and others in enforcement of contract disputes, especially where one party to a contract (the NCAA) is a virtual monopoly and, as a result, the parties do not have equal bargaining power. Since all major colleges need to be members of the NCAA, there is little choice but for colleges and universities to join and remain as members of the NCAA and subscribe to NCAA rules and regulations.

> National major college sports brings recognition, pride and loyalty to the college, encourages alumni and other contributions [and candidly, the legislature admits],

> . . . participation in national sports brings in revenue to the university that helps to fund its various programs.

Illinois colleges and universities must belong to a National Collegiate Athletic Association composed of schools of a similar size and standing to those colleges and universities in the State in order for Illinois colleges and universities to compete on a national level in major college sports.

These associations have rules governing admissions, eligibility, academic status and financial aide. All colleges must abide by those rules.

Enforcement procedures are highly significant and must be fair to the accused. State institutions that are regulated by collegiate athletic associations are engaged in state action due the collegiate athletic associations in regulating those institutions.

Disciplinary procedures in collegiate athletic associations are a matter of public interest and the public policy of the State of Illinois mandates that procedures be fair to the university or college, its employees, its students and the communities involved.

The personal and professional lives and aspirations of students and those involved in administering athletic programs on behalf of the universities are at risk when collegiate athletic associations prosecute violations or alleged violations of rules.

Disruption of a university or college athletic program may have serious consequences including affecting the amount of taxpayer support that must be provided to the institution. In addition, an institution's reputation is a source of pride to the State and the State has a profound interest in protecting that reputation.

Arbitrary and capricious penalties may result if fairness and due process are not utilized in association proceedings. As a result, the unwarranted destruction of reputations of not only institutions but individuals in the State may occur.

The revenue derived by various communities in the State generated by college athletic programs is an interest that the State has a policy to protect.
—(Collegiate Athletic Association Compliance Enforcement Procedures Act, Illinois, 1991)

And, last, but definitely not least, in the words of the Illinois legislature:

The present procedures of collegiate athletic associations do not reflect the principle that one is innocent until proven guilty. Because of such potentially serious and far-reaching consequences, the procedures used to determine whether a violation of substantive association rules has occurred should reflect greater fairness and due process considerations than now apply and should provide for a speedier determination than at present of whether a violation of association rules has occurred.
—(Collegiate Athletic Association Compliance Enforcement Procedures Act, Illinois, 1991)

In 1992, the Knight Foundation Commission on Intercollegiate Athletics published its long-awaited report that discussed a number of issues involving the NCAA and regulations, including the issue of statutory regulation of intercollegiate athletics:

. . . four states already have enacted legislation to lay aside existing NCAA enforcement rules; comparable legislation is pending in six others. Their immediate effect, within each of the various states, is to virtually forbid the NCAA from enforcing any of its rules without court action. Left unchallenged, these measures threaten to kill nationwide collegiate competition.

Although these statutes appear to involve narrow issues of compliance or legislative support for local institutions, they go right to the heart of what athletic competition—Little League, intercollegiate, or professional—is all about. . . .

In this regard, a fundamental obligation of sports administration is maintaining oversight of the rules, changing them as participants agree, and enforcing compliance in the event of violation. If national governing bodies for intercollegiate athletics cannot ensure fair play through common compliance procedures across 50 States and the District of Columbia, nationwide intercollegiate competition as we have known it will not survive.

—*(Report of the Knight Foundation Commission on Intercollegiate Athletics,*
March 1992)

During the period from 1990-1992, Florida, Illinois, Nebraska, and Nevada enacted statutes regulating the NCAA's actions. Since that time, the Nevada law was declared unconstitutional by the courts (*National Collegiate Athletic Association v. Miller* 1993), and Florida's statute was repealed effective January 2003.

In the case of the Nevada statute, one year after the release of the Knight Report, the United States Court of Appeals for the Ninth Circuit declared the Nevada statute regulating the NCAA to be in violation of the Commerce Clause of the United States Constitution, because the law was found to regulate activity, not only in Nevada but elsewhere, and was thus a total infringement on the Commerce Clause of the Constitution which reserves to Congress the power to regulate Commerce with foreign Nations and among the several States.

The statute also violated the contracts clause of the Constitution, which prohibits any state from enacting any law impairing the obligation of contracts.

The Court concluded that, under Nevada's statute regulating the NCAA, the NCAA would need to follow the Nevada statute's dictates in all states and this was an impermissible burden on the NCAA, noting that the State of Nevada's authority ". . . goes to the heart of the NCAA and threatens to tear that heart out." (*NCAA v. Miller*). The Court analogized the disruption to the NCAA as follows: "Procedural changes at the border of every state would as surely disrupt the NCAA as changes in train length at each state's border would disrupt a railroad." The Court concluded that since only Congress can regulate interstate commerce, and the NCAA engages in interstate commerce, the Nevada statute was unenforceable. Thus, the future of similar statutes is uncertain at best.

In June 2001, the Knight Commission issued a new report, after conducting a number of hearings during 2000 and 2001. The Commission concluded that college athletics is in need of major reforms, focusing on academics, commercialization, and gambling, concluding that, "the NCAA cannot independently do what needs to be done. Its dual mission of keeping sports clean while generating millions of dollars in broadcasting revenue from member institutions creates a near-irreconcilable conflict." (Press Release, John S. and James L. Knight Foundation, June 26, 2001).

UNITED STATES OLYMPIC COMMITTEE AND NATIONAL GOVERNING BODIES

On a national and, in a sense, international scale lies the ultimate governing body: the United States Olympic Committee (USOC). The International Olympic Committee (IOC) coordinates the efforts of the USOC and all other member nations Olympic organizations to provide a framework for Olympic competition. In addition, the IOC recognizes more than two dozen international "federations," each of which exercises control and publishes rules for various sports played on the Olympic level.

In 1978, amateur athletics in the United States were the beneficiaries of an active Congress, which enacted legislation popularly known as "The Amateur Sports Act of 1978." The act gave legal recognition to the concept of **international amateur athletic competition**: defined as any amateur athletic competition between U.S. athletes and athletes representing any foreign country. The act went on to recognize the **national governing bodies** (NGB), as they are designated by the USOC, thereby giving each NGB its statutory niche in establishing rules and regulations for fostering competition.

According to this law each NGB is charged with nine duties:

1. to develop interest and participation throughout the United States and be responsible to the persons and amateur sports organizations it represents,
2. to coordinate with other organizations to minimize scheduling conflicts,
3. to take into account the opinions of amateur athletes in rendering policy decisions and keep the athletes informed of those policy decisions,
4. to promptly review requests of amateur sports organizations or other persons for sanctions to hold or sponsor competitions, within or outside the United States,
5. to allow athletes to compete in international amateur athletic competition conducted by the NGB,
6. to "provide equitable support and encouragement for participation by women where separate programs for male and female athletes are conducted on a national basis,"
7. to encourage and support amateur sports for individuals with disabilities and to expand opportunities for those individuals to participate in all athletic competition,
8. to render technical information on physical training, equipment design, coaching, and performance analysis, and
9. to encourage and support research, development, and dissemination of information in the areas of sports medicine and sports safety

—(The Amateur Sports Act of 1978).

In short, the act gave the USOC, through the force of law, exclusive jurisdiction over all matters pertaining to U.S. participation in the Olympic Games and the Pan American Games. Coupled with this power was the authority to resolve disputes and foster equal opportunity for all to participate. For their part, organizations selected to be NGBs are given more or less exclusive positions because there is only one recognized NGB for each Olympic sport. The law requires an NGB to:

1. have as its purpose the advancement of amateur athletic competition and, to that end, be incorporated as a nonprofit corporation and maintain the wherewithal to fulfill its purposes,

2. submit a copy of its corporate charter and by-laws and such additional information as the USOC may require,

3. submit to arbitration any disputes as to eligibility of any athlete, coach, trainer, manager, administrator, or official or any disputes regarding its recognition as a governing body,

4. be a member of not more than one international sports federation that governs a sport played in the Olympic or Pan American Games and that exercises independent control over its sport,

5. demonstrate that membership is open to any individual or amateur sports organization in the sport governed,

6. refrain from discrimination on the basis of race, color, religion, age, sex, or national origin to provide equal opportunity to participate,

7. provide fair notice and opportunity for a hearing to any party before declaring him or her ineligible to participate;

8. be governed by persons who are selected to govern without regard to race, color, religion, national origin, or sex;

9. demonstrate that no less than 20 percent of the voting members of its governing board of directors are either actively engaged in amateur competition in the particular sport or have represented the United States in international athletic competition in the sport within the preceding 10 years,

10. provide for reasonable direct representation on its board that reflects "the nature, scope, quality, and strength of the programs and competitions of such amateur sports organizations in relation to all other programs and competitions in such sport in the United States" (36 U.S.C. 391),

11. demonstrate that none of its officers are also officers of any other NGB,

12. provide procedures for prompt and equitable dispute resolution,

13. have eligibility criteria relating to amateur status that are no more restrictive than criteria utilized by the corresponding international sports federation, and

14. demonstrate that it can meet all responsibilities imposed on NGBs by the law.

—(The Amateur Sports Act of 1978).

The significance of the act for the practitioner is, quite simply, that the authority of the NGBs is no longer grounded in any voluntarily or consensual milieu, but rather that it has become a creature of statute. The Amateur Sports Act has survived numerous challenges in the courts throughout the federal circuits.

In October of 1998, Congress enacted significant amendments to the Amateur Sports Act. The amendments concerned dispute resolution and access to the courts, participation of athletes with disabilities, and certain intellectual property rights. Most significantly in terms of the legal system, the Amateur Sports Act, as amended in 1998, prohibits the granting of injunctive relief against the USOC in litigation involving the opportunity to participate in either the Olympic, Paralympic, or Pan-American Games within a 21-day period before the beginning of the games [36 USC § 220509(a)]. If the Constitution and by-laws of the USOC cannot provide for the resolution of a controversy over whether or not an athlete may participate before the beginning of the games, courts will not intervene. In addition, arbitrators impaneled by the USOC may award money damages to an aggrieved athlete as well as direct the governing body to allow the athlete to participate. Other amendments include the requirement that the USOC engage an "athlete ombudsman" who can advise participants regarding technical matters of by-laws and rules.

As to athletes with disabilities, the amended law mandates that the USOC serve on the International Paralympic Committee. The USOC also may now designate national governing bodies for Paralympic sports.

An important provision of the amended law delegates original jurisdiction to the federal courts while providing that the amendments do not *create* a private right of action to anyone to bring a lawsuit under the Act.

CASE STUDIES

CASE 12.1 AMATEURISM

Ron Behagan was a University of Minnesota All-American basketball player who went on to a professional career in the National Basketball Association. After several seasons, he traveled to Italy where, although paid for his skills on the hardwood, he played for an "amateur" league, in accordance with the rules of the international basketball governing body, Federation International de Basketball Amateur (FIBA).

The FIBA rules govern U.S. amateur basketball players, who are bound by their NGB, the Amateur Basketball Association of the United States of America (ABA/USA). ABA/USA is the United States' delegate to FIBA; thus, Behagan's participation was governed by the rules established by both these governing bodies.

One of those rules provides that U.S. players playing in foreign countries must qualify as amateurs. This qualification involves obtaining an ABA/USA travel permit and a license issued by FIBA. Although FIBA rules permitted U.S. professional basketball players to reinstate their amateur status once, but not more than once, in a lifetime, Behagan was apparently ignorant of the rule. After he played one season as a paid "amateur" in Italy, Behagan returned to the United States and played for the Washington Bullets in the spring of 1980.

Thereafter, Behagan returned to Italy, signed a contract with the Italian team for which he had played the prior season, but failed to apply for reinstatement. When FIBA advised the Italian basketball team that their U.S. star was ineligible because he had violated FIBA rules, the team in turn told Behagan that they would not honor his contract for the forthcoming season. Ron Behagan was unable to change FIBA's mind and brought suit in the U.S. District Court for the District of Colorado, charging that FIBA and ABA/USA violated federal antitrust laws, interfered with his contract of employment, and caused him to lose his job without due process.

Federal and state antitrust laws date back to the Sherman Anti-Trust Act (1890), a federal law that made illegal contracts, combinations, and conspiracies that restrain trade. Professional sports organizations are exposed to antitrust laws on a much broader scale (see *Amateur Softball Association of America v. United States, 1972; Board of Regents, University of Oklahoma v. NCAA, 71983; and Association for Intercollegiate Athletics for Women v. NCAA*, 1984).

Ron Behagan won his case against ABA/USA and its executive director, William Wall, after settling out of court with FIBA. But the Tenth Circuit Court of Appeals reversed the judgment and dismissed the lawsuit against the governing body. In its ruling, the court rejected Behagan's claim that the defendants violated federal antitrust laws by monopolizing competition because, as the court stated:

The Act also makes clear that Congress intended an NGB to exercise monolithic control over its particular amateur sport, including coordinating with appropriate international sports federations and controlling amateur eligibility for Americans that participate in that sport. . . . Although the Amateur Sports Act does not contain an explicit statement exempting action taken under its direction from the federal antitrust laws . . . we find that *the directives* of the Act make the intent of Congress sufficiently clear.

The Supreme Court has stated that the Amateur Sports Act was intended to correct the disorganization and the serious factional disputes that seemed to plague amateur sports in the United States. Behagan complains of exactly that action which the Act directs—the monolithic control of an amateur sport by the NGB for the sport and by the appropriate international sports federation of which the NGB is a member. This truth is underscored by the fact that the ABA/USA could not be authorized under the Act unless it maintained exactly that degree of control over its sport that Behagan alleges as an antitrust violation. *(Behagan v. Amateur Basketball Association of the United States of America,* 1989)

Perhaps more important, the Circuit Court of Appeals, following *San Francisco Arts & Athletics* (1987), held that the U.S. Olympic Committee did not engage in state action such as to trigger the requirement for due process of law in Behagan's case.

[Adapted from *Behagan v. Amateur Basketball Association of the United States of America,* 884 F.2d 524 (C.C.A. 10 1989)]

CASE 12.2 ELIGIBILITY DISPUTE BETWEEN A NATIONAL GOVERNING BODY AND A STATE HIGH SCHOOL ATHLETIC ASSOCIATION

Around the time that Ron Behagan's case was being decided (see Case 12.1), three high school students named David Burrows, Kyle Hetrnan, and Oreluwa Mahoney played high school soccer in Montgomery County, Ohio. David played for his public high school team, Kyle for his parochial school team, and Oreluwa for his private school team. All three students also played on independent teams organized through the Ohio South Youth Soccer Association, Inc. This nonprofit organization was a member of the United States Youth Soccer Association, which in turn is a division of the United States Soccer Federation (USSF). USSF, like ABA/USA for basketball, is the national governing body for soccer. This means that amateur soccer not under the control of high school or college governing bodies is governed, for purposes of international competition, by the USSF, under the authority of the Amateur Sports Act.

The Ohio High School Athletic Association, a state interscholastic athletic association composed of public, parochial, and private schools in the state of Ohio and responsible for administering interscholastic athletics in the state, changed its by-laws to make students who had played soccer on an independent team during the spring of 1988 and thereafter ineligible to compete in high school soccer. Suit was brought in the U.S. District Court for the Southern District of Ohio against the Ohio High School Athletic

Association, not only in the names of the three high school students, but by the Ohio Youth Soccer Association, Inc., and its related associations on behalf of approximately 15,000 high school students in Ohio who played soccer in 1987.

In this clash between a constituent organization of a national governing body, whose authority was derived from an act of Congress, and a state high school athletic association, a voluntary group composed of public, private, and parochial schools and given the power to regulate the interscholastic athletics of virtually all the public schools and many of the private and parochial schools in the state, the Sixth Circuit Court of Appeals compared the Ohio High School Athletic Association to the NCAA in that both associations have public, parochial, and private scholastic institutions as members, and membership is voluntary. The court also reasoned that "both organizations promulgate and apply rules to promote and protect amateur sports competitions among their respective members" (*Burrows v. Ohio High School Athletic Association*, 1989, p. 125).

Thus, even though the plaintiffs and the defendant in the lawsuit had agreed that the Ohio High School Athletic Association was indeed a state actor for purposes of constitutional law, the court rejected that analysis. Even so, the court said, whether the Ohio High School Athletic Association was a state actor or not, the regulation embodied in the by-law change that the interscholastic association made was certainly a valid exercise of its authority. The court reminded the parties that the state high school association did not prevent the plaintiffs from playing soccer on independent teams, but merely prevents those who have previously played on a high school team regulated by the Ohio High School Athletic Association from again playing on those teams "if, in the interim, they have participated in independent outdoor soccer during the school year" (*Burrows*, p. 126).

Finally, the court rejected the NGB Youth Soccer Association's argument that the Amateur Sports Act prohibited a state high school athletic association from interfering with the authority of a national governing body that was qualified under the federal statute rules and regulations. In rejecting this argument, the court of appeals cited the exclusive jurisdiction, under the Amateur Sports Act, of other amateur sports organizations that restrict participation to a specific class of athletes "such as high school students" (36 U.S.C. Section 396).

[Adapted from *Burrows v. Ohio High School Athletic Association*, 891 F.2d 122 (6th Cir. 1989)]

CASE 12.3 AN ATHLETIC CONFERENCE AS A STATE ACTOR

Jim Stanley was the head football coach of Oklahoma State University, a member of the Big Eight Conference. The conference is a football league composed of Oklahoma State University and seven other state universities in neighboring states. These institutions are all publicly funded. The conference is in turn a member of the NCAA, another voluntary association consisting of several hundred colleges and universities across the country.

The conference, in joining the NCAA, agreed to be bound by the NCAA's rules and regulations. Member schools are also bound to obey any conference rules and regulations that are more restrictive than the NCAA's rules. According to conference rules, the head football coach is responsible for any violation of recruiting rules. In June 1982, Coach Stanley was contacted by a representative of the Big Eight Conference and told that an investigation was in progress concerning the Oklahoma State University football program. No further details of the investigation were given to Coach Stanley. Several months later, the Commissioner of the Big Eight Conference, Charles Nein, prepared a report from information gathered by his representatives and investigators, one of whom had spoken with Coach Stanley several months before. Approximately 50 people had been interviewed for the report, which contained statements from some of the people interviewed to the effect that Coach Stanley had spent various amounts of money that had been funneled by other persons named in the report to members of the university's football team.

Under the rules of the Big Eight Conference, any member college may be ordered to show cause why it should not be further disciplined in the event of violations of conference or NCAA rules if either governing body maintains that the university did not take sufficient action. Coach Stanley knew that the conference could virtually force additional disciplinary action upon an institution that would prevent a coach from being hired as coach by any member institution in the country. Thus, the effect of disciplinary action imposed by either the conference or the NCAA could well be to "blackball" a head coach from remaining a head coach or being hired as a head coach of any college or university that is a member of the NCAA.

Without a job in the only career he knew and, worse yet, facing the prospect that he would never be hired to coach college football again, Jim Stanley sued the Big Eight Conference to prevent the conference from conducting any hearing of charges against him without due process of law.

Because all schools in the conference were publicly funded universities, and because these universities had delegated to the Big Eight Conference the function of supervising their athletic programs, the conference was a state actor and due process protections of the U.S. Constitution applied. Coach Stanley would have his day in court, and instead of a hearing conducted solely on the basis of a "report" containing statements and conclusions of dozens of witnesses whom Coach Stanley would not have had the opportunity to confront in his defense, Coach Stanley would have a hearing with live witnesses whom Mr. Stanley, through his attorney, could cross-examine.

[*Stanley v. The Big Eight Conference*, 463 F.Supp 1978 (W.D. Missouri 1978)]

CASE 12.4 ATHLETIC CONFERENCES AND DUE PROCESS

On January 28, 1972, Ron Behagan (see also Case 12.1) was in his junior year at the University of Minnesota. Ron and his teammate, Marvin "Corky" Taylor, became involved in a slight disagreement with Ohio State's Luke Witte during a basketball game, which resulted in the Big Ten Conference suspending Ron Behagan and Marvin Taylor for the remainder of the season. The fight on the basketball court was followed by a second, more genteel battle in the U.S. District Court for the District of Minnesota. In this case the court recognized the economic value of intercollegiate athletics for those who participate:

> In these days when juniors in college are able to suspend their formal educational training in exchange for multimillion dollar contracts to turn professional, this Court takes judicial notice of the fact that, to many, the chance to display their athletic prowess in college stadiums and arenas throughout the country is worth more in economic terms than the chance to get a college education.

It is well recognized that the opportunity to receive an education is an interest of such substantial importance that it cannot be impaired without minimum standards of due process

—(*Behagan v. Intercollegiate Conference of Faculty Representatives*, 1972, p. 604).

After criticizing the Big Ten Conference for not having any written procedures to deal with disciplinary situations, Judge Larson found that the investigation that had resulted in the suspension had been conducted in a manner contrary to both procedural and substantive due process. The court noted that the handbook did provide for the athletic directors imposing the penalty to appear in person at the meeting at which the commissioner's report is made and for charged athletes to appear to defend themselves. This provision, however, did not provide for due process in the eyes of the court.

Although Big Ten regulations as they existed at the time empowered the commissioner of the conference to promote the conference's general welfare, the court ruled that a temporary suspension of a student athlete must immediately be followed by notice and hearing by the students suspended. In addition, the students must be apprised of the commissioner's report on which the suspension is based and be given an opportunity to defend themselves. Judge Larson concluded:

This was never done. Any report which was made to the Directors of Athletics at their January 21, 1972, meeting is as yet undisclosed, and it is undisputed that none of the participants were ever appraised [sic] of the meetings, let alone offered an opportunity to speak in their own defense.

It is elemental that action beyond the scope of a body's own procedural regulations is a violation of due process of law.

—(*Behagan v. Intercollegiate Conference of Faculty Representatives*, 1972, p. 606).

As a result, the defendant Big Ten Conference was given about three days to hold a hearing according to various due process guidelines that were set forth by the court. Plaintiffs Ron Behagan and Marvin Taylor were to be given written notice of the time and place of the hearing at least two days in advance. The notice was to specify the exact charges against each and the grounds under which they would be penalized. Although the court did not require that the plaintiffs have the right to cross-examine witnesses in the Behagan case, it did require the presentation of testimony and that both sides of the story be heard. Plaintiffs were to be given a list of all the witnesses appearing and were to receive a copy of the athletic director's written report. Finally, the court indicated that the hearing should be tape recorded and that the tapes should be made available to the plaintiffs if they were to appeal, as they were entitled to do according to the Big Ten handbook.

[Adapted from *Behagan v. Intercollegiate Conference of Faculty Representatives*, 346 F. Supp. 602 (D. Minn. 1972)]

CASE 12.5 ASSOCIATION DISCIPLINARY RULES

Plaintiff Christensen, a well-known local soccer player, took up coaching youth soccer by joining the Michigan State Youth Soccer Association. Christensen was suspended by the association for six months following complaints regarding his behavior at youth soccer games. Following his suspension, Christensen brought suit for breach of contract, tortious interference with contractual relations, fraud, and violation of due process guarantees. After he started his lawsuit, Christensen was apparently hired as head coach of the Detroit Wheels professional soccer club—and then "unhired" when the professional team was apprised of his suspension from coaching youth soccer. The plaintiff also sought a declaratory judgment, so that he would be permitted to continue to coach youth soccer.

Christensen claimed that the defendant association failed to conform to its "first time offender" penalty, failed to forward copies of officials' game reports to the appropriate persons, failed to hold a hearing at the site of the alleged misconduct, and failed to convene the hearing in a timely manner, all in alleged violation of the Association's rules.

In addition, Christensen claimed he was not afforded due process with respect to the association's actions. Finally, he alleged fraud, claiming that the Association assured him that his suspension would not affect his employment and that he relied to his detriment on those representations.

The Court of Appeals of Michigan found no evidence of fraudulent representations on the part of the defendants; no evidence that the association's reasonable hearing procedures weren't carried out; and no evidence that plaintiff exhausted his administrative internal remedies within the association. Nor was this plaintiff, suing a private voluntary association, the beneficiary of protection afforded by the 5th Amendment to the United States Constitution. The court stated that "there is no provision of law that imposes upon private associations the same panoply of procedural rules imposed on public entities by the due process clauses."

Rather, the court instructed that the United States and the Michigan Constitution due process provisions create a distinction between things that are public and things that are private. The Association involved was private (i.e., not a state actor). Beyond that, the court found, as a fact, that plaintiff was provided with notice of the charges, a fair hearing, and the opportunity to defend himself and that these procedures would comply with requirements of due process even if the United States and Michigan Constitutions applied.

The Christensen case illustrates the general rule of deference to the legal authority of a sports association to regulate the conduct of the competition and the coaches and athletes who compete.

CASE 12.6 ATHLETE'S CHALLENGE OF PRIVATE ASSOCIATION

A temporary restraining order granted against a youth hockey association ordering the association to release a 12-year-old athlete from his obligation to play for a particular team forsaking certain other teams was vacated by the Appellate Court of Illinois in *Lee v. Snyder*, at 673 N.E.2d 1136. The 12-year-old hockey player was required, as were his teammates, to sign agreements requiring an exclusive commitment to a certain team, thus barring participation on a team of lesser skilled players sponsored by the same organization and, in fact, most other teams.

A few weeks later, plaintiff filed a grievance pursuant to the by-laws of the association asking to be relieved from the obligations of his contract, citing several personal reasons why he did not want to be bound to play for the team he signed up with. The reasons ranged from the location of the team's practices and the times of the games to his school work and the fact that he might get on a team that was at a higher level of competition. In addition, the athlete and his parents maintained that the facts of the obligations entailed with playing for team Illinois—the team he signed up for— were misrepresented by the association staff. The committee of the association charged with hearing grievances denied the grievance. Under the by-laws, an appeal was permissible to the organization's board of directors. An appeal hearing was held with the same result. A temporary restraining order was issued mandating another team within the organization to allow the plaintiff to try out and skate with the club pending further order of the court and enjoining the state hockey association from penalizing either the local hockey team or the plaintiff. On hearing for the permanent injunction, the same relief was granted, prohibiting any sanctions to be imposed on anyone and permitting the plaintiff to play on any team that would have him. An appeal was taken.

The Appellate Court of Illinois cited a litany of case law to the effect that the noninterference rule should be applied, where the association is proceeding in accordance with rules so long as it is exercising its power consistently within those rules and the member is treated in a fundamentally fair fashion. Then, while noting exceptions to the rule of noninterference for fraud, collusion, and arbitrariness or some property or economic right that implicates due process, Justice Cahill, writing for a three-judge panel, waxed philosophical as he vacated the injunction, thus ending the lawsuit brought by the 12-year-old plaintiff and his parents:

> We are aware of the elaborate and minutely governed structures that have evolved to oversee everything from pre-school soccer leagues to the international monolith that is little league baseball. Judges who recall summer pickup games on the prairie with a lopsided ball wrapped in black friction tape and winter hockey matches with a stone for a puck on a frozen sanitary canal are probably the wrong people to exercise judicial restraint in a case such as this. The quarrels that erupt in an era when every aspect of a childhood game is encrusted with a bureaucratic rule written by an adult seem ripe for judicial intervention.
>
> The temptation to intervene, to scold and then sermonize on the joys of childhood, with dark reference to adults who spoil the fun, is strong. It swirls up from a desire to revisit the prairie and the canal. The irony is that the same desire motivates those who volunteer to coach little league and to form amateur hockey leagues.
>
> —(*Lee v. Snyder*)

CHAPTER SUMMARY

Governing bodies derive their authority in one or both of two ways:

1. With the consent of members of the governing body with the tacit or express imprimatur of government. (Members may be institutional, as in the case of the University of Las Vegas at Nevada's membership in the NCAA, or individual, such as the membership of Michelle Kwan in the United States Figure Skating Association.)
2. From an enactment of a state legislature or an act of Congress, the most notable example being the Amateur Sports Act of 1978, which vested authority in the U.S.

Olympic Committee and which, in turn, vested authority in sport-specific national governing bodies whose authority is clearly established by the Act and which, in turn, vested authority in sport-specific national governing bodies whose authority is clearly established by the Act.

Litigation frequently arises when:

1. individual members of an organization challenge a rule or enforcement proceeding taken against them by their own organizations, either on the ground of deprivation of their legal constitutional rights, or on the ground that their organizations did not follow their own rules in imposing a sanction or penalty,
2. individuals challenge rulings or actions of their associations that are mandated by their association's memberships in a larger association, or
3. individual student athletes enrolled in educational institutions challenge decisions of governing bodies of which their schools or colleges are members.

Although each of these situations presents a different fact pattern, a common issue to all such litigation is the origin of the body's authority and the proper and lawful exercise of that authority. These, then, are the primary questions at the threshold of virtually all court challenges to the authority of governing bodies in sport.

Whatever the reasons, it is abundantly clear that today's administrators, athletic directors, and coaches cannot afford to ignore the increasing interaction of our legal system with the bodies that govern sport. Populations participating in sport and athletic programs are clearly more cognizant of their legal rights and less content to follow, without challenge, the authority of coaches, administrations, and governing bodies. In addition, the universally acknowledged ascension of sports into "big business" precipitates more, not less, government intervention and corresponding interaction with the legal system. Therefore, as a matter of economics and good management, athletic administrators today simply must be aware of the legal consequences of their actions and those of their staffs.

The natural consequence of government intervention, the increased susceptibility to litigation, and the ever-increasing complexity of association, conference, and subgroup affiliations is the possibility of conflict, power struggles, and political maneuvering that require administrators to be fully aware of their legal environments. Finally, the legislative process that has witnessed the proliferation of statutes, the purpose of which is to redress perceived wrongs and allow everyone to participate, has landed full force in the sports arena. The athletic administrator must now be prepared to deal with the legal rights and responsibilities of an ever-increasing superstructure of governing bodies, organizations, chapter groups, sport-specific and special interest spin-offs, and their progeny.

KEY TERMS

By-laws
Compelling state interest

Contract
Federal antitrust laws
Fundamental rights
International amateur athletic competition
National governing bodies
Rational basis
State actors
Strict scrutiny
Suspect classifications
Voluntary associations

QUESTIONS FOR DISCUSSION

1. Distinguish between voluntary and legislatively mandated governing bodies and give examples of each.
2. Enumerate the factors that render a governing body a state actor and give examples of the types of governing bodies that are state actors.
3. Discuss how governing bodies, both voluntary and government sponsored, can defend their disciplinary actions in court.
4. Discuss the legal significance of the "contract" into which members of governing bodies enter.
5. What fundamental rights are most frequently associated with litigation against governing bodies?
6. Identify two instances in which courts are likely to interfere in the internal decisions of governing bodies.
7. Describe the relationship between governing bodies for sport-specific activities and educational institutions.
8. Describe the circumstances under which government is most likely to pass laws limiting the power of governing bodies.
9. Identify the set of rules that every governing body must follow so that its actions will be sustained in a court of law.

REFERENCES

Amateur Softball Association of America v. United States, 467 F.2d 312 (10th Cir. 1972).

Amateur Sports Act of 1978, 36 U.S.C. s. 371-396 (1978).

Association for Intercollegiate Athletics for Women v. NCAA, 588 F. Supp. 487, *aff_d,* 735 F.2d 577 (D.C. Cir. 1984).

B.C. v. Cumherland Regional School District, 220 N.J. Super. 214, 531 A.2d 1059 (1987).

Behagan v. Amateur Basketball Association of the United States of America, 884 F.2d 524 (10th Cir. 1989).

Behagen v. Intercollegiate Conference of Faculty Representatives, 346 F. Supp. 602 (D. Minn. 1972).

Black, M. (1990). *Black's Law Dictionary* (6th ed.). St. Paul: West.

Board of Regents, University of Oklahoma v. NCAA, 561 P.2d 449 (Okla. 1983).

Burrows v. Ohio High School Athletic Association, 891 F.2d 122 (6th Cir. 1989).

Christensen v. Michigan State Youth Soccer Association, 553 N.W. 2d 638 (1996).

Collegiate Athletic Association Compliance Enforcement Procedures Act, Illinois and Florida, c. 260, s. 1 (s. 240.5341 et seq.) (1991).

Goss v. Lopez, 419 U.S. 565 (1975).

In Re United States EX REL Missouri State High School Activities Association, 682 F.2d 147 (8th Cir. 1982).

Johnson, C. (1992, April 13). The rules of the game. *U.S. News and World Report,* pp. 60-62.

Kite v. Marshall, 661 F.2d 1022 (1981).

Lee v. Snyder, 673 N.E.2d 1136 (1996).

Mozingo v. Oklahoma Secondary School Activities Association, 575 P.2d 1379 (Okla. 1978).

NAACP v. Button, 371 U.S. 415, 433, 83 S. Ct. 328, 9 L.Ed.2d 405 (1963).

NCAA Division I Operating Manual. (1991). National Collegiate Athletic Association, Overland Park, Kansas, 1991.

NCAA v. Kansas Department of Revenue, 245 Kan. 553, 781 P.2d 726 (1989).

NCAA v. Tarkanian, 488 U.S. 179 (1988).

Nebraska Laws 397 (1990).

Nevada Revised Statutes, § 398 (1991).

New Jersey Statutes Annotated (1979). 18A:11-3.

NJSIAA By-laws (1991).

Prince v. Cohen, 715 F.2d, 87, 93 (1983).

Report of the Knight Foundation Commission on Intercollegiate Athletics. (1992, March). Charlotte, NC: Knight Foundation.

Sidle v. Majors, 264 Indiana 206, 341 N.E. 2d 733 (1976).

University Interscholastic League v. North Dallas Chamber of Commerce Soccer Association, 693 S.W. 2d 513 (Tex. Ct.App. 1985).

ADDITIONAL READINGS

Arnold, D.E. (1983). *Legal considerations in the administration of public school physical education and athletic programs.* Springfield, IL: Charles C. Thomas.

Johnson, A.T., & Frey, J.H. (1985). *Government and sport.* Totowa, NJ: Rowman & Allanheld.

National Federation Handbook. (1971). Kansas City: National Federation of State High School Associations.

Rapp, JR. (1984). *Educational law.* New York: Matthew Bender.

Sharp, L.A. (1990). *Sport law.* National Organization on Legal Problems of Education.

Valente, W,D. (1985). *Education law.* St. Paul: West.

Yasser, R., McCurdy, J.R., & Goplerud, C.P. (1990). *Sports law.* Cincinnati: Anderson.

PART V

Legal Responsibility for Participant Safety

CHAPTER 13

BASIC PRINCIPLES AND CONCEPTS OF TORT LIABILITY

John was a star pitcher for his high school baseball team. Although he was only a junior, he was already the object of much attention from professional scouts and college recruiters. In the late spring of his junior year, the football coach suggested that John's speed, coordination, and height would make him a natural receiver, even though he had never played organized football. John decided to try out for football in the fall.

From the first day of fall practice, John was used exclusively as a wide receiver. To help him develop his offensive skills and techniques, the coaches released him from all defensive drills and provided him instead with extra practice on pass routes and receiving. The lone exception to this procedure occurred during the second week of practice when John and several other players were given a five-minute explanation of proper tackling technique, after which John made one tackle under the supervision of the coach. Immediately after he had accomplished the tackle, John was once again directed to practice his receiving skills.

As the season progressed, John's skills improved rapidly, and by the third game he was the starting wide receiver as well as a punt and kickoff return specialist. In the fourth quarter of the fifth game of the season, John ran a pass route to the right side of the field. The ball was thrown to the left and was intercepted by a member of the opposing team. John came across the field toward the ball carrier, lowered his head, and made the tackle, preventing a long return.

As the ensuing pileup was cleared, it became obvious that John had suffered an injury. The game was delayed for over 30 minutes as medical personnel carefully ministered to John and moved him to the waiting ambulance. John had suffered a fractured cervical vertebrae with a severance of the spinal column, resulting in permanent quadriplegia. A long period of intensive medical treatment, followed by the need for nearly constant medical care and costly modifications to the family home, resulted in a financial drain far beyond the means of John's family, who ultimately sought the advice of an attorney.

Although in the past, John's injury would most probably have been classified as bad luck, this is no longer the case. Athletes and their families are becoming increasingly aware of their legal rights and consequently more willing to seek compensation through the courts. In this case, John's attorney alleged that the coaches, the team trainer, and the company that manufactured John's helmet all failed in their obligations to provide for John's safety and therefore should thus be held liable for his injuries.

After a lengthy process of litigation, the trainer and helmet manufacturer were found not to have been guilty of negligence. The coaches, on the other hand, were found to have been negligent for their failure to prepare John properly for the foreseeable eventuality that he would be required to attempt a tackle. John was awarded compensatory damages in the amount of $4.25 million.

LEARNING OBJECTIVES

Upon completion of this chapter, the student will be able to

1. enumerate and explain the factors that underlie the recent growth in personal injury litigation in sport,
2. list the elements of negligence and give examples of their application in programs of sport and physical activity,
3. discuss the applications of the various legal defenses and give examples of how each might apply to specific situations,
4. develop effective releases and participation agreements for specific sports or activities, and
5. explain the importance of record keeping and public relations in the legal process.

ROOTS OF THE LIABILITY EXPLOSION

The recent propensity for litigation among North Americans in general and the sporting community in particular has been strongly affected by factors that are mostly beyond the influence of the sport and physical activity profession. These factors include the following:

1. **Insurance shortfalls.** When someone suffers an accidental injury, the medical and hospital insurance available may not cover all of the treatment and rehabilitation costs. When this occurs, the injured party has only two alternatives: absorb the financial burden or seek redress through the courts.
2. **The right to sue.** Under American civil law, any person can sue another person at any time, for practically any reason. Although this simplistic analysis ignores the legal complexities as well as the possible variations in outcome, the fact remains that the right to initiate a lawsuit is, for the most part, guaranteed.

3. **Doctrine of entitlement.** It is not surprising that jurors, typically people untrained in justice issues, tend to view litigation involving an injured person in humanistic terms. They see a person who, through no apparent personal fault, has suffered a painful and costly injury. They feel, quite understandably, that someone should help to bear the financial burden that has resulted. The problem is that the only "someone" currently available is the one being sued. This sense of the need for compensation—in essence a humanitarian desire to help the needy—can to some degree slant the perceptions of otherwise unbiased jurors.

4. **Settlements.** A settlement is a financial agreement to a lawsuit reached between the opposing parties. In agreeing to a settlement, neither party admits guilt nor claims victory. They simply agree that it is more desirable to accept negotiated financial arrangements than to pursue the matter any further. The overwhelming majority of all liability suits end in settlements.

    It is not difficult to see that the cumulative effect of these factors predisposes us to litigation. An injured person has a financial loss and a legal right to pursue the matter, and he or she realizes that most people who do so gain at least some compensation through a negotiated settlement. In sport and recreation, the problem is further complicated by an additional factor.

5. **The myth of being risk-free.** It is impossible to conduct a program of physical activity that is entirely safe. If you think this is a gross overstatement, consider the following: The usual connotation of the word *safe* involves freedom from risk, harm, or injury. This condition is, however, contrary to the very nature of physical activity. As long as one or more persons are allowed to move, particularly when this movement includes physical contact, competition with others, and perhaps the use of equipment and apparatus, there exists the threat of danger, harm, or loss.

Table 13.1 shows the extent of estimated injuries during 1997 alone in selected areas of sport and physical activity. Although we can and should do everything reasonably in our power to reduce the number and severity of injuries, we must at the same time also recognize that, despite our very best efforts, some injuries will occur.

Unfortunately, each injury must be recognized as a potential lawsuit. We've seen that it is impossible to remove all risk from physical activities; and for many participants, the very element of controlled risk (or the perception of risk) is part of the enjoyment of the sporting experience. It probably would be unwise to entirely eliminate every element of danger, even if it were possible to do so. The remaining activities would be so sterile and unchallenging that no one would bother with them.

This fact is not, however, an excuse for allowing unreasonable or unnecessary risks to exist. The prudent coach or teacher takes all reasonable steps to remove the dangers in any given activity and then answers this question: Does the value of the activity significantly outweigh the risk that remains? When the answer is yes, the risks can be viewed as both reasonable and controlled, and the activity may be conducted. Where the answer is no, however, the prudent teacher or coach will either make further modifications to the activity or eliminate it entirely.

TABLE 13.1
ESTIMATED SPORTS-RELATED, MEDICALLY-ATTENDED
INJURIES DURING CALENDAR YEAR 1997

Sport	Medically attended injuries
Basketball	644,921
Touch and tackle football	334,420
Baseball and softball	326,714
Roller skating and in-line skating	153,023
Soccer	148,913
Exercising with weights or equipment	86,024
Swimming	83,772
Ice hockey	77,491
Volleyball	67,340
Wrestling	39,829
Golf	39,473
Gymnastics	33,373
Tennis	22,294
Racquetball, squash, and paddleball	10,438
Street or roller hockey	10,028
Field hockey	4,830
Archery	3,213
Total	2,086,096

Source: U.S. Consumer Products Safety Commission/National Injury Information Clearinghouse, 1999.

TORTS AND INTENTIONAL TORTS

A **tort** is a civil wrong for which an individual may seek recompense through the courts. A negligent tort arises when a loss occurs as a result of another person's failure to meet a legal duty or obligation properly. There is no requirement to show conscious deliberation or intent on the part of the defendant. The failure is often entirely inadvertent.

An intentional tort, on the other hand, results from an act that the defendant consciously decided to do. Assault and defamation are forms of intentional torts discussed elsewhere in this text. The overwhelming majority of torts involving sport and physical activity focus on the alleged negligence of the person or persons in charge.

ELEMENTS OF NEGLIGENCE

While access to the courts is a hallmark of a free society that enables all persons to seek the power of government to right injustices and be compensated for injuries caused by others, that freedom is a separate concept from the principals and precedents of law that determine under what circumstances one person may be liable for injuring another person.

Common misconceptions regarding access to the courts and tort liability run the gamut of possibilities. There is a widespread belief—augmented by advertising and anecdotal evidence—that the right to recovery in tort is predicated upon (1) the fact of an injury alone and (2) that the amount of recovery is predicated solely on the seriousness of the injury. At the other end of the spectrum are those who believe that injuries arising in the course of sport and physical activity programs are somehow immune from litigation as they are "part of the game" and not compensable in a court of law. Neither extreme, of course, is accurate.

Negligence is essentially either failing to do something that a reasonable, prudent person would have done under the same or similar circumstances or doing something that a reasonable, prudent and up-to-date person would not have done. Negligence may therefore arise from an act of omission or commission. To meet the legal requirements for proving liability for negligence, the plaintiff must show all the following elements:

1. **Duty.** Every civil action for personal injury must show that the **defendant** (person being sued) owed a duty of care to the **plaintiff** (injured party). If the injured party was an athlete on a team, a student in a class, or a participant in a program, the duty of the coach, teacher, or administrator under whose direction or supervision the program was run is virtually indisputable.
2. **Breach.** This is the error or omission that forms the basis of the complaint. The issue is essentially whether or not the defendant failed to act reasonably under the particular circumstances involved. The yardstick by which a jury would be asked to determine whether a breach existed is the standards of the profession as applied to the circumstances in question. Normally expert testimony is required to provide the factual basis for the necessary determination. For example, a Little League coach would not necessarily be expected to act as an intercollegiate coach would, but would be expected to act as a reasonable, prudent and up-to-date Little League coach.

    Additionally, there must be proof that the defendant should have been able to predict the possibility of an injury under the circumstances in question. It is not necessary to show that the specific injury suffered by the plaintiff was predictable under the circumstances. All that needs to be shown is that a reasonable person should have realized that *someone* might suffer *some* type of injury. This requirement is known as **foreseeability.**
3. **Loss.** The breach must have resulted in damages or losses to the plaintiff's person, property or interest.

4. **Proximate cause.** The fact that the defendant negligently breached a duty owed to the plaintiff is not sufficient grounds for a successful lawsuit. The plaintiff must prove that the particular injury for which compensation is sought was actually caused or aggravated by the defendant's negligent act (see Cases 14.1 and 14.2).

In summary, the success of a negligence claim is dependent upon the plaintiff's ability to prove that the defendant owed a duty of care; that the defendant acted unreasonably in breaching that duty; that the plaintiff suffered an injury or loss; and finally, that the defendant's act or omission caused or aggravated the injury or loss. Note that nothing in these elements is predicated upon the severity of the injury. The fact that a person is seriously, or even fatally, injured does not mean that an actionable negligence claim exists under the law absent the elements of duty, breach and proximate cause.

ORDINARY vs. GROSS NEGLIGENCE

In some circumstances an alleged negligent act or omission is believed to be so extreme as to merit special consideration by the courts. When a person with a legal duty of care fails to exercise even slight diligence in the fulfillment of a duty, the court may sustain a claim for **gross negligence.** A finding of gross negligence differs only in degree from ordinary negligence but carries more severe legal consequences. Most immunity laws, for instance, do not offer protection from allegations of gross negligence. Similarly, the courts will disregard the protections of a waiver in the face of gross negligence. Finally, gross negligence exposes a defendant to the possibility of punitive damages.

LEGAL DEFENSES AGAINST CLAIMS OF NEGLIGENCE

A number of legal concepts and professional procedures can be used to help formulate a defense against claims of negligence. Although these procedures are of unquestioned importance in the litigation process, their application to the daily activities of coaching and teaching is sometimes overlooked. It must be remembered that these defenses can only be of value to the degree that they are supported by the routine and faithful application of the administrative and instructional procedures upon which they rely.

GOVERNMENTAL IMMUNITY

Traditionally, all states were protected by Sovereign Immunity which prevented them from being sued for torts of negligence. This immunity barred liability claims against the governmental entities; although not, in most cases, against their officers, agents or employees individually. Sovereign Immunity has been gradually eroded based on the belief that broad immunity protection is unfair to injured parties.

The federal and state governments have now instituted varying degrees of **tort claims legislation** which allows injured parties to sue the governmental entities within more or less limited circumstances. For instance, most tort claims provisions allow suit for negligence in **ministerial acts** but bar claims involving **discretionary acts.** A ministerial act is one which involves the management and control of the day-to-day activities of government while a discretionary act involves judgmental decision-making functions. For example, the issues of whether and where to construct a new tennis facility would normally be considered discretionary functions and, thus would be immune from negligence. The actions of the governmental employees with regard to the maintenance and management of the tennis facility, on the other hand, would in most cases be seen as a ministerial function and, thus, subject to negligence claims.

VOLUNTEER IMMUNITY STATUTES

In the last decade, federal and state legislation limiting or circumscribing liability for volunteers in sport and physical activity programs has become ubiquitous. Every state has at least one statute dealing with volunteer liability. In addition, the Volunteer Protection Act of 1997 preempts inconsistent state law except where a state law provides additional liability immunity for volunteers. States are allowed under the federal law to opt-out of the federal law under certain conditions.

All volunteer immunity statutes contain numerous exceptions. The most common of these exceptions is that willful and intentional conduct, and in many cases, gross negligence negates immunity. Thus, a volunteer who intentionally, willfully or recklessly causes an injury to another may not be immune under either state or federal law.

GOOD SAMARITAN LAWS

Good Samaritan legislation has been enacted in many states in an effort to encourage individuals to assist others in need of help when they are under no obligation to do so. The concept is that by removing the threat of liability for ordinary negligence, individuals will be less reluctant to "get involved." It is important to recognize, however, that Good Samaritan Laws do not offer any form of protection for persons who have a duty of care for the individual in need. Therefore, coaches or teachers who fail to administer prompt and proper first aid to students or athletes for whom they are responsible would not be protected by Good Samaritan Laws.

RELEASES

A **release** or **waiver** is a type of contract signed by participants or, in the case of minors, by their parents as well. In the release, the participants or their parents absolve the coach or teacher from liability if an injury occurs as a result of the specified activity. Such documents are seldom considered legally valid for absolving a defendant of responsibility for school-related programs or for minors for the following reasons:

1. The courts are generally reluctant to grant individuals pre-event protection from the consequences of their own negligent actions.
2. No person can legally waive the rights of another. Parents therefore cannot waive the rights of their children.
3. It is extremely difficult to enforce contracts executed by minors because they can be voided at anytime by the minor: even after an injury has occurred (see chapter 10).

4. The requirement that one execute a release to participate in a public program is commonly held to be a violation of public policy and is therefore invalid.

However, a release can be a valuable legal document for programs involving adults, especially those conducted within the private sector, because adults may waive their rights under certain circumstances. Chief among these are the following:

1. Reasonable options are present. In the private sector, adults can usually find a wide variety of program options. Furthermore, because private programs are not supported by their tax dollars, adults have the option not to be involved or not to support them.
2. The adults are aware of, understand, and appreciate their risks and responsibilities for the program or activity.

PARTICIPATION AGREEMENT

A **participation agreement** is another type of formal document indicating that the participant or the participant's parents

-   understand and appreciate the risks involved in the activity;
-   know the safety rules and procedures, understand their importance, and agree to comply with them; and
-   specifically request that the person be allowed to participate in the activity.

A properly drafted participation agreement must do the following:

-   Be clearly and explicitly worded.
-   Clearly explain the nature of the activity and the prerequisite skills or level of physical ability.
-   Identify the rules that must be followed.
-   State in detail the possible dangers inherent in the activity and the consequences to the participant should an accident occur (This should include the specific types of injuries that may be encountered and, if appropriate, the possibility of paralysis and death.)
-   Require the participant to indicate that she possesses the requisite skills and level of physical condition.
-   Include a statement wherein the participant agrees to assume the risks inherent in the activity.

Although a properly designed participation agreement cannot offer absolute protection from a lawsuit, it can help establish contributory or comparative negligence. The draft in Figure 13.1 can form the basis for a participation agreement. Remember that all such documents should be specific to the activity and situation in question and should be reviewed by an attorney. Additionally, it is generally advisable to include a release with the participation agreement.

FIGURE 13.1
AGREEMENT TO PARTICIPATE

I realize that _____ is a vigorous physical activity that involves
            (name of sport)

<u>*(Characterize the elements of the activity: e.g., height, flight, and rotation; violent*</u>
<u>*body contact; rapid directional change.)*</u>

_____

_____

I understand that participation in _____ involves certain inherent
risks and   *(name of sport)*

that, regardless of the precautions taken _____

                              (name of organization providing program)

or the participants, some injuries may occur. These injuries might include, but
are not limited to:

    1. *(Give examples, being sure to*
    2. *include the most common and*
    3. *most severe injuries; e.g. blind-*
    4. *ness, quadriplegia, death.)*

These injuries may result from hazards such as:

    1. *(List circumstances that might bring about the types of injuries cited*
    2. *above. Again, be sure to include the most common hazards; e.g., being*
    3. *struck by a racquet or ball, making initial contact with head while*
    4. *blocking or tackling.)*

The likelihood of such injuries may be lessened by adhering to the following
safety rules:

    1.
    2.
    3.

FIGURE 13.1 CONTD.
AGREEMENT TO PARTICIPATE

4.

5.

In order to properly protect my own safety and that of my fellow participants, I agree to follow these rules as well as any others that may be given by my (coach/instructor).

Further, in recognition of the importance of shared responsibility for safety, I agree to immediately report any noted deviations from the safety rules as well as any observed hazardous conditions or equipment to my (coach/instructor).

I further certify that my present level of physical condition is consistent with the demands of active participation in _____. Following is a full

(name of sport)

 and complete list of all of my known health conditions that might affect my ability to participate.

I have carefully read the foregoing document. I have had the opportunity to ask questions and have them answered. I am confident that I fully know, understand, and appreciate the risks involved in active participation in

_____ and I am voluntarily requesting permission to participate.

(name of sport)

_____

_____

_____

Signature   *Date*

CONTRIBUTORY AND COMPARATIVE NEGLIGENCE

Under the principle of **contributory negligence,** acts or omissions by the plaintiff that fall below the standard of ordinary care and that contribute to the cause or aggravation of the injury complained of may prevent the plaintiff from legally recovering damages from the defendant. In other words, if the negligent actions of the plaintiff in any way helped to cause or aggravate the injury complained of, the plaintiff cannot win the lawsuit regardless of the negligence of the defendant teacher or coach.

For instance, a gymnastics coach might have a rule that forbids any athlete to attempt any skill unless a spotter is present. The coach faithfully enforces this rule and issues reprimands immediately whenever violations are noted. If on a given day one athlete attempts several back handsprings without a spotter and ultimately falls and sustains a serious injury, the principle of contributory negligence would probably prevent the athlete from successfully pursuing a negligence suit. The injured athlete knew, or should have known, that unspotted back handsprings were improper and in contravention of established rules. The athlete failed to take the ordinary actions reasonably expected under the circumstances and thus must accept the legal responsibility for the injury which ensued.

Most states, however, currently apply the more equitable principle of **comparative negligence.** In a situation involving comparative negligence, the jury is asked to determine the relative degree of responsibility of the plaintiff and the defendant(s). The amount of damages that the plaintiff could recover would then be decreased by the athlete's percentage of responsibility. If, for instance, athlete Barnes sued Coach Thompson for $100,000 in compensatory damages, and if Barnes was found to be comparatively negligent in the amount of 20%, the maximum award would be 80% of $100,000, or $80,000.

Some states maintain a threshold beyond which the plaintiff is barred from recovery. This threshold, where applied, is usually around 50%. In other words, if athlete Barnes is found to be more responsible for the injury than coach Thompson, in some states Barnes would not be eligible for any compensatory damages (see also Case 13.3). Table 13.2 illustrates the application of contributory and comparative negligence to several hypothetical jury awards.

TABLE 13.2

RELATIVE EFFECTS OF CONTRIBUTORY AND COMPARATIVE NEGLIGENCE ON COMPENSATORY AWARDS FOR DAMAGES

Plaintiff	Percent of Responsibility for Own Injury	Damages Sought	Maximum Award if Contributory Negligence Applies	Maximum Award if Comparitive Negligence Applies
David Strange	15%	$100,000	$0	$85,000
Mary Bishop	45%	$750,000	$0	$412,500
Alicia Ames	0%	$250,000	$250,000	$250,000

OPEN AND OBVIOUS

Those who conduct or supervise programs of sport and physical activity are not required to be insurers of the safety of the participants. Risks of participating in an activity which are open and obvious are, by and large, the responsibility of the participant. If one elects to take part in an activity or a game conducted on a surface that has obstructions such as a drainpipe, depressions or a fence, these **open and obvious** risks are often held to be the responsibility of the participant. Generally, the more mature and the more knowledgeable the participant, the greater the responsibility for open and obvious conditions.

ASSUMPTION OF RISK

It is often said that persons who take part in vigorous physical activities must recognize the possibility that they could suffer an injury during the course of their participation. They must therefore assume the risk of any injuries that are normally associated with participation in that activity. However, **assumption of risk** has little absolute value as a legal defense.

As a general rule, participants cannot be expected to assume a risk of which they are unaware or which they are required to undertake. It is incumbent upon the teacher or coach, therefore, to warn participants of the risks of any activity and to teach them reasonably effective procedures for reducing or eliminating the dangers associated with those risks. If no such warning and instruction is provided, and the participants have no prior independent knowledge of the risks involved, then they assume nothing. Consider, on the other hand, a participant who has been warned of the dangers and provided with reasonable instruction and feedback to help reduce or eliminate them. The participant willingly engages in the activity and subsequently does something contrary to the learned procedure and thereby suffers an injury despite thorough preparation. The issue is really one of contributory or comparative negligence. In either case the assumption of risk terminology has no direct value as a separate defense.

ACT OF GOD

Certain types of accidents are sometimes referred to as having occurred as a result of an **act of God.** Like assumption of risk, this term has little absolute value as a legal defense.

If, for instance, a golf class was being conducted on a large field and one of the students was struck and badly injured by a bolt of lightning, one might argue that the lightning was an act of God and therefore beyond the reasonable control of the teacher. The real issue, however, is whether or not the accident was foreseeable. Foreseeability is one of the elements defined earlier in this chapter that must be proven to successfully establish a negligence claim.

Therefore, if the accident occurred on an otherwise beautiful day with no warning of an approaching thunderstorm, or if the teacher had curtailed activities and taken reasonable steps to protect the students from a sudden storm, then there would probably be no cause for a claim of negligence. If, on the other hand, the teacher saw lightning and heard thunder but estimated the storm to have been a safe distance away and directed the students to continue practicing for the few minutes remaining in the class, then a jury might decide that the incident in question was foreseeable and therefore preventable. The issue is whether or not the incident in question was foreseeable. The act of God terminology is really excess verbal baggage.

MANAGEMENT GUIDELINES: EFFECTIVE RECORD KEEPING IMPROVES DEFENSIBILITY

Although effective documentation and record keeping are certainly not technical legal defenses, they can be of inestimable value in preparing an effective defense against claims of negligence. Effective documentation actually serves a dual function: First, it is an important component of sound program planning and organization that can lead to the development and delivery of safer activities. Second, if routinely and regularly maintained, it provides a written record of procedures followed and actions taken that can refresh recollection of past events and serve as factual evidence in the event of a lawsuit. Lawsuits usually extend over a period of several years, and few people can remember for that length of time the details of any given event or of the events that preceded it to be able to furnish the kind of information likely to be requested by attorneys for both the plaintiff and the defendant. Only a strong commitment to effective record keeping can spare a defendant from an embarrassing series of "I don't knows" and "I don't remember's" at the time of trial.

Beyond the previously discussed releases, participation agreements and warnings, written materials commonly requested as evidence in a lawsuit include the following:

1. *Lesson plans* help to provide evidence of thought and preparation prior to the delivery of a given lesson. Well-developed plans are no less valuable for coaches than for teachers because they can provide clear evidence of how subject matter was organized, what warm-up and safety procedures were included, the learning sequence, and so forth.

2. *Curriculum and unit plans* show how the activity in question fits into the overall instructional unit. They are particularly useful in establishing the validity of any given activity and the sequence of preparatory activities and lead-ups.

3. *Rosters and attendance records* can help establish the plaintiff's experience by documenting participation in important preliminary classes, meetings, or practices.

4. *Testing and screening results* are valuable tools for establishing the plaintiff's readiness for the activity in question. Careful screening and testing records can provide factual documentation of the plaintiff's previous achievements and thus justify participation at the next reasonable level. At the same time, they provide inferential testimony regarding the level of care exercised by the instructor or coach in determining participant readiness.

5. *Emergency action plans* help document a coach or instructor's readiness for foreseeable emergencies and the soundness of the procedures followed. Moreover, they help guarantee appropriate responses when emergencies arise.

6. *Participation agreements* provide documentary evidence that the plaintiff understood and accepted both the risks of the activity and the obligation to exercise reasonable care.

7. *Maintenance/inspection checklists and reports* for both facilities and equipment provide written confirmation of continuing efforts to maintain the level of safety and function that the appropriate professional standards call for.

8. *Incident reports* provide documentary evidence regarding the exact circumstances surrounding an injury, the names and statements of witnesses, emergency procedures followed, and the nature and results of any follow-up. Figure 13.2 is an example of an effective incident report form you may use as a model.

FIGURE 13.2
INCIDENT REPORT

Name of injured athlete: _____

Date of injury: _____ Time of injury: _____

Nature of injury: _____

Describe the accident: (Include exact location, nature of the activity, sequence of

activities/events preceding the injury, and all other pertinent facts.) _____

First aid/medical treatment: (Describe procedures followed.) _____

Names and addresses of witnesses: (Append written statements from witnesses where

appropriate.) _____

_____

Follow-up:(Medical diagnosis, visitation, etc.) _____

Comments: (This is an appropriate place to include any statement by the injured party

that indicated his or her own careless or wrongful actions. In completing the form,

however, report only facts and direct statements, not your opinions or those of other

observers.) _____

Date of report:_____ Signature: _____

MANAGEMENT GUIDELINES: PUBLIC RELATIONS HELP REDUCE THE DESIRE TO SUE

Strong, positive public relations is an extremely valuable tool for preventing law-suits that is often overlooked. Although positive public relations may have little or no impact on the legal outcome of lawsuits once they have been brought, it most certainly helps determine whether or not injured persons or their parents initiate one. As a general rule, people are reluctant to sue persons who they like and care about and who they think like them and are sincerely concerned about their welfare and satisfaction. Conversely, they are often quick to strike out against people they do not like or who they think do not like or care about them. It is important, therefore, that all people who administer and deliver programs give parents and participants the impression that they are skilled, caring professionals who are willing to go out of their way to ensure the safety and satisfaction of the participants. This is not a matter of pretense or slick marketing but of honest, open communication. It must begin with the very first introduction and continue well beyond the conclusion of the activity or event. Most importantly, it must not stop when the participant is pulled out of the activity due to accident or illness.

CASE STUDIES

CASE 13.1   PROXIMATE CAUSE

JoAnn Samuels, age 8, was a member of the Springwood Angels soccer team. It was raining heavily on the day of her regularly scheduled practice, so her coach, Alex Wilson, secured permission to use the gymnasium of Pineville Elementary School. The gymnasium was a typical elementary facility that measured approximately 50 ft by 90 ft with masonry walls, a wooden floor, and a stage at one end.

Near the conclusion of the practice, the coach informed the children that they would have a relay race. The group was divided into four teams, and the children were told to run the length of the gym, tag the wall, and return to the starting line where they would tag their teammate. The starting line was painted on the floor and was 3 ft from the masonry wall.

Although competition and excitement levels were relatively high, the children were well controlled and held to their waiting positions throughout the contest. When JoAnn ran her leg of the relay, her team and one other were competing very closely for the lead. As she completed her leg of the relay and made the tag, she stumbled and fell, striking the end wall and fracturing her shoulder.

Alex Wilson was negligent in the manner in which he planned and conducted the practice session in question. His organization of the relay race was significantly below the accepted standards of practice, and JoAnn Samuels was seriously injured as a result. The jury, in finding Wilson negligent, discounted his argument that JoAnn should have exercised greater care for her own welfare by slowing down before she reached the finish line and awarded full compensatory damages to the plaintiff.

This case illustrates the problems associated with rainy day activities that have not been carefully planned in advance. Although Coach Wilson was well prepared for his scheduled outdoor activity, he had not thought out the modifications that might be necessary if the weather forced a move indoors. Like many individuals forced into similar positions, he elected to play a few simple games and lead-up activities.

Perhaps if Mr. Wilson had realized that games have been found to be one of the leading sources of negligence suits ñ ahead of such activities as soccer, gymnastics, baseball, and football ñ he would have exercised more care in the planning process. Like many others, however, Mr. Wilson fell into the trap of taking a simple activity for granted. He combined a relatively safe relay with an otherwise safe facility in a manner that created an improper and easily avoidable risk of harm to the participants. The result was a painful injury and a costly negligence suit.

Because he was unprepared for the possibility of a rainout, Alex Wilson had not thought carefully about the nature and organization of the games he conducted on the date of the accident. He therefore ignored the normal provisions for safety zones and the avoidance of walls and other potentially hazardous obstructions. Instead he directed the children to run into a wall at one end of the gym and to complete the race at a line 3 ft away from the wall at the other end. Certainly he should have been able to anticipate the fact that, especially in a competitive event, the children would be running at or near full speed when they reached each of the walls. It would, in fact, be illogical to expect that a child would slow down prior to the finish line and thus risk losing the race and incurring the wrath of her peers. The risk of injury was not only foreseeable but probable.

The professional impropriety of the decision to utilize the Pineville facility in the manner described is compounded by the fact that it was easily avoidable. The simplest and most commonly employed alternative would have been to shorten the race by 15 to 20 ft and to place traffic cones, tape marks, or some other designators at the new stopping and turning points. The athletes would then have had a safe turning radius and a reasonable distance after the designated finish line in which to decelerate and regain their equilibrium. Providing the necessary margin of safety in this way would not have detracted significantly from the nature or value of the game.

[Based on a case adjudicated in the lower courts.]

CASE 13.2 PROXIMATE CAUSE

Stephen Latley is a physical education teacher in Carson Elementary School. He has been teaching at Carson for 12 years and is thoroughly familiar with the school and the students in it. The gymnasium in which he teaches is 78 ft in length, with a stage at one end and a solid tile wall at the other.

Mr. Latley knows from long experience that many of the children in his classes will seize any opportunity they can to run to the stage and do a sliding dive along the smoothly polished stage floor. This is especially true of the fifth and sixth grade boys who fit the chest-high stage ideal for a running takeoff from the gymnasium floor. For this reason, Mr. Latley exercises great care to keep his students a safe distance from the stage throughout the course of his class activities.

Six months ago he was conducting a relay race for the fourth graders. He placed a tape line on the floor 16 ft from the stage to serve as the starting point. The children were directed to run to the far wall, tag it, and return to tag the next person on their team, who was to be waiting at the starting line with one foot on the taped line. The students were reminded of the hazardous nature of running into the stage and were warned of the possibility of injury if they did so. Further, Mr. Latley told them that they were to walk to the rear of their team after the tag and immediately assume a seated position away from the stage. Failure to comply with this rule would result in disqualification.

As Jimmy Morton completed his leg of the relay, he tagged his teammate and continued running at full speed directly toward the stage. He timed his jump incorrectly and struck the edge of the stage, suffering serious injury. Jimmy's father instituted a lawsuit, naming Stephen Latley as a defendant. Mr. Latley was understandably quite concerned about this suit and wondered whether there was anything more he could or should have done to prevent the injury.

This case is very similar to Samuels v. Wilson (Case 13.1). Like JoAnn Samuels in the earlier case, Jimmy Morton was injured when he struck a major obstruction at the conclusion of a relay race. Mr. Latley, like Coach Wilson in the Samuels case, failed to meet the standard of care expected of a prudent professional in the same or similar circumstances. Unlike Coach Wilson, however, Mr. Latley was not held legally responsible for the injuries sustained by the child entrusted to his care. The essential difference between these two cases brings the concept of proximate cause into focus.

Mr. Latley directed his students to race to the far wall of the gymnasium, tag it, and return to the starting point. This was entirely improper and fell significantly below accepted standards. Simply put, walls are not intended to be turning or stopping points. The risk of injury is far too great to be acceptable because it can be avoided easily. However, Mr. Latley was fortunate that none of his students were injured while approaching or turning at the far wall.

Jimmy Morton was injured at the conclusion of the race. Mr. Latley had provided thorough instruction and warnings about the dangers of running into the stage. Moreover he had provided an ample amount of space between the start/finish line and the stage. In this regard, his actions were fully in compliance with the best practices in the field. There was in fact nothing more that he could or should have done to ensure his students' safety at that end of the floor.

Mr. Latley improperly directed his students to run into a wall, but because that act did not cause or aggravate the injury sustained by Jimmy Morton, he was not held liable for damages arising from the incident. If, however, someone had been injured at the turning point, the results would almost surely have been quite different.

[Based on a case adjudicated in the lower courts]

CASE 13.3 CONTRIBUTORY AND COMPARATIVE NEGLIGENCE

Mary Wells was a 14-year-old student in the eighth grade at Marsten Junior High School. At the time of the incident that gave rise to this lawsuit, Mary was participating in a required physical education class under the direction of George Bailey, a certified teacher. The class of approximately 25 boys and girls had been divided into four teams, and two whiffleball games were being conducted. Each game used one half of the gymnasium, which measured approximately 85 ft by 100 ft. Mr. Bailey was dividing his attention between the two games by alternately facing and focusing on each game.

One of Mary's teammates was at bat, and Mary and another student were chatting as they awaited their turns at bat. Mary was standing approximately 6 ft behind home plate in the 8 o'clock position. As the batter swung at a pitched ball, the bat slipped from his hands and struck Mary in the eye, causing serious injury. At the time of the accident, Mr. Bailey was on the opposite side of the gymnasium with his back toward the game in which Mary Wells was participating. Mr. Bailey testified, however, that all students had been warned to stand against the gymnasium wall (approximately 20 ft from home plate) while waiting for their turns at bat. He stated that, in his opinion, Mary would not have been injured if she had simply followed these directions. The jury found Mr. Bailey negligent but decreased Mary's award by 30% based on her comparative negligence.

The fundamental causative factors in this injury are those of improper supervision and organization of the class in question. Mr. Bailey's failure to organize and control both segments of his class effectively was entirely improper and precipitated this unnecessary injury.

The importance of proper supervision and class organization as tools for reducing student injuries and the responsibilities of teachers in that regard have been well documented in the professional literature and have been a fundamental component of teacher education programs for many years. The failure to provide for effective supervision and organization is therefore a deviation from the standard of care that one would expect from a reasonable teacher.

Mr. Bailey should have positioned himself so that he could see all of the players and provide effective general supervision. By alternately giving his full attention to one game at a time, he was also alternately ignoring one half of the students for whom he was responsible. Coaches and teachers must position themselves in locations that allow them to see all the participants and should maintain this visual contact as they move through the area. Generally this would mean moving around the perimeter of the playing area and trying to stay in close proximity to the areas of greatest danger.

Mary Wells was standing in an inappropriate area. Her location was far too close to the batter and clearly at variance with the position Mr. Bailey had set in his rules. Moreover, while Mary was chatting with a classmate, it is unlikely that she was attentive enough to react to a sudden hazard such as a slipped or thrown bat. If Mr. Bailey had seen Mary's position, he would have (or at least should have) taken corrective action that would have prevented this injury. Because he was looking in the opposite direction, he neither saw nor corrected the problem, and Mary Wells was injured as a result.

The jury's decision to assign comparative negligence to Mary was due to her violation of Mr. Bailey's rule regarding appropriate waiting positions. Mr. Bailey had emphasized the dangers of standing too near the batter and had set safe guidelines for where students should stand. This was a critical factor in determining comparative negligence and reduced George Bailey's responsibility in proportion to the jury's perception of Mary's responsibility.

[Based on a case adjudicated in the lower courts]

CHAPTER SUMMARY

The threat of a lawsuit arising from an injury suffered by a participant has had a major impact on sport and physical activity programs. Although it is practically impossible to completely eliminate risk, you can reduce the likelihood of lawsuits and improve your chances of winning those that cannot be prevented by understanding the legal requirements to support a negligence claim, the legal defenses available, and the nature and importance of record keeping and public relations.

KEY TERMS

Act of God
Assumption of risk
Breach
Comparative negligence
Contributory negligence
Damages
Defendant
Doctrine of entitlement
Duty
Foreseeability
Good Samaritan Laws
Governmental Immunity
Gross Negligence
Insurance shortfalls
Loss
Myth of being risk-free
Negligence
Open and obvious
Participation agreement
Plaintiff
Proximate cause
Release
The right to sue
Tort claims legislation
Settlements
Tort
Volunteer immunity statutes
Waiver

QUESTIONS FOR DISCUSSION

1. Many of the factors that underlie the so-called "liability explosion" are beyond the control of those involved in the development and delivery of sport and physical activity programs. However, actions can be taken to reduce insurance short-falls, reduce the desire of injured participants to pursue legal action, and increase one's ability to defend against claims that may be brought. Discuss alternative strategies to achieve these ends and include appropriate activity-specific examples.

2. Name and explain the four basic elements that a plaintiff must prove to win a negligence suit.

3. Develop activity-specific examples of informed consent documents and incident reports. Review those developed by your classmates and share suggestions for modification and improvement.

4. For each of the following circumstances, give three practical examples of an accident or injury situation.
    a. There was a breach of duty but no proximate cause.
    b. There was a breach of duty and comparative negligence.
    c. The incident was not foreseeable.

ADDITIONAL READINGS

Carpenter, L.J. (2000). *Legal concepts in sport: A primer.* Champaign, IL: Sagamore.

Champion, W.T., Jr. (1990). *Fundamentals of sports law.* Deerfield, IL/New York, NY/Rochester, NY: CBC—The Lawyers Co-operative Publishing Company.

Clement, A. (1988). *Law in sport and physical activity.* Indianapolis: Benchmark Press.

Cotton, D.J., & Cotton, M.B. (1996). *Waivers and releases for the health and fitness club industry.* Statesboro, GA: Sport Risk Consulting.

Cotten, D.J., & Wilde, T.J. (1997). *Sport law for sport managers.* Dubuque, IA: Kendall/Hunt.

Peterson, J.A. (1987). *Risk management for park, recreation and leisure services.* Champaign, IL: Management Learning Laboratories.

van der Smissen, B. (1990). *Legal liability and risk management for public and private entities* (Vols. I-II). Cincinnati: Anderson.

Wong, G.M. (1994). *Essentials of amateur sports law.* Westport, CT: Praeger Publishers.

Yasser, R., McCurdy, J.R., Goplerud, C.P., & Weston, M.A. (2000). *Sports law—cases and materials.* Cincinnati, OH: Anderson.

CHAPTER 14

THE STANDARD OF CARE IN SPORTS AND PHYSICAL ACTIVITIES

Melissa Herman, a sophomore member of the cheerleading squad at Southernmost High School, is suing for injuries she sustained while performing a two-person mount at a soccer game. The skill in question, a step-up to a shoulder straddle, had been taught by the coach, Jane Quinn, and was part of the only routine that the cheerleaders had been directed to perform that day.

On the date the injury occurred, considerable rain had fallen, and the start of the game had been delayed. Ms. Quinn sent the cheerleading squad to the field, but she did not attend. No instructions or warnings were provided regarding precautions or modifications appropriate for wet ground surfaces. At approximately 4:30 P.M., the cheerleaders began their first stunt of the day. As Melissa Herman was negotiating the step-up to the straddle position, her partner slipped on the wet grass. Both girls fell to the ground, and Melissa fractured her left arm.

Two key questions need to be answered in order to determine Coach Quinn's potential liability regarding the injuries sustained by Melissa Herman: (1) What is the standard of care expected of a reasonably prudent cheerleading supervisor? And (2) did Coach Quinn fall below this standard?

The American Association of Cheerleading coaches and advisers (AACCA) has published the *AACCA Cheerleading Safety Manual* (George, 1990), which clearly outlines the responsibilities of cheerleading coaches and supervisors for the development and delivery of safe and productive activities. Portions of the text that apply directly to this case spell out in detail the requirements for adequate supervision and a safe performing environment and the obligation of the supervisor to make activity modifications when inclement weather causes risk to rise above normal limits. This text would be a persuasive piece of documentary evidence at the time of trial.

The alleged actions of Jane Quinn in connection with this incident fell significantly below the articulated standard. Through her failure to effectively supervise and direct the girls for whom she was responsible, an activity was conducted that exposed the cheerleaders to an improper and otherwise avoidable risk. If Ms. Quinn had properly executed her duties, it is reasonable to assume that she would have noted the danger and modified or eliminated the activity. Under such circumstances, her actions would have been in compliance with AACCA guidelines, and Melissa Herman probably would not have been injured. Moreover, if Ms. Quinn had complied with the standards and, despite her best efforts, Melissa Herman had still suffered an injury, the same standards used to condemn her would have become her strongest defense argument.

LEARNING OBJECTIVES

Upon completion of this chapter, the student will be able to:

1. define the nature and importance of effective supervision, appropriate selection and conduct of activities, and safe environmental conditions,
2. differentiate between general and specific supervision and give examples of each, and
3. enumerate guidelines to reduce the risk of injuries attributable to faulty supervision, inappropriate selection or conduct of the activities, and unsafe facilities and to provide activity specific examples of their application.

MAJOR AREAS OF RESPONSIBILITY

Most sport-related lawsuits allege that the defendant teacher or coach breached the standard of care by failing to fulfill professional duties in one or more of these three major areas:

1. The responsibility to provide effective supervision
2. The responsibility to provide appropriate and well-conducted activities
3. The responsibility to provide safe and appropriate environmental conditions.

A survey of over 400 recent lawsuits (Table 14.1) found that 23 percent of plaintiffs had argued that the primary cause of their injuries was faulty supervision on the part of the defendant, 24 percent alleged there had been inappropriate selection or conduct of the activities, and 53 percent claimed their injuries resulted from unsafe environmental conditions. Note that these results have been generalized across all levels of activity and that the relative likelihood of a lawsuit in each of the three primary areas of responsibility appears to vary depending on whether the activity is recreational, instructional, or an organized competitive sport. Table 14.1 illustrates the differences in the results when these levels of activity are viewed separately.

For purposes of the survey, the following operational definitions were used:

- Instructional programs are those with an assigned teacher or leader. These programs could occur in a school, club, or any other setting.
- Teams are situations in which athletes are under the structured control of a coach. This includes interscholastic and intercollegiate sports, organized clubs, and private groups. It does not include the more informally structured intramural or recreational teams in which a player may assume some role in organizational leadership.
- Recreational activities refer to all of the less-structured circumstances not covered in the other two categories. They include children on a playground, participants at a racquet or health club who are not involved in an instructional event, and players in most adult softball leagues.

By examining Table 14.1, you can see that the condition of the environment is the largest source of negligence claims in recreational programs, and that proper selection and conduct of the activity is the primary concern in instructional activities. Finally, it is important to recognize that, regardless of the level of activity, it's possible to identify most controllable injury-causing factors by carefully analyzing the areas of supervision, selection and conduct of the activity, and environmental conditions.

TABLE 14.1
SURVEY OF LAWSUITS BY ACTIVITY LEVEL

Responsibility allegedly breached	Recreation	Instruction	Teams	Number of cases	Ptg.
Supervision	40	36	22	98	23%
Selection and conduct of activities	16	58	29	103	24%
Failure to provide a safe environment	151	43	33	227	53%
Total number of cases	207	137	84	428	
Percentages	48%	32%	20%		

SUPERVISION

Because careful supervision can prevent many needless injuries, failure to fulfill one's supervisory responsibilities properly is alleged to be at least a contributing factor in most negligence suits. **Supervision** can be defined as the quality and quantity of control exerted by teachers or coaches over the individuals for whom they are responsible. Thus, the number of supervisory personnel assigned to a group must be sufficient to effectively control the group in question, and the supervisors must have the training and skills necessary to fulfill their assigned duties.

The issue of **qualitative supervision** is of far greater legal concern to administrative personnel than to those directly involved in delivering programs and services. Although greater levels of training and certification are likely to provide teachers or coaches with the skills and knowledge necessary to conduct a safer program or activity, they would not protect them from the legal results of their own negligence. For example, if an athlete is injured due to the coach's failure to fulfill his legal responsibilities for her care, the coach will probably be found guilty of negligence regardless of his credentials.

The potential liability of the coach's employer or supervisor, however, is a different matter that relates to the civil law concept known as **respondeat superior,** whereby employers or supervisors may be held legally responsible for the work-related actions of their employees. Thus, supervisors of a coach accused of negligence may well face legal action. In this situation employers face a form of **vicarious liability,** whereby their legal responsibilities to supervise and, within reason, to control the actions of their employees place them in the position of being to some degree indirectly responsible for an incident over which they had no direct control.

Additional legal complications can arise when employers fail to exercise reasonable diligence in the selection and training of their employees. Consider two identical gymnastics classes, each with 25 students and one instructor. The instructor for Class A is a certified teacher with extensive experience as a gymnastics instructor who received safety training and certification from the U.S. Gymnastics Federation. The instructor for Class B is a former national collegiate gymnastics champion who has had no specific training as a coach or teacher. In each class a student attempted to perform a very difficult skill several times without the aid of mats or spotters. The instructors either ignored or did not see these violations of approved safety procedure. Not surprisingly, the students each suffered serious injury.

In each instance, the instructors were negligent, and differences in their credentials and qualifications did not affect the outcome of the lawsuit against them. In each case, however, the program administrator was also named as a defendant. Because both administrators performed all other aspects of their duties properly, only the administrator responsible for Class B was found negligent. The plaintiff successfully argued that the administrator in charge of Class B should have realized that an instructor who lacked the training appropriate for the assigned responsibilities would be likely to make an otherwise avoidable error that could foreseeably result in an injury. This is referred to as **negligent hiring** (see Chapter 11 for a discussion of negligent hiring as well as issues related to negligent supervision of employees).

The issue of **quantitative supervision** is different from that of qualitative supervision. Certainly the question of the number and assignment of supervisors is a purely administrative matter, but it is seldom the source of a lawsuit in and of itself. Most activities lack guidelines regarding the appropriate instructor/student ratio. Regardless of the activity, most administrators tend to do their best to provide a reasonable number of supervisory personnel. Improper quantitative supervision is of greater concern for the individual teacher or coach. The issue for them is not necessarily one of absolute numbers, however, but of the relative degree of attention and effectiveness exhibited by the supervisor.

The individual teacher or coach is responsible for two types of supervision: general and specific. **General supervision** requires an overview of the entire group. The supervisor must keep all of the participants within sight, be alert for dangers or deviations from accepted procedure, and be ready to intervene quickly and resolve any problems noted.

When problems or dangers are noted, the supervisor must shift to specific supervision. **Specific supervision** is the term applied to the direct interaction between the teacher or coach and one or more students. Specific supervision is required when a deviation from prescribed procedures is noted or when a student demonstrates a need for additional assistance or attention.

It's important to recognize, however, that the need to move to specific supervision does not remove the obligation to maintain general supervisory control over the remainder of the group. The supervisor cannot (as in Figure 14.1) become so engrossed in meeting the needs of one or two students that he fails to detect and eliminate a hazardous situation that has arisen in another area of the gym.

The question of how much specific supervision may be required for any given group is a function of the participants' ages and skill levels and their ability to understand and appreciate the risks and consequences of their own actions. Generally, as the participants' ages and abilities increase, it's reasonable to expect longer periods of productive activity with only general supervision.

MANAGEMENT GUIDELINES: SUPERVISION

Routine observance of the following guidelines and principles can help prevent injuries and subsequent lawsuits associated with supervisory shortcomings.

1. *Take all reasonable steps to keep supervisory/instructional skills and certifications at the highest possible level.* Keep abreast of the best practices in the field to reduce the chance of risk or harm to the participants and to provide clear evidence of your readiness to teach, coach, or supervise the activity.
2. *Organize participants to facilitate effective supervision.* Move about the area to maximize contact with participants, being careful to minimize instances in which some person or persons are out of your direct line of vision.
3. *Don't leave individuals or groups unsupervised.* You cannot solve problems or eliminate hazards you don't see because you're taking a telephone call in the office or gathering equipment from a closet.

FIGURE 14.1

Although this coach is providing excellent specific supervision for one athlete, he is neglecting his duty to provide general supervision for all.

4. *Establish, post, explain, and enforce general behavioral and safety rules for the gym, fields, locker rooms, and all areas where activities may be conducted.* Figure 14.2 shows an effective set of rules posted in a fitness center.

5. *Secure facilities and equipment when not being used.* If facilities are open and the equipment is accessible, people can be expected to enter and use them. It's also reasonable to predict that if these facilities and equipment are used in the absence of proper supervision and guidance, the likelihood of an accidental injury will increase greatly. Gymnastic equipment, fitness centers, porta-pits, etc., present an invitation to dangerous activity. They can, therefore, be viewed as a type of **attractive nuisance** and thus impose an obligation to either supervise their use or to take reasonable steps to limit their accessibility (see Case 14.1).

6. *Be prepared to render immediate and effective first aid when necessary.* In the event of an emergency, the supervisor must take appropriate actions to sustain life or prevent further harm until emergency personnel arrive to take over (see Case 14.4).

7. *Develop emergency procedures to be followed in the event of an accident or injury.* While these guidelines should be specific to the particular group and area in question, the School and Community Safety Society of America has provided an excellent analysis of the elements essential to all emergency action plans (see Figure 14.3).

FIGURE 14.2

Clearly worded and posted safety rules help prevent accidents and increase the legal responsibility of the participants.

8. *Remember that supervisors must maintain control of their classes or teams and spectators to guide their actions and to detect and correct inappropriate behaviors.* Never allow the actions of one individual or one group to endanger others or to detract from the effectiveness of the learning environment.

SELECTION AND CONDUCT OF THE ACTIVITIES

Regardless of the nature or level of the program, teachers, recreation leaders, coaches, and administrators are expected to select or allow activities that are reasonable for the ability levels of the individuals involved. Courts generally recognize and accept the concept that, with few exceptions, no activity is inherently unsafe in and of itself.

The question then is whether the participant was physically, mentally, and emotionally ready for the demands of the activity so that she or he should have been able to execute it safely. In the event of an injury, therefore, one question frequently asked is whether it was reasonable to allow the injured person to attempt the particular skill involved.

FIGURE 14.3
EMERGENCY PLAN COMPONENTS

Who does what when?
Who is the designated first responder?
What level of certification and/or training should they have?
Who assists? How?
Who supervises the rest of the group?
What are the levels of authority?
What types of in-house training and testing are provided for the staff?
Emergency equipment
What is available?
Where is it located?
How will it be accessed?
Communication
How? With what? Where is it?
Who calls whom? Include numbers
When are the calls made?
What is the order of contact of key individuals?
What if one of the people called is not there?
Staff debriefing
Who does what? When?
Forms management
Who completes what forms?
When?
How? (best done initially in draft form)
How many copies are sent to whom?
Where are records retained?
How long are records retained?
Follow-up
When is follow-up done and by whom?
What will be done? (e.g., calls or visits to injured persons, checking insurance payments, checking disposition of matter by police)

This question is relevant only to the person who was injured; the fact that the rest of the team could perform the skill or that it was a generally accepted activity for individuals at the grade level in question will not suffice (see Case 14.2). The supervisor must be prepared through appropriate forms of skill testing and successful lead-up activities to document the fact that the injured participant was indeed equal to the demands of the activity that resulted in the injury.

That was certainly not the case in Mr. Dolan's sixth grade physical education class a few years ago. The class had been practicing for a gymnastics exhibition for six weeks. Part of the show involved simple vaults performed in rapid-fire fashion by each member of the class. Mr. Dolan's students had all been performing the vaults for some time and had spent two weeks working up to the rapid-fire routine.

Mary Worth and her family had just moved into town, and she was enrolled in Mr. Dolan's class two weeks before the show. Mr. Dolan, who was preoccupied with preparations for the show, welcomed Mary to his class and told her to join the group activities. After conducting a brief warm-up, the students moved to the horse, where they began with a squat vault.

When her turn came, Mary, who had never before attempted a vault, struck the horse and suffered a serious knee injury. Although the squat vault was a safe and proper activity for Mr. Dolan's class, it was not appropriate for Mary Worth. In his haste, Mr. Dolan neglected to ascertain her readiness and failed to provide the kind of instruction that might have enabled her to succeed at the vault. If Mary Worth's parents elect to seek compensation through the courts, there is every reason to expect they'll be successful.

In addition to selecting appropriate activities, the teacher or coach is expected to provide **instruction** that is both accurate in its detail and presented in a manner that maximizes the likelihood of the participants' success. This instruction should include not only information regarding the techniques of successful performance but **warnings** regarding any potentially hazardous elements of the activity and guidelines for minimizing these risks.

However, to be effective these instructions must be augmented by accurate and detailed **feedback.** The simple act of telling a person how to perform a physical skill in no way guarantees success. Successful performance requires practice supplemented by accurate feedback and remediation. Without these elements, athletes may perform to the best of their ability and may believe they have been successful, although the actual performance may have been lacking in one or more respects. Performance discrepancies that are perpetuated can retard progress and, in some cases, pose a risk of injury. Eliminating such problems through a continuous process of evaluation and feedback is essential to the development of a safe and successful program and to legal defensibility.

Even athletes physically capable of performing the skills necessary for success may face unnecessary and improper risk of injury if they are mismatched with their opponents. A **mismatch** is an inequity in size, strength, or ability of competitors that, if not properly controlled, can increase the risk of injury to the undermatched athlete. Teams and classes should be organized to minimize the risks associated with mismatching in activities involving physical contact (see Case 14.3).

Remember, however, that mismatching is a function of size, strength, and ability, not gender. With the advent of Title IX (See chapter 8), some professionals became concerned with what they perceived as the inevitable mismatching of boys and girls. This concern has no basis in law or professional logic. A 100-pound girl injured in a collision with a 160-pound boy is no more or less mismatched than a 100-pound boy injured when he collides with a 160-pound girl. The 60-lb. mismatch in the preceding two examples is entirely unrelated to the gender of the participants, and the requirement for equitable and safe balancing of the competitors existed long before Title IX was instituted.

A further means of reducing risk and the potential severity of injuries is through providing appropriate **protective measures.** These measures include the use of spotters for safety in gymnastics and weight training and the use of protective devices and apparatus designed to protect participants in many sports, including catchers' masks, landing mats, and shin pads. Protective measures such as these are essential to safe participation, and failure to use them within a program of instruction or competition constitutes a violation of proper professional procedure that could result in a lawsuit if that failure is shown to have caused an injury.

MANAGEMENT GUIDELINES:
SELECTION AND CONDUCT OF THE ACTIVITIES

Observing the following general guidelines and principles will help reduce the incidence of unnecessary risks and the likelihood of lawsuits related to negligence:

1. *Allow only activities that are within the reasonable ability levels of the participants.*
2. *Learning and performance readiness varies from one individual to the next.* Implementing and documenting screening and pretesting procedures and providing individualized progressions and lead-ups significantly increase both learning and safety.
3. *Thorough planning of lessons and practices is essential both to success in learning skills and to legal defensibility in the event of a lawsuit.* Written plans can provide documentary evidence of sequential learning experiences, attention to critical safety factors, and organizational details as well as the nature and extent of warnings provided.
4. *All activities should contribute to the educational objectives of the program.* Too many injuries occur in activities implemented simply to fill time or that bear no relationship to the goals of the program. Such injuries are both unnecessary and difficult to justify.
5. *Prepare alternative plans for activities that are subject to weather conditions or frequent uncontrollable modifications.* Regardless of how well you have planned for an outdoor lesson, if rain forces the activity indoors, the only real issue of concern will be how well you have planned for the indoor activity that you are now forced to conduct.
6. *Develop routine procedures for excusing students or athletes from class or practice due to medical complaints or injuries.* Equally important are procedures for resuming participation after an injury or extended illness. As a general rule, persons who have been seen by a doctor or who have missed several practices for medical reasons should not be readmitted without medical clearance (see Case 14.5).
7. *If a participant expresses strong fear, insecurity, or reluctance to participate, do not force the issue.* The role of the teacher or coach is to help the participant develop confidence, which is predicated upon successful experiences that are most likely to occur when the participant believes he or she can succeed. Moreover, when a participant says "I cannot do this" or "I'm afraid to try," the supervisor has just been informed by the best expert imaginable that the participant is not equal to the task. If the

supervisor forces the participant to try, and he or she suffers an injury, the supervisor must be prepared to shoulder both the moral responsibility and the legal consequences.

8. *Provide any and all protective measures and devices appropriate to the activity and require their routine use.* If adequate and appropriate safety measures cannot be provided for some reason, then make plans to reduce the hazard by modifying the activity (see Case 14.6).

9. *In contact sports, carefully organize the group to reduce the likelihood and extent of mismatch situations.* Perhaps the worst form of mismatch is when the supervisor participates with the athletes. To be effective, demonstrations should be done at reduced speed and under controlled circumstances. Moreover, it's virtually impossible to play and supervise the entire group simultaneously. Given these facts, playing with the individuals you are supposed to be supervising can only be viewed as a breach of professional responsibility.

10. *Not all risks can be eliminated.* Thus, the role of the program deliverer is to carefully examine all elements of the program to take all reasonable steps to remove or control identifiable risks and to make a conscious judgment as to whether the value of the activity significantly outweighs the risk that remains. If the identified values significantly outweigh the risks that cannot be controlled, the activity can and probably should be conducted. If this is not the case, however, the activity must be modified or discontinued.

ENVIRONMENTAL CONDITIONS

Even a well-designed and carefully supervised activity can prove unsafe if you fail to properly control factors related to the **environmental conditions**: the facilities and equipment involved. As professionals, we bear a responsibility to recognize environmental conditions that expose participants to unreasonable risks. This is referred to as the concept of **notice. Constructive notice** of defects in the environment is derived from the obligation to routinely inspect facilities and equipment before use. On the other hand, when a defect has been reported or otherwise brought to the teacher's or coach's attention, a coach or teacher is said to have **actual notice.** In either case, the coach or teacher is clearly responsible for correcting the defect or reducing the risk of injury through other means such as modifying the activity or applying protective measures.

Before using any given facility or piece of equipment, the teacher or coach should carefully inspect it to be sure that it is free of observable defects or hazards. If problems exist, appropriate remedial actions should be taken. If a coach or teacher fails to fulfill this duty and an injury occurs as a result of an environmental defect that proper inspection would have disclosed, an unpleasant lawsuit may ensue.

Although most teachers and coaches exercise reasonable care in terms of preactivity inspections, too many carelessly create additional hazards by the manner in which they use otherwise safe facilities. Jane Samuels, for instance, directed her third grade class to run a short race across the gym. The finish line was a painted line on the floor four feet from the wall. The class was told that the first three finishers would represent the third grade in the 40-yard dash to be conducted at the upcoming school field day.

Jimmy Tomkins was first across the finish line, but he broke both wrists when he slammed into the wall. The gym was not unsafe in and of itself. Certainly a short sprint is not a particularly hazardous activity, either. The problem is that in conducting the activity Ms. Samuels failed to consider the critical importance of a **buffer zone,** or safety area, between the designated finish line and the wall, in which her students could decelerate and stop. Other examples of environmental hazards created by those who are responsible for conducting activities include:

- relay races in which running lanes and turning directions are not clearly identified,
- the use of equipment that requires a level of skill beyond that of the participants (e.g., high beams and bars for beginning gymnasts), and
- the use of improper substitute equipment (e.g., stones, candy wrappers, and trees as bases).

MANAGEMENT GUIDELINES:
ENVIRONMENTAL CONDITIONS

Here are some principles and guidelines for reducing the likelihood of injuries caused by unsafe environmental conditions.

1. *Begin each day with an inspection of the facilities and equipment to be used.* Note and correct any hazards or deficiencies. Pay particular attention to surface irregularities, slipperiness, and the presence of inappropriate or dangerous materials, and the function and security of all components and fittings. Remember that little that can be said to justify an injury that occurs as a result of an environmental hazard that could and probably would have been uncovered through a reasonably conscientious inspection. Conditions such as those found in Figure 14.4 should not be tolerated.

2. *If environmental hazards are detected but cannot be immediately corrected, take actions to isolate the area or equipment until repairs can be completed.* Put the damaged equipment away, mark off the unsafe area to warn participants, modify the activity, or do whatever else may be necessary to provide a safe environment.

3. *Teach participants to perform basic safety inspections of the equipment they'll be using and require them to do so as part of their daily routine.* This procedure should supplement rather than take the place of inspections by the person in charge and should virtually eliminate the dangers and the potential liability associated with equipment failure.

4. *Don't allow running activities to be conducted on a slippery or badly uneven surface.* Similarly, be sure that all participants have footwear appropriate to the activity and the surface conditions (see Case 14.7).

5. *When selecting equipment or playing areas, be sure that they meet or exceed applicable safety standards.* Keep in mind that size and weight guidelines for many facilities and equipment are meant to promote uniformity, not safety. Thus, it's not necessarily dangerous or improper to shorten a playing field or to use a larger or smaller ball. Shortening the area of unobstructed space between a sideline and the nearest obstruction, on the other hand, may very well increase risk of injury and thus should be avoided (see Case 14.8).

FIGURE 14.4

The careless placement of equipment, tables, or chairs presents a hazardous situation that could result in a painful injury and a costly lawsuit.

CASE STUDIES

CASE 14.1 SUPERVISION AFTER PRACTICE

Tom Clark was a member of the track team at Douglass High School. After practice, Tom and several of his teammates were in the gymnasium awaiting their rides home. While waiting, the boys began playing on mats left on the floor of the gym. The boys had been engaging in general horseplay and friendly wrestling for approximately 20 minutes without supervision at the time of the accident in question. Tom was being chased by several boys and ran out of the gym and into an adjacent hallway. While running toward an exterior door, Tom extended his hand, which slipped off the opening bar and through a glass panel. He has instituted a lawsuit against his coaches for damages resulting from the injuries he sustained.

Tom Clark's injury was the direct and easily avoidable result of the improper supervision provided by his coaches. Their failure to meet their responsibility to provide effective supervision and to control the behavior of their athletes not only allowed but invited horseplay.

This is especially the case in light of the presence of a wrestling mat. Such equipment, when not properly secured or supervised, serves as an open invitation to roughhousing and horseplay.

The need for effective supervision increases significantly in the presence of mats, weights, gymnastic equipment, or other inviting paraphernalia that tend to be dangerous if used improperly and not controlled.

All teachers, coaches, and administrators must wrestle with the question of how best to deal with students or athletes who are dropped off early or picked up late or who simply wait for their friends before or after a scheduled activity. Although there is no single best solution, here are some guidelines for minimizing the dangers and maximizing your legal defensibility in the event of a lawsuit.

1. Provide ongoing general supervision for all participants.
2. Notify parents and participants in writing of the times during which supervision will be provided.
3. Extend actual scheduling of supervisors at least 15 minutes before and after the announced times to allow time to deal with early arrivals and late pick-ups. For example, if parents have been told that practice will conclude at 4:30 P.M. and that no supervisors will be present after 5:00 P.M., schedule supervisors to be on duty until at least 5:15 P.M. so that if a problem arises outside of the posted hours it will be clear that the staff went beyond their acknowledged responsibilities and that the students and/or their parents failed to meet theirs.
4. Secure all equipment when not in use.
5. Establish and enforce rules of conduct for locker rooms and waiting areas.

Remember that the legal and moral responsibility to supervise and control students or athletes is not restricted to the time limits of actual class or practice. Failure to recognize and account for that fact may result in a lawsuit similar to the one brought against Tom Clark's coaches.

[Based on a case adjudicated in the lower courts]

CASE 14.2 PARTICIPANT READINESS AND PROTECTIVE MEASURES

Victor Lindsay was a fourth grade student in Holmes Elementary School who was participating in a physical education class conducted by Vivian Hansen. Ms. Hansen had set up several stations throughout the gymnasium, including two balance beams, a vaulting box, a mat station for tumbling, and parallel bars. Ms. Hansen provided instruction and demonstration for the entire class at the parallel bars and then divided the class among all of the stations. Victor went to the vaulting box. When he attempted to jump over it, he stumbled and fell, suffering a fractured arm.

Victor's mother contacted an attorney, who immediately discussed the case with an expert in gymnastics safety. The expert requested the following additional information:

1. What was the nature and extent of previous instruction and/or screening with regard to vaulting?
2. What kind of spotting was provided?
3. What kind of matting was provided?
4. What was the teacher doing at the time of the incident?

During the course of the discovery process, the attorney learned the following:

1. The class had received its first introduction to vaulting on the previous day. The teacher taught and demonstrated the approach, the squat-on-jump-off, and the squat. After the group instruction, Ms. Hansen remained at the box while students rotated among the stations. During this time she spotted and provided individual assistance.
2. Ms. Hansen has no recollection of whether Victor or his group got to the box on that day, nor does she have any recollection of whether she had ever seen Victor vault prior to his injury.
3. Although the initial instruction regarding vaulting included a statement indicating the importance of spotting, no one was spotting at the vaulting station at the time of the accident.
4. The landing area at the vaulting station was covered with a 1-1/2 inch folding mat.

Vaulting is an accepted component of a gymnastics program and is commonly taught in schools and clubs throughout North America. As with any skill involving height and flight, however, it can be dangerous if not conducted properly. Ms. Hansen ignored several essential safety factors in the conduct of the class in question. To the degree that some or all of these factors are seen as having caused or aggravated Victor Lindsay's injury, she will probably be found liable for the damages that ensued.

The primary reference point for the establishment of standards appropriate to the teaching of gymnastics is the *USA Gymnastics Safety Handbook* (1998). This source and several other authoritative references clearly indicate the critical importance of learning skills slowly and in a progressive manner. The background and readiness of the performer are critical to learning.

Ms. Hansen had little if any knowledge of Victor's ability. She had provided only the most minimal instruction with regard to the specific vaults in question, and (at least insofar as the evidence shows) she had not provided any planned experiences to develop body awareness, landing techniques, or falling skills. Her students were, it appears, unprepared to cope with the physical tasks she placed before them. This situation would be expected to increase the likelihood of falls among the students.

Despite the increased likelihood of falls, however, Ms. Hansen provided only a basic tumbling mat in the landing area. This is well below the standards for competition and ignores the reasonable guidelines of the profession that underscore the importance of soft training mats for providing a safe learning environment for beginners.

Further, although she claims to have told the children that spotters were important to their safety in vaulting, there appears to have been little if any training in the techniques and procedures involved, and at least during the 5 to 10 minutes preceding Victor's injury, she failed to notice and correct the fact that no one was spotting at the vaulting station. Surely if she had been providing effective general supervision she should have noticed and remedied this lapse, which was not a simple and sudden one-time omission but a consistent behavior pattern exhibited over a time period that was more than sufficient to allow instructional intervention and correction.

In summary, Vivian Hansen created a situation in which underprepared fourth graders were allowed to perform activities involving height and flight without the benefit of the safety matting and spotting normally required. It would be difficult to create a scenario more conducive to injury. An otherwise safe and valuable educational experience was allowed to degenerate into a high-risk situation that ultimately caused a costly negligence claim.

[Based on a case adjudicated in the lower courts]

CASE 14.3 ACTIVITY SELECTION AND PROXIMATE CAUSE

Richard Banding, a high school sophomore, was injured while participating in an introductory wrestling unit conducted by his physical education teacher, Paul Adams. After three classes of instruction and practice on basic skills, the students were divided into weight classes, and an in-class double elimination tournament was conducted. The tournament was concluded after five classes, by which time each student had wrestled at least twice.

On the ninth class day, Mr. Adams announced that the class would begin a tag-team wrestling tournament. In this contest, two wrestlers would be paired off in the center of the mat. From this point they would attempt to force their opponent toward their team's side of the mat so that a teammate could be tagged. The tagged teammate would then replace the person who tagged him and continue the contest against the adversary, who would remain on the mat until he tagged one of his own teammates or was pinned.

Richard Banding was wrestling for the Blue team. His opponent, Anthony Carmino, had worked him over to the Red team's side of the mat. When Anthony tagged his teammate, several others piled on top of the two wrestlers, and Richard suffered an injury.

This case is particularly interesting because, although there may have been negligence in the selection and conduct of the activity, the negligence does not appear to be the proximate cause of Richard Banding's injury.

Tag-team wrestling is used in the professional arena. It has no valid association with the sport of amateur wrestling as it is properly taught and practiced in the public schools. Worse, neither the lesson plans nor the curriculum guide supplied by Paul Adams, the teacher, made any reference to tag-team wrestling. Both call for instruction and practice followed by a class tournament. It would appear therefore that the activity was unplanned and instituted to fill at least one of the remaining two days in the two-week unit.

The tag-team activity carries a number of risks not normally associated with the wrestling activity. Most notable among these is the potential for a mismatch. Instead of pairings based on size and skill, this activity pairs participants based on which person one of the wrestlers tags. To be successful, the wrestler should try to tag someone who is far superior to his present opponent. The possible catastrophic results of such a situation should be fairly obvious to even the most naive observer.

In this case, the risk of the activity itself was compounded by failure to provide sufficient instructional and practice time to develop the skills and techniques necessary to engage safely in competitive wrestling. Even a cursory perusal of any of the accepted resources on wrestling or wrestling safety would indicate that match wrestling requires a level of skill and understanding that simply could not be developed in three class periods.

The most interesting aspect of this case, however, is that although these are valid points that represent an unusual risk of injury and are negligent acts, they do not appear to be the cause of the injury. Richard Banding was injured when several wrestlers jumped on him and his opponent. As inappropriate as tag-team wrestling may have been, there is no indication that group pile-ons were part of the design and no evidence to indicate that such behavior had ever before occurred or been tolerated by the teacher. Therefore, the injury would appear to be the result of a sudden, one-time event that may have been beyond the reasonable prediction or control of the teacher.

If the jury accepts this premise, then it must accept that the teacher's specific acts of negligence did not cause the injuries; so Paul Adams should not be held liable for damages. If, on the other hand, student witnesses testify that horseplay and piling on were common during the activity or that Mr. Adams failed to clearly define the tag/exchange procedure and they therefore thought that more than one wrestler could simultaneously enter the contest, then a causal relationship could be established.

A further point that could be stressed eloquently and that could therefore prove quite persuasive in this case is the nature of the contest itself. The only referent the students would have had for tag-team wrestling beyond what their teacher told them is what they had seen in the professional arena. The level of stylized violence and exaggerated disregard for the rules exhibited at that level make it difficult to consider professional wrestling as a sport. Given that background, it should be expected that, unless the strictest rules and closest supervisory control are applied, a tag-team contest among high school students would almost certainly begin to degenerate to the behavioral example set at the professional level. Therefore, although the specific piling-on incident that caused Richard Banding's injury may not have been predictable, it would have been only a matter of time before some form of unsafe behavior was demonstrated.

Choosing such a pointless activity, even though there may be a reasonable technical defense, opens both the choice of activity and the general level of professionalism to such strong attack that, in the eyes of a jury, the defendant could be held responsible for any damages that resulted. It was precisely this point that contributed to the defense's decision to offer a relatively large pretrial settlement in this case.

[Based on a case settled prior to trial]

CASE 14.4 INJURY IDENTIFICATION AND CARE

Margaret Downing suffered an injury to her hand and fingers during the final minutes of a junior varsity basketball game—her hand and fingers were very painful, and one finger appeared slightly displaced. Margaret's coach, Rick Westman, acknowledged the injury and directed Margaret to sit on the bench. No first aid was provided, and no medical assistance was summoned.

The game resumed with a substitute filling Margaret's position. But with less than a minute to play and the outcome of the game still very much in doubt, Mr. Westman directed Margaret to reenter the game. On the ensuing play, the ball was thrown to Margaret; she attempted to catch it and suffered further damage to her injured hand.

After the game, the parent of a teammate noticed Margaret's fingers, which were by this time more noticeably displaced and bleeding slightly. The parent suggested medical examination to the coach. Mr. Westman, however, was preparing to supervise the varsity game, scheduled to begin in a few minutes. Margaret waited unattended and without first aid throughout the varsity game, after which she was transported back to the school parking lot and dismissed with the team. When she arrived home her parents saw the injury and transported Margaret to a hospital emergency room, where a compound fracture was diagnosed and treated. Margaret's enraged parents initiated a lawsuit almost immediately.

This case is a callous and blatant example of a coach's neglect for player welfare and safety. All coaches are expected to know basic first-aid procedures for injuries common to their sports. Furthermore, every coach should have established procedures for obtaining medical assistance for injured team members, both at home and away. When Margaret Downing initially suffered her injury, her coach should have at least provided immobilization, applied cold, and sought proper medical attention. Under no circumstances should she have been allowed to reenter the game.

Whether Rick Westman's action in returning Margaret to play was the result of a lapse of attention in the heat of a close contest, a misdiagnosis of her injury, or a conscious decision to run the risk in an attempt to win the game, the consequence was the same. The injury was exacerbated, and Margaret's parents were understandably infuriated.

This parental anger is noteworthy, as anger frequently results in legal action that otherwise might not have been taken. Also worthy of note is the relative ease with which the question of proximate cause could be handled. This is often not the case in first aid-related lawsuits. When an individual is injured, there is some level of initial damage. To win a lawsuit alleging improper first aid, it is necessary to prove that the actions or inactions of the defendant caused the initial injury to worsen. This medical question is often difficult and highly disputable. Coach Westman, however, put Margaret back into the game, and the first pass thrown to her changed slightly displaced fingers to a compound fracture. The failure to properly react to an initial injury very clearly resulted in a worsening of her condition. Little could be done to defend the coach's actions from either a legal or a moral standpoint.

Coaches or teachers must be sure to stay current and confident in their first-aid skills. They must also be sure that their team or organization has an effective set of procedures for the routine management of accidents, whether in practice or contests, at home or on the road. As with everything a coach or teacher does, these procedures should clearly state and demonstrate the attitude that "when in doubt as to which course of action to pursue, the well-being of the child must always be given precedence."

[Based on a case adjudicated in the lower courts]

CASE 14.5 READINESS: RETURN FROM INJURY

Donna Marino was a high school student who had been under a doctor's care for recurring knee problems. During the course of her freshman and sophomore years she had been under the care of a doctor who pursued conservative treatments. The doctor had written a letter to the school requesting that Donna be excused from all physical activity for a two-month period during her sophomore year and had thereafter directed her to refrain from any activities that placed excessive strain on her knee. On three occasions after the two-month excuse period, the school nurse excused Donna from physical education classes because of pain and swelling in her knee.

In mid-April of her sophomore year, Donna once again experienced pain and swelling in her knee and was extremely reluctant to participate in her scheduled physical education class. She related these facts to her teacher, Jeanne Lewis, who told her to dress for activity. After getting dressed, Donna again told Ms. Lewis that she felt her knee was too weak and painful to participate, but Ms. Lewis told her that unless she performed the activity of the day, she would not pass physical education.

The activity of the day was a shuttle run that was being timed for grading purposes. Shortly before she was to perform the run, Donna again reminded Ms. Lewis, who had been her teacher throughout the year, of her knee problem and asked to be excused. Ms. Lewis again refused, indicating the need for documented grading data. Donna reluctantly attempted the shuttle run and fell during one of the turns when her knee gave out. Later that evening she underwent reconstructive knee surgery. Some time later, her parents filed suit on her behalf against her teacher, Jeanne Lewis.

It is theoretically conceivable that Donna's knee problem would have required surgery under any circumstances. It is even possible that the surgery should not have been put off as long as it was and that the shuttle run did little to exacerbate the already existing injury. In fact, these are theories that the defendant asked the jury to consider.

However, the jury also considered the facts with which they were confronted. Donna had a clear history of knee problems. Throughout the year both her own physician and the school nurse had frequently excused her from physical education, often for extended periods, to aid in her recovery and to avoid exacerbating the problem. Jeanne Lewis was aware of Donna's problem, and Donna had addressed her several times on the date in question and asked to be excused. A shuttle run is a vigorous running activity requiring explosive starts, stops, and directional changes. This particular event was being conducted and timed under the pressure of a grade. Given these facts and the irrefutable presence of a severe injury, the swift and generous award that Donna received is not difficult to understand.

Many programs have well-developed guidelines for considering excuses from activity. The best of these routinely send all students who ask to be excused to the school nurse, who examines them and determines whether to excuse them for the day. A note is sent to the parents informing them of the problem and suggesting that they be alert to the possible need for medical attention if it continues. Persistent problems or those that extend beyond a few days require referral to a physician. This policy displays clear concern for the students' welfare and avoids unjustified excuses by alerting parents to the fact that their children are missing important educational experiences.

Unfortunately, no policy of any kind was in effect at the time of Donna Marino's injury. Instead, her teacher took upon herself the role of medical diagnostician and concluded that Donna should participate in the shuttle run. In forcing Donna Marino to participate in an activity that clearly placed great strain on her knee, against her will and despite her complaints of knee pain and swelling, Ms. Lewis displayed both a lack of sound professional judgment and a total disregard for the welfare of a student entrusted to her care. Such behavior is diametrically opposed to accepted standards of professional conduct and must be expected to result in needless injuries and costly legal actions.

[Based on a case adjudicated in the lower courts]

CASE 14.6 PROTECTIVE MEASURES

Tina Fraser was a 16-year-old member of the junior varsity softball team at Bathgate Regional High School. She and her teammates were taking batting practice with the aid of an automatic pitching machine. The coach, Ellen Ames, directed Tina to feed balls into the machine, which was pitching balls to a batter at the plate. The fielders were shagging the balls and throwing them to another player, who stood about 15 feet from Tina and was flipping Tina the balls to load into the machine. The school had a safety screen for use with the machine, but Coach Ames had elected not to use it. In fact, when the other equipment was being brought to the field, one of the players asked whether the screen should be brought out as well. The coach answered that it would not be necessary. During the course of the batting practice, one of the batters hit a line drive that struck Tina on the nose, fracturing the nasal spine and causing profuse bleeding. Several surgeries were required to correct the damage caused by the injury.

This injury was the direct and easily avoidable result of Coach Ames's deliberate disregard for the necessary provisions of safety. When she assigned Tina Fraser the task of feeding balls into the pitching machine, she placed her in one of the most dangerous positions on the field. Tina was required to divide her attention among the tasks of feeding balls into the machine, receiving balls returned from the field, and protecting herself from batted balls. The latter responsibility, however, could and should have been eliminated by the presence of an appropriate protective screen.

The risk of injury from a line drive back to the pitcher's mound, especially during batting practice, and the necessity of protecting players from this hazard have been well documented in professional literature. Screens are commonly employed during batting practice to protect the person on the mound from the possibility of being struck by a batted ball. They can be purchased commercially or locally manufactured for use with machine or player pitching. Although such a screen was available at Bathgate Regional High School on the date in question, Coach Ames had elected not to use it.

Coaches are obligated to anticipate the hazards involved in an activity and to take any and all reasonable precautions necessary to ensure the safety and well-being of their athletes. Consequently, it's virtually impossible to justify this injury as an unforeseeable accident. This was not a simple error of omission: Coach Ames made a conscious decision to omit the use of an important safety device that was readily available.

In fact, Ellen Ames would have been no less responsible for the safety of her athletes if no screen had been available. She would have been expected to structure and organize the drill in a manner that eliminated or at least minimized the risk to the person or persons on the mound. But the failure to use an effective and readily available safety device is virtually indefensible.

Remember that teachers or coaches should provide safety equipment and require its use. Post reminders for the staff as well as for the participants to make sure they are aware of the importance of protective equipment and that they use it routinely. Such measures serve a dual purpose: they help reduce the risk of injuries, and they help establish the shared responsibility of the participant to adhere to reasonable safety procedures.

[Based on a case settled before trial]

CASE 14.7 FIELD CONDITIONS

Carl Flynn was in the seventh grade at Millwick Junior High School. On October 15, as part of his regularly assigned physical education class, Carl was directed to take part in a game of touch football. After a brief warm-up indoors, teams were selected and the class was led outdoors.

This was the first day on which the football activity was conducted. No instructions were given, the rules were not explained, and no warnings or safety provisions were discussed.

The game was played on a poorly maintained field located behind the school that was strewn with stones and glass. The grass in many areas of the field was worn away, leaving bare ground, and erosion from water runoff had caused even greater surface irregularities. The condition of the field on the date in question was worsened by the weather, which was cloudy and damp, producing muddy conditions and general slipperiness. During the game, Carl attempted to tag an offensive player, lost his footing, and fell, suffering serious injury to his knee.

Although failure to provide adequate instruction and warnings and some reasonable discussion of safety provisions deviates from proper professional practice, it is not the focus of this particular lawsuit. Carl Flynn was not injured because of these factors. The condition of the playing field on October 15 is the only factor that can be shown to have directly caused or aggravated the injury that Carl Flynn sustained on that date. His attorney therefore based his claim on the alleged failure of the teacher and the school to provide a safe playing environment. But had Carl or some other student suffered an injury due to a lack of skill or understanding that might have been prevented by proper instruction, then the focus of the primary complaint would have been readjusted to reflect the results of the additional areas of negligence.

There is little question that the field behind Millwick Junior High School was unsuitable for the conduct of a vigorous running activity such as touch football. The surface irregularities were sufficient in and of themselves to expose the students to unnecessary risk of injury. When these preexisting surface problems are compounded by the addition of surface moisture, the resultant mud and slippery grass clearly invite falls and injuries like Carl Flynn's.

This case illustrates the problems that can arise when a teacher, coach, or administrative authority fails to demonstrate adequate concern for the quality and safety of the playing surface on which running activities are conducted. It should also serve as a warning to anyone who might be under the mistaken impression that a lower standard of safety can be applied to fields used for instructional classes than for those used by varsity teams. Although the level of amenities such as bleachers, benches, painted lines, and official goalposts can definitely be lowered for instructional classes, the same cannot be said for the level of safety.

All participants, regardless of the level of their involvement, have a right to expect that the facilities they use will be as safe as reasonably possible at the time of their use. If, as in the case of Carl Flynn, a substandard facility is found to be the cause of an injury, the individuals responsible for that occurrence must recognize the very real possibility that they will be held liable for the resultant damages. In this case, generous settlements were reached on behalf of the defendant teacher and school district prior to trial.

[Based on a case settled before trial]

CASE 14.8 BUFFER ZONES

John Sanderson was seriously injured while playing in an intramural basketball game at Morrisville High School when he ran into an unpadded cinderblock wall after a driving lay-up. Although there was a regulation basketball court in the center of the gymnasium, intramurals were conducted on three smaller courts that ran across the gym and perpendicular to the long axis of the regulation court. The backboard involved in this particular incident was four feet from the cinderblock wall.

This case brings up the conflict between the valid and commendable desire to maximize participation and the necessity to provide a safe playing environment. On the one hand, the individuals in charge recognized that using the large regulation basketball court would greatly limit the number of games possible in a given time period. They decided that intramural games could be conducted on courts that were both shorter and narrower than the prescribed minimum for varsity sports. In this decision they were entirely correct: There is absolutely nothing wrong with reducing the size of a playing area for practice, instruction, or less formal games provided that safety is not unreasonably compromised. Shortening the length and width of the basketball court for intramurals would therefore be a sound decision provided the reductions were not so drastic as to result in overcrowding, an unlikely though not impossible scenario.

In this case, however, important safety factors were also drastically reduced. All guidelines for basketball safety indicate the importance of a reasonable amount of unobstructed space between the backboard and the nearest obstruction. Although the exact amount of space recommended varies depending upon the source and the level of activity, four feet, is well below even the most minimal standard. Moreover, most sources recommend padding walls located behind a basket. This would be particularly important in a case such as this one, in which the distance between the backboard or end line and the wall was already substandard.

When laying out courts and fields, it's perfectly reasonable and often more productive to modify the size of the playing area. But unless the game itself is modified, the need will remain for safety zones between the playing areas and around their perimeter that are wide enough to prevent injury to the players. On the other hand, if a safe buffer zone cannot be provided, the only reasonable option is to find another playing area or to modify the game itself.

Because the intramural supervisors at Morrisville High School failed to provide a reasonable safety area at the end of the court on which John Sanderson was injured, they were found guilty of negligence and ordered to compensate John for his losses.

[Based on a case adjudicated in the lower courts]

CHAPTER SUMMARY

The professional responsibility to provide an appropriate standard of care for participants in sport and physical activity encompasses three general areas: the provision of adequate supervision, proper selection and conduct of the activities, and safe environmental conditions. This chapter presented specific behavioral guidelines that can effectively reduce the risks associated with these areas regardless of the specific nature and level of the activity involved. To be most effective, however, the guidelines must be considered in the context of the published standards and recommendations that apply to the specific activity in question. Thus, general recommendations for a buffer zone, for instance, can be translated into the 25 feet of space recommended between a baseline and the nearest obstruction on a softball field.

KEY TERMS

Actual notice
Attractive nuisance
Buffer zones
Constructive notice
Emergency action plans
Environmental conditions
Feedback
General supervision
Instruction
Mismatch
Negligent hiring
Protective measures
Qualitative supervision
Quantitative supervision
Respondeat superior
Specific supervision
Supervision
Vicarious liability
Warnings

QUESTIONS FOR DISCUSSION

1. Name and define the three primary areas of responsibility with regard to the standard of care in sport and physical activity.
2. Give activity-specific examples to illustrate negligence associated with the following concepts:
    a. general vs. specific supervision
    b. *respondeat superior*
    c. inadequate instruction or feedback
    d. mismatch
    e. unsafe environmental condition
    f. actual notice
3. In each example given above, change one factor other than the occurrence of the injury itself so that, although an injury still occurs, it is unlikely that the person in charge would lose a negligence suit.
4. Given a particular activity, develop a series of guidelines in checklist form to reduce the risk of injuries due to faulty supervision, inappropriate selection and/or conduct of the activity, and unsafe facilities.
5. Modify the facts of Case 14.2 so that the teacher, Vivian Hansen, is not negligent.

REFERENCES

George, G.S. (Ed.) (1990). *AACCA cheerleading safety manual.* Memphis: The UCA Publications Department, p. 25.

George, G.S. (1990). *USGF gymnastics safety manual.* Indianapolis: USGF Publications.

Parker, D. (1993). Wrestling. In N.J. Dougherty (Ed.), *Principles of safety in physical education and sport.* Reston, VA: AAHPERD Publications.

ADDITIONAL READINGS

Note: One essential source of information is the official rule book of the particular sport in question. The rules provide both directives and recommendations, many of which are essential to safe play and legal defensibility.

The following additional sources exemplify the types of materials and organizations which are of great value in seeking to identify standards and guidelines for the safe conduct of specific sports and activities.

American Alliance for Health, Physical Education, Recreation and Dance, Reston, Virginia. http://www.aahperd.org

American College of Sports Medicine, Indianapolis, Indiana. http://www.acsm.org

American Association of Cheerleading Coaches and Advisors, Memphis, Tennessee. http://www.aacca.org

Borkowski, R.P. (1998). *The school sports safety handbook.* Horsham, PA: LRP Publications.

Dougherty, N.J. IV (Ed.) (1998). *Outdoor recreation safety.* Champaign, IL: Human Kinetics.

Dougherty, N.J. (Ed.). (1993). *Principles of safety in physical education and sport.* Reston, VA: AAHPERD.

Gabriel, J. (Ed.). (1999). *U.S. Diving safety training for competitive diving coaches.* Indianapolis, IN: US Diving, Inc.

McIntyre, S., Goltsman, S.M. & Kline, L. (1997). *Safety first checklist.* Berkeley, CA: MIG Communications.

National Swimming Pool Foundation, Merrick, New York. http://www.nspf.com

Project Adventure, Inc., Hamilton, Massachusetts. http://www.pa.org

Sawyer, T.H., Goldfine, B., Hypes, M.G., LaRue, R.L., & Seidler, T. (1999). *Facilities planning for physical activity and sport–Guidelines for development.* Dubuque, IA: Kendall/Hunt Publishing Company.

School and Community Safety Society of America, AAALF, Reston, Virginia. *Safety notebook.* 1-800-213-7193 xt. 432.

Tharrett, S.J., & Peterson, J.A. (1997). *ACSM's health/fitness facility standards and guidelines,* 2nd edition. Champaign, IL: Human Kinetics.

U.S. Consumer Products Safety Commission. *A handbook for public playground safety.* Washington, D.C.: Author.

U.S.A. gymnastics safety handbook for gymnastics and other sport activities (1998), Indianapolis, IN: USA Gymnastics Publications.

CHAPTER 15

RESPONSIBILITIES OF GAME OFFICIALS

JANE SAILOR V. CLAMPETT TOWNSHIP ET AL.

Clampett field was the best high school baseball facility in the county. The field was generally well designed and well maintained and was the site of all home games for the high school baseball team. Last year the Clampett High School softball team reached the finals of the state championships and was asked to host the final game. The decision was made that, because of the high quality of the field and the large permanent seating capacity, Clampett field would be adapted for softball play. The base paths were shortened from 90 feet to 60 feet, as required for softball play.

In the bottom of the second inning, a short pop fly was hit down the right field line. As the first baseman pursued the ball, she appeared to stumble and fall. She had stepped into the hole surrounding the fixed anchor for the first base used by the baseball team. No caps or covers had been applied when the base was removed and, as a result, when she stepped in the hole her foot caught and twisted between the anchoring stake and the ground. She suffered a severely fractured ankle.

The injured athlete, through her parents, sued Clampett Township and its agents for maintaining the field in a condition that she claimed was improper and unsafe. She also sued the umpires officiating the game. Citing the American Softball Association rule that gives the plate umpire the responsibility of determining the fitness of the grounds for the game, the plaintiff argued that the umpires should have examined the field, noted the hazardous condition, and had the problem corrected before play began.

LEARNING OBJECTIVES

Upon completion of this chapter, the student will be able to:

1.   explain the duty that a game official owes to an athlete through application of the concepts of contractual duty of care and duty to control,
2.   explain how the courts would seek to determine if an injury was the foreseeable result of a breach in the reasonably expected standard of care,
3.   describe the application of the but-for test in determining the proximate cause of an injury sustained by an athlete as the alleged result of a referee's negligence,
4.   give examples of situations that could give rise to claims of negligence due to an official's actions or omissions with regard to environmental conditions, inappropriate activities, and inadequate supervision.

THE OFFICIAL AS DEFENDANT

Game officials have been named as defendants in lawsuits where rough play, fights, and spectator violence have resulted in injuries to participants or spectators.

Liability for negligence on the part of officials and coaches is governed by principles that govern civil liability generally. Officials, to be held liable in the event of an injury to a player or spectator, must be shown to have violated a duty owed by them to the injured player or spectator. Second, that violation of duty, consisting of an action or failure to act, must bear a causal relationship to the injury. Third, the injury caused by the official's actions or failure to act must have been reasonably foreseeable. Fourth, the conduct of the official must be unreasonable in light of what a reasonable official would be expected to do or refrain from doing under all the circumstances present.

Once the competition starts, the primary responsibility for the ultimate safe conduct of the contest devolves upon the official, who is more directly involved with the control and flow of the game.

Officials who fail to intelligently and firmly enforce rules regarding player contact, opponent baiting, and unsporting conduct are placing themselves in a position of high legal exposure. By *not* penalizing player infractions early in the contest, the official, in effect, places a stamp of approval on prohibited conduct and in so doing makes allegations of negligence by a participant who is later injured possible to sustain. Officials have the authority and the obligation to effectuate negative reinforcement for prohibited and dangerous acts by penalizing participants for such infractions. If appropriate penalties and sanctions are not imposed by the official at the time of violations and injury results, the officials may be liable.

Consider a situation where a player throws and lands an elbow at the guarding opposing player in full view of the official. Instead of calling a foul, the official, within earshot of all concerned, tells the player involved that "the next time you throw an elbow, I'll call a foul." The official has just informed everyone involved that (1) the official has witnessed a dangerous violation and has chosen not to penalize the player for it, which is in dereliction of an official's duties and responsibilities, and (2) the official is on notice that the player involved entertains a propensity for violent conduct.

Game officials have been named as defendants in cases involving players injured in any number of contexts. Officials have been sued by basketball players for allegedly not calling enough fouls to deter rough play. They have been sued by football players for failing to penalize rules infractions designed to promote player safety. Baseball umpires have been sued for failing to suspend the game during inclement weather conditions. And officials in all these sports have been sued for failing to take measures to prevent injuries due to dangerous conditions existing on a field or playing surface and areas. Since officials have virtually complete control of most sporting events once the competition begins, it's clear that liability may attach when officials fail to properly execute their duties in enforcing playing rules and controlling the actions of players and coaches.

The potential liability of officials can best be understood when examined in the context of the basic aspects of tort law: duty, standard of care, foreseeability, and proximate cause.

DUTY

The duty that an official owes to a participating athlete rests largely on two legal concepts: **contractual duty of care** and the **duty to control**. When a contractual duty is performed in a negligent manner, there exists the possibility of a tort action for recovery of the damages that may result. Although the participating athletes do not, as a general rule, share in the process of contracting for referees and officials, their safety and welfare is clearly recognized as the **end or aim** of the contract. Thus, the contractual relationship between the official and the hiring authority is seen as establishing a legal foundation for liability (duty) in the event that the official should fail to effectively fulfill prescribed duties regarding participant safety. In addition to the responsibilities imposed by a formal contract, the rules of most sports place officials in a position of authority over coaches and athletes. The rules of most sports, for instance, charge the official with the responsibility of ascertaining the playability of the field, penalizing identified illegal or unsafe behaviors, and ejecting from the game those individuals whose conduct flagrantly deviates from the prescribed limits. Officials, therefore, are able to exert a degree of control over the actions and conduct of the athletes and, thus, may bear a legal obligation to do so.

STANDARD OF CARE

Having established that the official owes a duty to exercise reasonable care in the control of an athletic contest and over its participants, one must next establish the standards of performance that he or she must meet in fulfilling this duty. The standard of care is that standard which a reasonably prudent individual would be expected to follow under the same or similar circumstances. In making this determination, courts give special consideration to training and qualifications beyond the ordinary and the effect that they might be expected to have on the actions of the official. The yardstick used in assessing the performance of an official, therefore, is not simply a person of ordinary prudence but a reasonably prudent *official* who must, by the rules of the sport itself, act in a specialized and skillful manner.

Sports officials are, almost universally, assigned the responsibility of ensuring that rules and regulations of the sport and the sanctioning body or league are enforced. These rules and regulations, then, become key elements in establishing the standard of care required of the official. A distinction should be made, however, between **rule enforcement** and **rule enactment**. While the referee is, without question, responsible for the enforcement of the rules and regulations of the contest, for the most part they have no direct control over the design and enactment of those rules. They are, therefore, bound to uphold the standards as designed. One notable exception to this situation, however, is where local ground rules are instituted. If a local ground rule creates an unreasonable risk of injury to the athletes and, if the official accepts and enforces this unsafe modification without question or modification, then the official must be prepared to share in the potential liability that could exist in the event of an injury.

FORESEEABILITY

Before an individual can be held responsible for damages suffered by another, the possibility of harm must be shown to have been reasonably predictable. In all sports, rules have been instituted for the protection of the participants. Rules regarding spearing and clipping in football, for instance, were enacted to reduce the risk of serious injury to the players. If these rules are not enforced diligently, the frequency of spearing and clipping will likely increase. As the frequency of these unsafe practices increases, the likelihood that a player will suffer an injury as a result of clipping or spearing also increases. While any given injury to some particular athlete may not have been predictable, the likelihood of *an* injury to *some* player most certainly was. Thus, the yardstick by which foreseeability is judged is whether the possibility of an injury should have been apparent to a prudent official acting under the same or similar circumstances. The specific accident or injury need not have been foreseeable.

PROXIMATE CAUSE

Given a breach of the duty to perform according to an accepted standard of care in a situation where some risk of harm was reasonably foreseeable, a fourth issue still remains to be resolved before an official can be held legally responsible for the harm suffered by an athlete. The negligent actions of the official must be shown to have been the proximate cause of the injury. While volumes have been written on the concept of proximate cause, for purposes of this discussion, the concept can be reduced to one rather simple question: Did the negligence of the defendant cause or aggravate the injury in question? If the answer to this question is no, then regardless of the amount of carelessness present, the injured athlete cannot recover damages for negligence from the official.

This question is often made more complex in the case of a referee, however, because of the intervention and actions of a third party. When one athlete is injured as a result of the actions of another, and an official is sued, the proximate cause issue revolves around the question of whether the actions of the player who caused the injury could reasonably have been controlled by the official. One way of addressing this question is seen in the use of the **but-for test.** That is, to hold all factors of the incident constant except for the alleged negligence and, thus, to determine whether, but for the negligence of the official, the injury would not have occurred.

Consider a football game. The quarterback drops back and throws a pass, which is completed. The defensive tackle delivers a vicious blow to the quarterback well after the completion, causing a serious injury. Because the officials were all concentrating on the completion and the subsequent touchdown run, no penalty was called for the late hit. The officials were remiss in their failure to penalize the actions of the tackle. If, however, they had seen and penalized the infraction, the quarterback still would have been injured. It's unlikely, then, that their failure to see or react to the safety violation could be held to be the proximate cause of the injury. If, on the other hand, the defensive tackle had been delivering late hits throughout the game and few if any had been penalized, the scenario changes considerably. Given the proper action of diligent enforcement and, if necessary, ejection, the likelihood of the dangerous act continuing decreases greatly. In this case, proper actions by the official might have made a difference and, thus, negligence can be held to be proximately related to the eventual injury.

EMPLOYMENT STATUS OF OFFICIALS

Officials are generally viewed as **independent contractors** rather than as employees of the schools or leagues that have contracted for their services or of the associations that may have trained or assigned them. This is an important distinction, as it significantly restricts the extent to which negligent actions of an official can be imputed to the school or league under the concept of *Respondeat Superior* (see Chapter 14).

The single most compelling feature in determining if a person is an employee or an independent contractor is the degree of control that the employer is able to exert over the person's actions. For this reason, the great majority of courts and agencies that have considered the question have determined that most game officials are independent contractors. Independent contractors are generally not subject to the control of the hiring authority but rather possess an independent skill or trade, pay their own expenses, supply their own equipment and clothing, and are compensated on a per-event basis.

In addition, while officials may generally be regarded as independent contractors for some purposes under the law, they may be deemed employees for other purposes, such as taxation or laws against discrimination.

Be that as it may, a school or a league that engages an official may still be liable to an injured participant should it be shown that the school or league failed to exercise reasonable care in selecting that official.

RESPONSIBILITIES OF OFFICIALS

Like teachers and coaches, game officials are responsible for enforcing rules regarding the safety of the facilities and equipment, the conformance of the activities to the rules, and the provision of effective supervision. The National Federation of State High School Association's officials' codes of ethics require referees and umpires to inform event management of conditions or situations that appear to be unreasonably hazardous, and to recognize emergency conditions that might arise during the course of a game. Their responsibilities in this regard are different, however, in that they are mostly limited to the time frame from shortly before to just after the actual contest or game.

FACILITIES AND EQUIPMENT

Officials are charged by the rules and officiating mechanics of most sports with the responsibility of determining the safety and appropriateness of the facilities and equipment used in a contest. In general, this would include the physical layout of the area, adherence of the equipment to appropriate specifications and standards, playability of the surface, and continued safety of the playing area during the contest. A gymnastics judge, for instance, is expected to note and correct a situation involving inadequate matting. A softball umpire is expected to correct a badly eroded base path or equipment left in the playing area. And a football referee should note and correct the absence of proper protective equipment and safe field marking devices.

Like coaches and teachers, the official is expected to respond to both actual and constructive notice. Coach or athlete complaints regarding facilities or equipment are examples of actual notice. Reasonably obvious deficiencies such as those revealed by the required performance of an appropriate pregame inspection constitute constructive notice. In both cases the official has a clear responsibility to take immediate and appropriate actions to safeguard the athletes involved.

APPROPRIATE ACTIVITIES

Like coaches, officials may be expected to shoulder some portion of the legal burden of insuring the appropriateness of the individual activities attempted by the athlete. Many elements of play are within the control of the officials during the game. If they overlook unsafe or illegal behaviors, it's reasonable to assume that those behaviors will continue and perhaps even increase in number. In football, for instance, the act of making primary contact with the head is both unsafe and illegal. If a player does this, whether by intent or by accident, and he is not injured or penalized, he will probably do it again. If one player appears to get away with a violation, it's only a matter of time before others will try. The results in terms of the safety of the players and the quality of the contest are obvious. Equally obvious is the fact that, to the degree that rules allow the official to control the actions of the players, the failure to effectively do so can result in legal action if and when an injury occurs as a result of inappropriate or illegal techniques or actions.

SUPERVISION

The official is expected to maintain reasonable control of the environmental conditions and the activities through the exercise of effective general and specific supervision. The officials must be alert with regard to their positioning in the playing area to ensure the best visual coverage of the action both on and away from the ball. For instance, in a field hockey game, an altercation started when two opposing players collided while attempting to gain control of a loose ball. The fight continued after the ball had moved downfield, resulting in an injury to one of the athletes. The officials, focusing their full attention on the ball, did not see or attempt to stop the problem until after the situation degenerated into a bench-clearing brawl. The alleged failure of the officials to intervene became the focus of a lawsuit where one primary issue was the time span between the initiation of the altercation and the injury and, correspondingly, the opportunity of the official to initiate reasonable corrective action.

AFTER AN INJURY

Officials bear a legal obligation to deal appropriately with injuries to participants as well as with hazardous situations and dangerous conditions.

Regarding player injury, officials need to be thoroughly familiar with the rules that govern stop of play and time-out procedures. In most situations, for instance, basketball officials must stop play following an injury only when the ball is dead or in control of the injured player's team or after the opponents of the injured player have completed a play. On the other hand, the official is required to stop play *immediately* when necessary to protect the injured player.

After stopping play, the official must determine if the player is in need of assistance. If the player is injured seriously enough so that play must be stopped, he or she will usually need to be substituted for, depending on the game rules. But in any event, it is the officials' responsibility to immediately summon adult personnel from the bench, in particular the head coach, who must then determine if a trainer or physician is required. Officials ought not to attempt to render first aid or medical treatment, nor should they discuss the cause of the injury with anyone. It's important that officials allow medical personnel the unfettered opportunity to determine if and when the player may be moved, regardless of the time of delay. Also, the officials must continue to supervise both teams. It's advisable to keep the teams separated and at or near their bench or team areas during the time-out.

SOMETIMES THE RULES AREN'T ENOUGH

Although most playing rules instruct game officials to interpret all rules with a view toward placing safety first, sometimes a situation does not appear to fall directly within the letter of the written rules. While in many ways this question is more a moral issue than a legal one, it's no less important. The critical point is that regardless of the potential

FIGURE 15.1

The rules of most sports enable the official to exert a degree of control over players actions and conduct. They may be liable for injuries that result from their failure to provide that standard of care.

for a lawsuit, the health and safety of the athlete must be the most important factor to be weighed in the decision-making process. If the likelihood of an injury is very remote, or the potential severity is very minor, then other factors such as the flow of the contest or the desires of the athletes or the coaches can be considered. As the potential likelihood and severity of an injury increases, however, so must the primacy of the safety issues. Remember: if you have to choose between an angry coach and a seriously injured athlete, there really is no choice. While the coach may cause a certain degree of annoyance and, perhaps, embarrassment; the failure to properly control the safety of the athletes can result in a serious injury and a costly litigation.

CASE STUDY 15.1—A QUESTIONABLE GROUND RULE

Derbyville High School was preparing to play a varsity football game against Gantley Township on the Derbyville Memorial Field. Before the start of the game, the head umpire informed both coaches that a trench dug in preparation for the installation of a sprinkler constituted a violation of the rules with regard to field design and was a safety hazard. The trench was approximately 1 foot deep, 2 feet wide, and 20 feet long. The trench ran away from the field on a perpendicular from the 20-yard line, beginning at a point about three feet outside the sidelines.

The coaches and the umpire agreed that, rather than postponing the game, the Derbyville coach would place someone near the trench to prevent anyone from stepping into the hole and that all plays in that area of the field would be initiated from either the center of the field or the hashmark on the opposite side.

During the second half of the game a punt sailed deep into Derbyville territory toward the trench. The receiver took the ball on a dead run moving toward the sidelines. He was hit almost immediately by a Gantley player, and their momentum carried them directly toward the trench. A uniformed Derbyville player who had been stationed near the trench in accordance with the pregame agreement tried to keep the athletes from going into the pit and was, himself, knocked into the pit. He suffered serious damage to his knee, which resulted in hospitalization and surgery.

In a subsequent lawsuit, the injured athlete cited the impropriety of the trench and the responsibilities of the Derbyville administrators and coaches to avoid such hazards. He also named the officials who had, according to the testimonial evidence, recognized the hazard and agreed to what the athlete claimed was an improper ground rule, which placed him in undue physical danger.

CASE STUDY 15.2—JOHN PLAYER V. ELWOOD UMPIRE

The Baywood Bombers were playing the Shorefront Sharks in the opening game of an adult softball league. During the bottom half of the first inning, a Baywood player hit a long fly ball to left center field. The Shorefront left and center fielders both pursued the ball and collided as they were about to make the catch. The left fielder suffered serious head and facial injuries as a result of the collision and instituted a lawsuit accusing both the league and the umpire involved in the game of negligence. It seems that the grass in the outfield ranged between four and eight inches in height, with clumps and bare spots scattered throughout the area. The injured player, through his expert, alleged that the umpire deviated from reasonable standards by (1) failing to inspect the playing field as specified in the rules of the Amateur Softball Association and (2) failing to comply with the rules of play and cancel the game in view of the hazardous condition of the outfield.

The expert for the defense had to concede that the field was, indeed, unfit for play at the time of the incident. Moreover, the plaintiff's expert was entirely correct in his assessment of the responsibility of the umpire regarding the safety and playability of the field. The umpire did owe a duty to the plaintiff and did fall short of acceptable standards in performing that duty. Moreover, it was reasonably foreseeable that an outfield in the condition described could lead to player injuries. Fortunately for the umpire, however, the issue of proximate cause was not so clear cut.

The defense expert pointed out that there was no testimony to indicate that this collision was, in fact, related to the condition of the playing surface. Neither player claimed to have slipped, tripped, or in any way been impeded by the grass. They simply failed to see and effectively react to one another. Given that, it is probably equally arguable that the grass slowed the runners and reduced the force of impact as it was that the grass somehow contributed to the problem. The case was ultimately settled for a nominal sum.

The umpire was, indeed, fortunate. Clearly duties had been breached. It just so happened that the particular injury in question was not directly attributable to the umpire's negligence. If it had been, the result would almost certainly have been quite different. More important, if the umpire had fulfilled the obligation to control the playability of the field, he or she probably would not have been named in the suit and even a nominal settlement could have been avoided.

CHAPTER SUMMARY

Sports officials are potentially liable for injuries that are alleged to have been related to the manner in which they fulfilled their responsibilities regarding the safety of the participants. Because of the specific requirements of the rules of the sport and the authority of officials to control the flow of the game itself, there exists a legal responsibility to exercise due care with regard to foreseeable hazards in the conduct of the game as well as in the environmental conditions under which the game is played.

KEY TERMS

But-for test
Contractual duty of care
Duty to control
End or aim
Independent contractor
Rule enforcement
Rule enactment

QUESTIONS FOR DISCUSSION

1. How can an athlete sue an official for violating a contractual obligation when that athlete did not sign, agree to, or, for that matter, even read the contract in question?
2. Explain the application of the "but-for" test in ascertaining proximate cause in cases involving game officials. Give activity specific examples of situations where officials would be held liable for injuries in question. Modify one or more factors so that, while the injury would still occur, the action or inaction of the official would no longer be a proximately causative factor.
3. Create sport-specific scenarios where either the rules of the game or the nature of the situation require the intervention of the game officials in order to reduce the potential for an injury. Explain actions that should be taken and outline the legal claims that might be lodged if an injury occurred as a result of a failure to act.

ADDITIONAL READINGS

Clement, Annie. (1988). *Law in Sport and Physical Activity*. Indianapolis, IN: Benchmark Press, Inc.

Goldberger, Alan S. (1984). *Sports officiating: A legal guide*. New York: Leisure Press.

CHAPTER 16

CIVIL REDRESS FOR VIOLENCE ON THE PLAYING FIELD

Barleycorn High and Parkside Tech, two ardent crosstown rivals, were contesting a varsity field hockey game. With approximately three minutes remaining in the second half and the score tied, a Barleycorn player, Jane Sharp, received a pass and was tripped by Ann Nelson, a defender from Parkside. The referee immediately signaled the penalty. After the referee's whistle, as Jane sat on the ground, Ann Nelson, whose momentum had carried her out of the penalty area, returned and kicked Jane in the side of the head, causing serious injury.

Jane and her parents have instituted a lawsuit against Ann for what they argued was a negligent deviation from reasonable and prudent standards of behavior. Specifically, they allege that Ann failed to provide due care for Jane's safety and welfare and failed to properly control her own emotions when she deliberately, willfully, and recklessly kicked Ann after completing the play. Ann Nelson claims that she was acting out of frustration and did not intend to harm Jane. Such suits are becoming increasingly common in the world of competitive sport.

LEARNING OBJECTIVES

Upon completion of this chapter, the student will be able to:

1. recognize the nature and importance of cases finding participants liable for violent acts,
2. articulate the alternative player conduct standards and the legal problems and issues associated with each,
3. give examples of the application of the "reckless disregard standard" to game situations, and

4.   identify situations in which a coach may be held legally responsible for a player's violent acts.

THE PLAYER AS A DEFENDANT

Julian Nabozny was the goalkeeper for his high school age soccer team in Winnetka, Illinois. Witnesses testified that Nabozny was standing within the penalty area when he went down onto one knee to receive a pass from a teammate. David Barnhill, a forward on the opposing team, pursued the ball into the penalty area and kicked Nabozny in the side of the head, causing permanent skull and brain damage. All the witnesses agreed that Barnhill had sufficient opportunity to avoid contact with the plaintiff and that Nabozny had remained within the penalty area throughout the encounter. The Federation Internationale de Football Association (FIFA) rules under which the game was played prohibit all players from making contact with the goalkeepers when they have possession of the ball within the penalty area. Nabozny, a minor, brought suit through his father against David Barnhill who he alleged had negligently caused his injuries (*Nabozny v. Barnhill, 1975*).

Although the theoretical liability of athletes who commit *intentional* acts is relatively obvious, their legal responsibility for acts of *negligence* (unintentional omissions or commissions) was far less clear at the time of the Nabozny case. In that case, the trial court granted the defendant's motion for a **directed verdict**, in which the judge finds for the defendant as a matter of law. The trial court ruled that Nabozny had assumed the risks inherent in the game of soccer. The court of appeals, however, reversed the decision of the lower court and remanded the case for a trial by jury. In so doing, the court created an exception to the established standard of ordinary care that:

> limited liability in contact sports and concluded that the law should not place unreasonable burdens on the free and vigorous participation in sports by our youth. However, we also believe that organized athletic competition does not exist in a vacuum. Rather, some of the restraints of civilization must accompany every athlete onto the playing field. One of the educational benefits of organized athletic competition to our youth is the development of discipline and self-control.

> Individual sports are advanced and competition enhanced by a comprehensive set of rules. Some rules secure the better playing of the game as a test of skill. Other rules are primarily designed to protect participants from serious injury.

> It is our opinion that a player is liable for injury in a tort action if his conduct is such that it is either deliberate, willful or with a reckless disregard for the safety of the other player so as to cause injury to that player, the same being a question of fact to be decided by a jury.

> —*(Nabozny v. Barnhill, 1975)*

Subsequent Illinois case law has extended the contact sports exclusion to include both formal and informal activities wherein physical contact is a reasonably expected aspect of the event. [*Landrum v. Gonzalez,* 1994 (recreational softball), *Keller v. Mols,* 1987 (backyard floor hockey), *Pfister v. Shusta,* 1995 (impromptu kick-the-can game).

The Nabozny decision made it clear that reckless and deliberate acts of violence will not be condoned by the courts and, in fact, that when they occur and an injury results, the injured party can seek compensation through the legal system. However, the manner in which the appellate decision was stated left some question as to the exact type of circumstances under which a defendant player could be held liable. Within the language of the Nabozny decision were three possible interpretations of the standards of conduct to which players could be held.

ORDINARY NEGLIGENCE STANDARD

Under an **ordinary negligence standard,** athletes are expected to refrain from unsafe conduct that is prohibited by playing rules or by reasonable standards of behavior. This standard is onerous, and the courts have been reluctant to follow it. Carried to the extreme, it would subject athletes who violate safety-related rules (for example, clipping, unnecessary roughness, high sticking) to potential lawsuits if their adversaries suffered injuries as a result. Such a stringent standard would be nearly impossible for athletes to meet and would probably cause even the best players to fear the possibility of spending more time in court than on the playing field.

The *Nabozny* court sought to avoid this problem by imposing the contact activity exclusion, but the question of exactly what constitutes a contact activity has, understandably, been the subject of subsequent judicial debate.

WILLFUL OR WANTON STANDARD

Under a **willful or wanton standard,** players are held liable if their actions indicate willful or wanton disregard for the welfare of others. Willful and wanton acts are more serious than simple negligent errors of omission or commission. At the risk of oversimplification, **wanton acts** are those in which individuals know that their actions or failures to act may very well result in injuries to others, but they go ahead and do it anyway. Although they do not really intend to hurt anyone, they know that an injury is a distinct possibility and make no reasonable attempt to prevent it.

Willful acts entail more of an intention. For example, athletes who deliberately make late hits to instill fear in their opponents or to take them out of the game are committing willful acts. Obviously, the distinction between willful and wanton acts requires some assessment of the defendant's state of mind at the time of the alleged violation. It's thus difficult to prove willful and wanton behavior in court, especially months or years after the incident, when even defendant athletes may not accurately recollect what was going through their minds at the time of the actions.

RECKLESS DISREGARD STANDARD

Based on the cases brought subsequent to the Nabozny decision, the standard of care required of an athlete moved toward a combination of the ordinary negligence and willful or wanton standards previously discussed. That is, athletes would normally be required to refrain from behavior that would constitute a **reckless disregard** for the safety of other players as prescribed by the rules of the game (*Bourque v. Duplechin, 1976; Ross v. Clouser,* 1982). This was seen as being both fair and within the athlete's reasonable control.

In the early 1990s, however, the Wisconsin Supreme Court affirmed by a four to three vote an award of $225,000 against an adult recreational soccer player who slid into an opponent to keep him from scoring a goal in an over-30 recreational league that prohibited sliding. The court reasoned that a simple negligence standard was sufficient to meet the legal rights of participants in recreational team sports *(Letsina v. West Bend, 1993).*

At about the same time, a New Jersey appeals court reversed a trial court decision adopting the reckless disregard standard, *Crawn v. Campo* (1993) involving an adult pickup softball game where Crawn, who was catching, was injured when Campo collided with him while attempting to score. The appeals court held that player vs. player lawsuits could most appropriately be decided under the ordinary negligence standard. In July of 1994, however, the New Jersey Supreme Court overturned the Appellate Decision, stating that:

> Our conclusion that a recklessness standard is the appropriate one to apply in the sports context is founded on more than a concern for a court's ability to discern adequately what constitutes reasonable conduct under the highly varied circumstances of informal sports activity. The heightened standard will more likely result in affixing liability for conduct that is clearly unreasonable and unacceptable from the perspective of those engaged in the sport yet leaving free from the supervision of the law the risk-laden conduct that is inherent in sports and more often than not assumed to be 'part of the game.'
>
> —(*Crawn v. Campo,* 1994, p. 508)

The Supreme Court of Connecticut reached a similar decision in a case involving participants in an adult coed soccer league, concluding that the defendant owed the plaintiff a duty to refrain from reckless or intentional conduct. This case is particularly interesting in that it involves players of different genders *(Jaworski v. Kiernan, 1997).*

It would appear that, in most jurisdictions, potential player liability will be measured against the reckless disregard standard in light of the accepted rules of the activity.

THE LEVEL OF ORGANIZATION

The reckless disregard standard applies to activities involving structured coaching and organized teams, but what about less structured activities such as intramurals and sandlot games? Although the same standards for civil behavior seem to apply in both an unstructured game and one with coaches and paid officials, an uncoached athlete's knowledge of safety rules and regulations can almost certainly be expected to be lower than that of a well-coached individual. Thus, the standard of behavior expected would normally be that of a reasonable individual of similar skill and knowledge rather than the higher level of a trained athlete (see Case 16.1).

THE PRESENCE OF OFFICIALS

Regardless of the skill and training of the athletes, how will these principles be applied to games in which no officials are used? If the game was organized by some authoritative body, as unofficiated intramurals and school activities are, it's at least theoretically possible that injured athletes could sue the organizers under the contention that the presence of effective officiating would have significantly reduced the likelihood of reckless and unsafe behavior.

But what of the offending athletes? Is there no recourse unless their actions are so blatant that they fall into the willful battery category and thus move beyond ordinary negligence? Current case law indicates that individuals who participate in unstructured games and contests should be expected to show the same level of care and concern for the safety and welfare of their opponents as formally trained athletes would. Their behavior on the field should conform to societal norms and the rules of the game as it is being played at the time. However, the degree to which the legal system can adjudicate alleged breaches of this standard effectively is, of necessity, highly fact-dependent and thus decided on a case-by-case basis in light of the testimonial evidence.

BEHAVIORS NOT COVERED BY RULES

What about behaviors that do not necessarily violate a safety rule but that are so violent or vicious that they may reasonably be argued to show at least a willful disregard for the safety of an opponent? We have all seen a tackle applied to a receiver immediately after a catch or a body check to an unsuspecting person that appeared far more vicious than necessary. If such an action resulted in an injury, would it be actionable in court? Here, the issue may hinge so heavily on the state of mind of the defendant as to be beyond the scope of law in any but the most extreme cases.

THE COACH AS INSTIGATOR

A final issue focuses not on the athletes themselves but on their coaches. What is the potential liability of coaches who teach and encourage intense, aggressive play from their athletes if any of their players go beyond the rules and spirit of the game and cause injury to their opponents?

The case of *Nydegger v. Don Bosco Prep High School* (1985) is an example of just such a situation. Kevin Nydegger was a high school soccer player in New Jersey. He filed a suit against the opposing coach and school for injuries he suffered during a game. Nydegger alleged that the opposing coach taught his players to compete in an "aggressive and intense manner" and that he engendered an attitude in which winning was all-important. During the trial, however, Nydegger failed to prove that the defendant coach had ever instructed his players to injure an opponent. In ruling in favor of the coach, the court put forth a conclusion that succinctly summarizes both the level of risk that athletes can reasonably be expected to accept and the point at which coaches must assume responsibility for pushing their players beyond reasonable aggressiveness.

> Those who participate in a sport such as soccer expect that there will be physical contact as a result of 22 young men running around a field 50 by 100 yards. Physical contact is not prohibited by the rules of soccer. Injuries do result. Those who participate are trained to play hard and aggressive. . . . A coach cannot be held responsible for the wrongful acts of his players unless he teaches them to do the wrongful act or instructs them to commit the act. . . . Teaching players to be intense and aggressive is an attribute. All sports and many adult activities require aggressiveness and intensity.
>
> —(*Nydegger v. Don Bosco Prep High School,* 1985)

Clearly coaches, no matter how careful and well intentioned, cannot guarantee that none of their players will go beyond reasonable aggressiveness and improperly cause injuries to their opponents. If such an event occurs, and if the behavior of the athlete is determined to be so flagrant as to exhibit a reckless or willful disregard for the safety of others, then the offending athlete may very well become the target of a negligence suit. If, on the other hand, it can be proved that the coach taught or encouraged athletes to go beyond the bounds of reasonable aggression and to use dangerous or illegal tactics, then the coach may be liable for the resultant injuries.

Although aggression and intensity are normal and often laudable by-products of athletic participation, the courts will not tolerate deliberate and willful behavior that defies the letter and the spirit of the rules or that is intended to cause injury to an opponent. If such behavior occurs, the injured player can, depending on the specific circumstances, bring suit against the player who caused the injury, that player's coach, or both.

CASE STUDY 16.1 SLIDING PLAYER ACCUSED OF NEGLIGENCE

Diane Black, age 19, was a catcher on the Bad News Bombers, a recreational softball team in Drayton Township. The league consisted of eight coed teams that played according to modified slow-pitch rules, which required four female players on the field at all times and allowed sliding. Diane Black was approximately 5 feet, 5 inches tall and weighed about 148 pounds.

On May 13, Diane was playing in her first league game of the season. During the fifth inning, Sam Nolan batted first and safely reached second base. The next batter hit a long fly ball to left center field, and Sam attempted to score. Sam was proceeding down the third base line when Diane received the throw from the outfield. She estimates that he was approximately 20 feet from her when she gained possession of the ball. Sam continued his approach and attempted to slide. In the course of his slide, some portion of Sam's body struck Diane, who fell to the ground and suffered what was eventually diagnosed as a fractured fibula.

Diane has instituted suit against Sam, alleging through her attorney and his expert witness that Sam (1) failed to exercise good judgment and control of his emotions in the interest of safety; (2) willfully, negligently, and recklessly injured Diane by sliding, even though she had gained possession of the ball approximately 20 feet before the point of contact; (3) failed to comply with the meaning and spirit of the rules by purposely and willfully running into Diane in an attempt to score a run; (4) failed to realize that he was physically larger than Diane and that a collision with her would cause injury; and (5) failed to fulfill his duty to avoid collisions with defensive players while running the bases.

This type of scenario in many ways tends to fuel the fires of paranoia regarding the so-called "litigation explosion." Viewed from the defendant's perspective, we see an instantaneous decision to slide rather than a deliberate decision to either run into the catcher or try to stop and turn back toward third while already running at full speed toward home. Because of this decision, the athlete is now embroiled in a time-consuming and emotionally draining lawsuit.

From the plaintiff's perspective, on the other hand, the injury caused a financial drain from both time lost from work and expenses for subsequent medical treatment and required her to give up her part-time graduate study. She certainly never expected any of these complications to arise when she agreed to spend a few hours a week playing softball.

Perhaps the most disconcerting viewpoint, however, is that of the average teacher or coach who sees a relatively commonplace occurrence that an attorney and an expert have portrayed as being willful, dangerous, and negligent and that is now the subject of a major lawsuit. They are likely to fear that if lawsuits are allowed to continue springing up from this sort of incident, there simply will be no one left who's willing to run the risk of playing in or conducting programs of sport.

It's important to recognize, however, that bringing a lawsuit and winning it are two distinctly different issues. Access to the courts is one of the hallmarks of a democratic society. Restrictions on the right to bring suits would prevent valid suits as well as those of less merit. On the other hand, if defendants and the insurance companies that represent them successfully defend those cases that are without merit, then neither plaintiffs nor their attorneys gain from suing and ultimately realize that undertaking weak cases is too risky. This seems to be the best and fairest way to control the threat of a continued "litigation explosion."

In the case of Diane Black, the court found that her injury was caused by playing errors and/or skill deficiencies that she and/or Sam Nolan committed. There was no evidence to support her allegations that Mr. Nolan's actions had been willful and deliberate. Ms. Black in fact testified during the course of her deposition that she did not believe that Sam had intentionally collided with her. Further, because sliding is a legitimate evasive technique that falls within both the letter and spirit of the rules, it's difficult to question its use in this particular situation.

Sam attempted to avoid a tag and to score a run by executing a slide. Diane attempted to avoid a run by standing within the basepath to apply the tag on the base runner. This is a simple matter of two relatively unskilled players executing complex motor skills in a very imprecise manner. Such collisions are not entirely uncommon among even highly skilled players but are even more likely to occur among recreational players. Although this fact argues strongly for the wisdom of no-sliding rules instituted by professionals who organize and supervise recreational leagues, it in no way imposes the burden of negligence upon unskilled participants who execute less than perfect slides. *[Based on a case adjudicated in the lower courts]*

CHAPTER SUMMARY

Recent case law has made it clear that an athlete injured by an opponent during the course of a game or contest can seek compensation through the courts. Yet to be fully determined, however, is the question of the standard of behavior against which a defendant player's actions are to be measured. It appears that the reckless disregard standard will emerge as the best compromise between the desire to encourage vigorous athletic competition and the rights of an athlete who has been injured by the allegedly wrongful actions of another player. It must also be recognized that coaches who encourage wrongful acts of aggression by their players may be liable for the results of their players' actions.

KEY TERMS

Directed verdict
Ordinary negligence standard
Reckless or willful disregard
Wanton acts
Willful acts
Willful or wanton standard

QUESTIONS FOR DISCUSSION

1. Discuss and expand on the following statement: although the Nabozny decision clearly articulated the rights of athletes to sue each other for injuries sustained as a result of their alleged negligence, it failed to define the specific types of behaviors that could reasonably precipitate such a lawsuit.
2. Give activity-specific examples of situations that could reasonably constitute breaches of the reckless disregard standard.
3. Give activity-specific examples of situations in which one athlete is injured by the aggressive or violent act of another, but a successful lawsuit is unlikely to result.
4. Devise a scenario whereby someone other than the offending athlete might reasonably be held liable for injuries resulting from player violence.
5. Change some facts in Case 16.1 so that Sam Nolan may indeed be held liable for Diane Black's injury.

REFERENCES

Bourque v. Duplechin, 331 So.2d 40 (La. app 1976).

Crawn v. Campo, 136 NJ 494, 1994.

Goldstein, L.A. (1976). Participant's liability for injury to a fellow participant in an organized athletic event. *Chicago-Kent Law Review,* 53, 97-108.

Jaworski v. Kiernan, 241 Conn. 399; 696 A.2d 332 (1997).

Keller v. Mols, 156 Ill. App.3d, 509 N.E.2d 584 (1987).

Landrum v. Gonzalez, 257 Ill. App.3d 942, 629 N.E.2d 710 (1994).

Letsina v. West Bend Mutual Insurance Co., 501 N.W.2d 28 (Wis 1993).

Nabozny v. Barnhill, 31 Ill. App.3d 212, 334 N.E.2d 258 (1975).

Nydegger v. Don Bosco Prep High School, 202 NJ Super. 535 (1985).

Pfister v. Shusta, 167 Ill. 2d 417, 657 N.E.2d 1013 (1995).

Ross v. Clouser, 637 S.W.2d 11 (Mo. 1982).

ADDITIONAL READINGS

Goldstein, L.A. (1976). Participant's liability for injury to a fellow participant in an organized athletic event. *Chicago-Kent Law Review,* 53, 97-108.

Horrow, R. (1985). Legislating against violence in sports. In H. Appenzeller (Ed.), *Sports and law: Contemporary issues* (pp. 53-60). Charlottesville, VA: The Michie Co.

Narol, M. (1991). Sports participation with limited litigation: The emerging Reckless Disregard Standard. *Seton Hall Journal of Sport Law,* 1, pp. 29-40.

APPENDIX

LEARNING OBJECTIVES

The student will be able to

1.　provide references to appropriate case or statutory law to support or refute the point addressed when given a legal problem;
2.　describe the technique for guaranteeing the currency of legal opinions;
3.　retrieve applicable case law when given a key number reference; and
4.　utilize the major research tools available to find statutes, regulations, and reported cases to support class assignments.

THE COMPLEXITY OF LEGAL RESEARCH

The law, to paraphrase the great jurist, Oliver Wendell Holmes, is the prophecy of what the courts will do. How, then, can you go about finding out what the courts have done? In addition to approximately 5 million reported cases in the United States to date, volumes of state and federal statutes, administrative codes, government agency regulations, rulings, and opinions all proliferate at a great rate.

The decisions of judges in the United States who have interpreted, shaped, and defined the law were first reported in 1658 (Jacobstein & Mersky, 1998). Decisions that find their way into the reporters, the bound volumes that line the stacks of law libraries, are published in the chronological sequence in which they are released by the court or the official reporter for publication.

To be sure, the decisions made by judges across America far outnumber published opinions. Nevertheless, approximately 140,000 cases find their way into U.S. law books every year (Jacobstein & Mersky, 1998). In addition, the 50 state legislatures and Congress together churn out approximately 50,000 pages of new or amended statutes each year. Federal, state, and administrative agencies produce a similar volume of rules, regulations, and commentary annually.

To complicate matters further, what may be "the law" for one purpose may not apply for another purpose. For example, a basketball referee may be an "independent contractor" for purposes of worker's compensation law but an "employee" for purposes of tort liability to a third party. In addition, what may be "the law" in one jurisdiction, or in one politically determined division of a jurisdiction, may not be the law 50 yards away in another jurisdiction or subdivision.

Finally, law is, to be sure, a movable feast. Today's law may be overturned tomorrow. Legislatures can and do repeal entire statutes, phrases, or exceptions. Immunities may be created by statute and then taken away. Judges declare statutes or regulations unconstitutional; appellate judges reverse their rulings; legislatures and Congress respond with still more enactments. Thus, legal research is in many ways a "work in progress."

FINDING THE LAW

Where, then, do we find the law? In all legal research of any kind, heed the maxim: A problem well stated is half solved. In other words, it is necessary to define as precisely as possible the issue to be researched and the facts that comprise the problem. Without all the facts of the issue being researched, it is impossible to find a satisfactory answer to the question, "What is the law that applies to the particular situation?" Once the facts have been identified, what next?

Everybody remembers from high school those social studies lessons that taught us "how a bill becomes a law." Visions of little cartoon like figures carting around a "bill" and toting it from the House of Representatives to the Senate to the President are fixed in every good student's mind! For those involved in the law of any activity, however, the business of how to go about finding that little bill that became a law is another matter.

Topical indexes to various subjects in the law are found in legal digests, about which more is forthcoming. But first, a word about the U.S. and State governments: Legislation enacted by Congress and by state legislatures deals with many issues in sport and physical activity.

Statutes passed by state legislatures are typically published as *slip laws* in booklet form and not generally or readily available to the public. When enough of these laws are assembled, a larger publication called *session laws* supersedes the slip law pamphlets and this version becomes the official statement of what the legislature has done.

Finally, the text of the session laws is republished as part of the statutory code of a particular state. At this point, grammatical errors are corrected, repealed provisions are deleted from text, cross- references are interposed and the new law is integrated into the numbering system established by the existing codification of the state's statutes.

FEDERAL LAWS

Acts of Congress are arranged according to subject matter in statutory codes and officially published under the title *United States Code.* The official *United States Code,* published by the United States Government, is also published in two commercially available annotated editions: The *United States Code Service* (USCS) and the *United States Code Annotated* (USCA). These two editions are the best sources to use when researching federal law. Each contains descriptive word indexes and annotations—brief capsules of cases interpreting the statutes.

These annotations contain citations—so the whole case can be easily located and read.

STATE LAWS

Like federal law, state statutes are typically arranged according to subject matter and published in fully annotated and indexed editions. Annotations in both federal and state statutes are important because the final wording of that "bill that becomes a law" is often the result of political compromise over phraseology that can leave everyone wondering about the meaning. They also frequently contain references to other legal resources and reference books that discuss the statutes being researched.

ADMINISTRATIVE CODES

Finally, federal and state administrative codes contain rules and regulations promulgated by government agencies whose authority is derived from the legislative bodies that created them. Many of these codes are quite lengthy and are of interest only to attorneys who appear before these agencies. Nevertheless, administrative codes are primary resources in the law, and the agencies who promulgate them have the authority to see that their regulations are carried out. An example of such an agency on the federal level would be the Equal Employment Opportunity Commission (EEOC).

FINDING COURT DECISIONS

After you have found citations to reported cases in legal digests and annotations to statutes, then what? How, and why, do some lawsuits ripen into reported cases while others languish in anonymity, never to be analyzed and digested for posterity? The answer is to be found in the internal mechanisms of our court systems and the procedures by which the decisions of courts are announced.

When a court is called upon to decide a case, that decision is communicated by the judge to the parties and the public in one of several possible ways. The method of communicating a court's decision differs according to the locality, the type of court (administrative agency tribunal, trial, or appellate), the preferences of individual judges, the type of controversy presented to the court, and the local rule or custom. The judge may:

- announce the court or administrative law decision from the bench without issuing a written decision;
- issue a written decision or order merely to inform the parties to the lawsuit of the judge's decision; or
- issue a written decision that articulates the facts and how the law applies to those facts so that it may serve as an instructive model for other judges and courts faced with similar legal controversies.

Although opinions of trial courts are not binding as precedent, or authority for decisions on other courts, they often serve as guiding lights to courts considering the same or similar fact patterns. A trial court is usually the first court to decide a lawsuit. Testimony and presentation of other evidence are customarily considered by this court, with or without a jury. Appellate courts, courts that consider appeals from rulings of trial courts and lower appellate courts (see chapter 2 for further information), render decisions that are binding upon lower courts within the same jurisdiction.

Nevertheless, the value of a judicial opinion, whether on the trial court or appellate level, is somewhat dependent on the skill of the judicial officer who renders it. In theory, a judicial opinion contains an accurate discussion of appropriate facts, a clear statement of the legal principles involved, an accurate analysis of the existing decisions that bear upon the case, and a well-reasoned conclusion of law upon which other courts and attorneys can rely. In practice, because judges' abilities vary widely, the quality of judicial writing varies widely. Further, not every written opinion is reported in the national reporter system.

In the federal court system, there are three types of written decisions:

1. Summary orders
2. Memorandum opinions
3. Full-dress opinions

Summary orders generally state the decision without delving into legal reasoning or analysis of prior authorities. These orders are usually not written for publication.

Memorandum opinions are somewhat more detailed than summary orders and may be published, although publication is not required.

Full-dress opinions contain detailed analyses of facts and legal principles to be articulated and developed from those facts. Legal authorities are cited. Full-dress opinions are generally reserved for those cases that raise either significant or novel issues of law. Due to the nature of our judicial system, appellate decisions—decisions of courts that hear appeals from the rulings of trial courts—are afforded more weight than trial decisions because they have precedential value for lower courts in their jurisdiction.

There are various rules and regulations in all federal circuits for deciding whether or not an opinion should be published. One such rule provides that:

> An opinion, memorandum, or other statement explaining the basis or judgment shall be published if it meets for this Court's action in issuing an order one or more of the following criteria:
> 1. With regard to a substantial issue it resolves, it is a case of first impression or the first case to present the issue in this Court;
> 2. It alters, modifies, or significantly clarifies a rule of law previously announced by the Court;
> 3 It calls attention to an existing rule of law that appears to have been generally overlooked;
> 5. It criticizes or questions existing law;
> 6. It resolves an apparent conflict in decisions within the circuit [one of 12 Federal jurisdictions in the United States] or creates a conflict with another circuit;
> 6. It reverses a published agency or District Court decision, or affirms a decision of a District Court upon grounds different from those set forth in the District Court's published opinion; or
> 7. It warrants publication in light of other factors that give it general public interest. (D.C. Circuit Rule 14[b])

Once an opinion is published, it is ripe for interpretation by the following groups:

- The parties to the lawsuit, one or more of whom may challenge the opinion by appealing to a higher court, where an attorney for each side will assert arguments as to why the opinion is erroneous and should be reversed, or why the opinion is correct and should be upheld
- The legal commentators who analyze and reanalyze the significance of opinions on issues that significantly affect a large number of people

- The class of individuals or institutions affected by the opinion who will, in most cases, glean their information from reports in the media or other secondary sources

READING AND UNDERSTANDING LEGAL OPINIONS

The best way to research legal opinions is to go right to the source and read them for yourself. To do so, you must know the various parts of an opinion. Typically the parts are presented in the following order:

- Names of the parties to the lawsuit
- Name of the court
- Date of the decision
- Brief summary of the case
- *Headnotes* reciting the various points mentioned in the case (see page 24)
- Names of the attorneys for the parties and the judge writing the opinion
- Opinion of the court

When you are reviewing the opinion of the court, you should be able to distinguish between its two parts: the dictum and the holding of the case. The holding is the precise statement of the law enunciated by the court in making the decision. The holding therefore includes the facts vital to the decision and states the scope of the decision. By contrast, the dictum discusses additional items the court found to be significant, but it is not necessarily intended to formulate law on the topic being discussed.

To compare the holding and the dictum, let's look at a case known as *Christian Brothers Institute of New Jersey*. In that case, the plaintiff, who operated a Catholic high school, sued an interscholastic league and all member schools after the league had denied several applications for membership. A complaint was originally filed with the New Jersey Division on Civil Rights. That action was settled by written agreement, with the league agreeing to open its membership rolls to private high schools and to entertain the plaintiff's future application if a vacancy for a team occurred in the league. While the agreement was being negotiated, a vacancy did occur and still another public high school was chosen for membership over the school operated by the plaintiff. Thereafter, the plaintiff filed a second complaint in the Superior Court of New Jersey, charging violation of its constitutional rights and the New Jersey Law Against Discrimination. The issue, then, was whether or not the agreement entered into between plaintiffs and defendants would bar the plaintiffs from having the matter decided by the Superior Court. The holding of the court was as follows:

> Plaintiff's election to pursue its grievance before the Division on Civil Rights operated to waive its right to pursue, in state court, other avenues of relief for the same grievance except through the appellate process.

> Such election, however, did not prevent plaintiff from obtaining judicial determination of its constitutional claims. *(Christian Brothers Institute of New Jersey v. No. N.J. Interscholastic League,* 86 N.J. 409, 1981)

The court said, by way of dictum, that the proper procedure was to raise these claims before the Appellate Division upon appeal from the adverse decision of the Division on Civil Rights.

While we hold that the trial court should have refused to hear this matter, it is also necessary to make some comment upon the court's findings of discrimination and violation of the equal protection guarantees. . . . It is clear that a rational basis can exist for an interscholastic league's decision to limit membership to public schools. . . . and that such a limitation does not result *per* se in a denial of equal protection under the Federal Constitution. . . . In any event, under the Conciliation Agreement, Defendant League has agreed to open its membership to nonpublic high schools so that the classification issue . . . is not a viable concern in this case. (86 N.J. 409, 1981, p. 418)

Thus, the holding of a case consists of only those facts that bear directly upon the court's decision based on those facts. Therefore, in researching a case for its value as *precedent,* look at the holding—that is, the court's answer to the questions presented to it by the parties. Keep in mind that due to the adversarial nature of the U.S. legal system, courts generally confine their decisions to the questions presented to them by the parties. Questions that parties to lawsuits *could* have raised in their litigation but chose not to may not be answered by the court and, if they are, would be part of the dictum, not the holding.

LOCATING AND REFERENCING LEGAL OPINIONS

The publication of written opinions and decisions of courts in the United States is dominated by the country's largest private law book publisher, the West Publishing Company of Eagan, Minnesota. Case reports from the 50 states and the federal court system are part of the West National Reporter System, which is linked according to subject matter by the West Key Number System, Headnote Analysis System, and American Digest System. All of these materials are duplicated by electronic research systems such as Westlaw, which are now widely used by attorneys and legal scholars.

For over 100 years, the National Reporter System has published the decisions of state courts primarily in series of volumes that group cases by geographical region. These reporters are known as the Atlantic, Northeastern, Northwestern, Pacific, Southwestern, Southeastern, and Southern Reporters. West also publishes opinions of state courts around the country as the *official* court reporter. Examples are *New Jersey Reports* and *New York Supplement.*

Decisions of federal courts are published in the Federal Reporter (now in its third edition and containing decisions of Federal Circuit Courts of Appeals) and the Federal Supplement, which contains decisions of Federal District Courts at the trial level. The federal judicial system is divided into 11 circuits and the District of Columbia's circuit court. Each circuit is made up of a number of federal district courts. Each state has one or more federal districts. For example, Delaware has one federal district. Missouri has two. Texas has four.

For purposes of *stare decisis,* the decision of an appellate court in the Ninth Circuit is not binding on an appellate court in the Third Circuit, or vice versa. Nevertheless, opinions from courts in different circuits are often cited by attorneys and found persuasive by courts in other circuits.

AMERICAN DIGEST SYSTEM

West's system of state, federal, regional, and national digests enables researchers to review cases standing for various principles in the law throughout the country. The digests contain brief summaries of various points of law in the decisions. They are laid out according to the key number system described in the next section.

West publishes a digest of United States Supreme Court decisions called the *Supreme Court Reporter*. These decisions are also published in a number of "unofficial" services. On a national basis, there is the massive *West Decennial Digest* system, which digests, according to the publisher, all federal cases decided since 1896 in 10-year increments. These digests are also tied to the key number system.

KEY NUMBER SYSTEM

The key number system works by assigning a consistent number to a principle of law throughout the U.S. court system, regardless of the jurisdiction or court. The key number system divides the body of legal knowledge into seven major categories and then divides each of those categories into about 450 specific legal topics. The seven major categories in the digest system are

1. persons,
2. property,
3. contracts,
4. torts,
5. crimes,
6. remedies, and
7. government.

The ever-increasing and evolving listing of the several hundred topics treated under one of the seven major categories is found in the front of the West digest volumes.

Theoretically, if you were to look up the key number for a specific legal concept in all the digests that have been published, you would find, hopefully, all reported cases on that principle of law. In practice, however, the key number system, like all indexing retrieval systems, is only as good as the person who did the indexing. Therefore, the alert student will not rely solely on the key number system to uncover all relevant authorities. Here are some examples of digest entries with key numbers:

> Monopolies 12 (6)Actions of the amateur basketball association in refusing to reinstate former professional basketball player's amateur status were exempt from the federal antitrust laws where monolithic control exerted by the association over its amateur sport was a direct result of congressional intent expressed in the Amateur Sports Act and the association could not be au thorized under the Act unless it maintained exactly that degree of control over its sport that was alleged as an antitrust violation. Sherman Anti-Trust Act, Section 1, 15 U.S.C.A. Section 1; 36 U.S.C.A. Sections 371-382b, 391-396, 391(a), (b) (4, 12), 393 (1, 7).

Constitutional Law 298.5 The amateur basketball association is a private rather than governmental actor and thus was not subject to the due process standards in refusing to reinstate professional basketball player's amateur status, even though it undertook to be the exclusive licensing authority for its sport and Congress, under the Amateur Sports Act, had bestowed on the association exclusive powers as a national governing body under the United States Olympic Committee. U.S.C.A. Const. Amend. 5; 36 U.S.C.A. Sections 371-383, 391-396. *(Behagan v. Amateur Basketball Association of the United States,* 1989)

Legal research, then, usually begins with a perusal of one or more of the resource digests that classify court opinions by locality (state or region), by forum (the type of tribunal deciding the lawsuit, such as Federal District Courts or a particular state's appellate court), or by subject matter within a particular jurisdiction. The information assembled in these digests is generally in the form of short vignettes of case opinions arranged by subject matter under either a topical index or the key number system. Cases that deal with more than one point of law (as most do) are cited under each appropriate topic or key number section.

The logical starting point for researching a point of law in the digests is the index, or the descriptive word index as it is called in most digests. For example, a case involving a state high school interscholastic athletic association may be digested under the general topic of "Schools." You may then find a principle of law under "Constitutional Law." A procedural point relating to the action of the judge may be listed under "Appeal and Error," and so on.

With a little practice, you can become proficient in smoking out the right descriptive words necessary to identify the focus of legal research. Often you'll find that a single case dealing with the general subject matter will cause the research to grow exponentially, as additional cases are cited, each with its own points of law and key numbers. Further research of the cases cited can help you narrow your focus.

Once you have determined the key numbers that most accurately describe the point of law you are researching, you can use the same numbers to find cases in any digest that uses the key number system, regardless of locality or forum.

HEADNOTE ANALYSIS SYSTEM

A word of caution, however, is in order: Every law student is warned—and you are too—that headnotes, the short summary written by the digest editor summarizing the point of law for which the case stands should not, *under any circumstances,* be relied on without reading the actual decision. The editor may be thinking something different from what the judge was when the judge wrote the summary; nor do all editors accurately digest each point of law articulated in each decision in the United States. Many a researcher has been led astray by headnotes that appeared to indicate that an issue had been decided one way when, in fact, the opposite was true. As one handbook states, "The authority is what the court said in the body of the decision, not what the editors of West say the court said" (Bledsoe, Johnson-Freese, & Slaughter, 1985, p. 7).

FINDING CASES IN CASE REPORTERS

The citation method used to identify cases is quite simple. Citations first list the names of the parties to the lawsuit that resulted in the decision. Usually the plaintiff's name is listed, followed by the abbreviation "v." or "vs." (meaning "versus"), and followed in turn by the name of the defendant or defendants and a series of numbers and letters. The first number tells you which volume in the set of reporters contains the decision. Next is an abbreviation of the title of the reporter, followed by the page number. Often the year in which the case was decided is provided as well.

For example, *University Interscholastic League v. North Dallas Chamber of Commerce Soccer Association,* 693 S.W.2d 513 (1985) is the citation of the lawsuit brought by the University Interscholastic League against the North Dallas Chamber of Commerce Soccer Association, which was decided in 1985 and reported in Volume 693 of West's *Southwestern Reporter Series,* 2nd edition, beginning on page 513.

Cases that are reported in more than one reporter have multiple citations. For example, the University Interscholastic League case could also be found at 251 Tex. Civ. App. 432.

In addition, if a case was appealed, and the decision of the Appellate Court was reported, the citation would indicate that fact. For example, *Ennis v. Bridger,* 41 F. Supp. 672, 674 (MD Pa. 1941), *aff'd.,* 129 F.2d 1019 (C.C.A 31942) means that this case was reported in Volume 41 of the reporter known as *Federal Supplement* (which contains decisions of the United States District Courts, the federal trial courts) on pages 672 and 674 and was decided in the United States District Court for the Middle District of Pennsylvania in 1941. It was subsequently appealed to the Third Circuit Court of Appeals, which decided the case in 1942, and was reported in Volume 129 of the *Federal Reporter,* 2nd edition (which contains the reported decisions of the Federal Circuit Courts of Appeals), starting on page 1019. The abbreviation *aff'd.* means that the decision that was reported in the first citation was *affirmed.* If a decision is modified or reversed, the abbreviations *mod.* or *rev'd.* are used.

Often in appellate courts, one or more judges on the panel hearing the case will write separate opinions. These opinions can be in the form of concurring opinions, which state that the judges agree with the result reached by the court, but for different reasons than the majority of the judges who decided the case, and the concurring judges wish to state their reasoning. There are also dissenting opinions, in which judges on the panel hearing the case disagree so strongly with the result that they feel compelled to render their views of the law as applied to the facts.

ENSURING UP-TO-DATE RESEARCH

In legal research, if you want to be the best and the brightest, you'd better be able to find the latest. That is to say, a court's decision that has since been overturned by a higher court in the jurisdiction is no longer of precedential value, and therefore is no longer the law. For this reason, your legal research project will not be complete until you Shepardize the relevant court decisions.

The process known as Shepardizing is named for the original publisher of *Shepard's Citations Volumes,* Frank Shepard, who started printing lists of cases that cited Illinois decisions in 1873. Shepardizing is accomplished by consulting the appropriate volume of *Shepard's Citation Volumes,* which reveal any case opinions that cite, overturn, comment on, or otherwise make reference to that case. The volumes list the reported cases from each official reporter in numerical order. Under each case is a list of cases that cite the opinion being researched. Similar volumes of Shepard's are published for many other legal authorities. The same information is also available on computer-assisted legal research systems. (For more information, see *How to Use Shepard's Citations,* 1976.)

Shepard's uses superscript code letters and symbols next to some citations to indicate whether the cited case reverses, mentions in dissent, modifies, or speaks to a particular point of law dealt with in that opinion. These codes also indicate whether the citation is the same case reproduced in a different set of reporters.

Shepard's also refers to headnote numbers assigned to the particular point of law to help researchers find the section of the opinion that is dealt with in the later case. This is especially helpful when Shepardizing a lengthy opinion that contains many points of law unrelated to the topic being researched. For example, a 27-page opinion dealing with the denial of an athlete's due process rights may contain statements of legal principles regarding contract rights, legal theories of awarding damages, and procedural errors of lower courts in admitting evidence. Only some of these areas may be of interest in any given research project. Therefore, you can save much time and effort by consulting only those cases cited in *Shepard's* that are denoted by the appropriate headnote number.

USING THE COMPUTER TO DO LEGAL RESEARCH

Electronic legal research in the United States is dominated by the leading publishers of law books, West Group's Westlaw Company and Reed-Elsevier's Lexis-Nexis Publishing, so that there is a natural congruity between printed material and electronic research. Computer assisted legal research can be accessed through the internet, as well as through proprietary software published by West, Lexis-Nexis, and others. Each system allows users to access a number of databases keyed to jurisdiction, subject matter, or a number of specialized "libraries" that are supported by menu-driven research systems. Each system allows documents (case reports, law journal articles, sections of encyclopedic treatises, and other material) to be retrieved by citation - or through the intuitive methods of Boolean Searching utilizing connectors. In addition, Westlaw and Lexis-Nexis users can pose a question in plain English: "natural language" searching.

Electronic legal research allows you to find both primary sources of law, including statutes, regulations, cases, and codes; and secondary sources of law, including, treatises, commentaries, encyclopedias, law reviews, and other publications. These materials are indexed in much greater depth and breadth than book based research. Both Westlaw and Lexis-Nexis utilize similar search methods which allow you to either ask a question in "natural language" (What is the measure of damages when a school breaches an employment contract?) or Boolean searching using terms, phrases, and connectors (damage! AND school AND/contract w/5 breach AND coach AND/NOT teacher). In addition, if you know the exact citation of a statute, regulation, case, or law review article, you can easily retrieve the full-text or summary of the document you want.

The so called "natural language" searches will take description of a legal quandary or question and isolate legal terms of art which will enable the server to search for "concepts." You can control the number of documents retrieved by your search and expand or narrow the scope by jurisdiction and type of database as needed. These search engines will retrieve documents in descending order of relevance.

Natural language searches generally use an electronic model to weigh the significance of each word in the question asked. By contrast, a Boolean search will, unless modified, only pull up documents that contain each word or term in the search. In addition, with electronic research, it is possible to view a statutory code's table of contents, just as you would in book research

By using some standard root expanders, symbols and universal characters, you can enable your Boolean search to retrieve "wild card" entries or documents containing different forms of the word or terms you have entered. You can also specify that certain words, phrases or terms need to be separated by not more than a given number of words or in the alternative, you can retrieve documents containing words, phrases, or terms located within the same paragraph or sentence.

You can also exclude documents containing certain words. For example, if you wanted to pull up cases involving injuries in soccer excluding youth soccer, you would formulate your search along the following lines: "injuries AND soccer AND player! AND (but not) youth." Searching can also be restricted by dates, courts, and proximity of one term to another.

Shepard's citations are available on Lexis-Nexis but since the Shepard's system is proprietary to Lexis-Nexis, it is not available on West. West, however, features its "Key-Cite," "Insta-Cite," and "Auto-Cite" services which the publisher says will retrieve cases citing the principal case.

Although details vary somewhat between the two major providers - and between professional and academic versions - the basics of Boolean and natural language searching are found in the tutorials and manuals for each legal research system and should be reviewed before beginning a search.

In short, electronic legal research can be used to pinpoint legal information in far greater detail and far more quickly than book research. Imagine being in a law library surrounded by books - but no computers - and attempting to find every case or statute in your state that mentions "basketball" and "injury" within 100 words of each other. This type of research is impossible utilizing only books, but is a "day in the park" with the proper electronic research tools.

ADDITIONAL RESOURCES

Rounding out the legal research tools are treatises, which are similar to textbooks that cover particular areas of the law. Treatises may be restricted to the treatment of one or several legal topics within a particular jurisdiction or may be national in scope. Newsletters and various periodicals that cover issues in sport and physical activity can also be useful resources. Consult a law librarian to find out which publications are currently available.

Other resources include Restatements: topical treatments of various areas of law that are not jurisdiction specific, the aim of which is to "restate" common law principles in an ongoing fashion. Restatements come in the following flavors that are most likely to be of interest to students of the law of sport and physical activity: Contracts, Torts, Agency, and Property. The restatements are published by the nonprofit American Law Institute and are widely cited by American courts, especially in cases for which no clear case law precedent exists.

Just as the rules of any sport largely depend upon definitions, so does the law. Therefore, law dictionaries and legal encyclopedias are vital to the success of any legal research project. West's *Black's Law Dictionary* is recommended from among the dozen or more law dictionaries and thesauri currently available. One of Black's useful features is that many of its definitions are *annotated* with key notes that guide the researcher to cases that illustrate the legal term. Do not underestimate the value of a good law dictionary.

The biggest and best legal encyclopedia is clearly West Publishing Company's 162-volume *Corpus Juris Secundum* (CJS). CJS has both a detailed table of contents before each major topic and a multivolume comprehensive index that makes it easy to use. It also cross-references topics to the key number system. Although the breadth of treatment of the topics in CJS may seem too detailed for nonlawyers, keep in mind that the authors attempt to render all aspects of American law within its pages. Therefore, comprehensively speaking, CJS can help you perform exhaustive research in a particular area of American law.

SUMMARY

When researching a legal topic, the first step is to assemble all the facts of the situation and define the legal concepts involved as precisely as possible. The law that relates to an issue may be found in one or more of the following: case reports, state or federal statutory codes, or in administrative codes, which contain the rules and regulations of certain government agencies.

In order to find reported cases whose precedent-setting decisions help describe the application of the law to a set of facts, look in West's state, federal, regional, and national digests or annotated statutes to review cases in which the legal issue in question has been tested. The logical place to start looking for cases would be in the digest's descriptive word index. Knowing the concept on which the case is based will lead you, via the index, to the page upon which short vignettes of relevant case opinions are arranged. It is important to know that principles of law are assigned a West key number. Looking up the key number of a specific concept in all published digests would, in theory, lead you to most published opinions on the precise topic you are researching. Therefore, you may use the key number associated with the first relevant court opinion you find in the digest to find other relevant opinions. Key number topics are divided into seven major categories and a listing of the topics treated under any one of the seven major categories is found in the front of the West digest volumes.

Because headnotes (the short summaries written by a digest's editor that summarize the point of law for which the case stands) are only as good as the editor who writes them, you will want to read actual decisions from the reporters of the National Reporter System. The National Reporter System publishes the decisions of state courts in a series of volumes that group cases by geographical region. Decisions of federal courts are published in the *Federal Reporter* and in the *Federal Supplement*. The citation of any case will give you the name of the reporter in which the case decision may be read and the page number on which the case appears. The citation will also show multiple listings for cases and whether or not the decision of the court was appealed. When reading a reported case, it is important to be able to recognize and distinguish the case's holding from the dictum.

If you already know the exact law you want to research, do the following;

A.   If you are attempting to locate a federal law, go to the *United States Code Annotated*. Title and section numbers appear on each volume. "Notes of Decisions" generally appear following the statutory material.

B.   If you are attempting to locate a state statute, go to the appropriate state statutory code. These codes may be indexed by subject matter and/or section numbers, subject matter and/or title and chapter numbers.

C.   To research a particular topic, consult the appropriate state digest. For federal law, consult West's Federal Practice Digest. All digests contain a "descriptive word index" or similar index that will point to cases construing specific words and terms.

D.   When doing any "book" research, always be sure to check pocket parts and supplement pamphlets for the latest information, as new cases and other source materials are continually being added. Practitioners who have working knowledge of the databases available can keep abreast of the latest developments in their field and use the law as a valuable management tool.

To ensure up-to-date research, you should "Shepardize" your findings by consulting *Shephard's Citation Volumes,* which reveal case opinions that cite, overturn, comment on, or otherwise make reference to the decision of the case you are researching. Finally, legal research can be rounded out by consulting other resources such as treatises, restatements, legal encyclopedias, or a good law dictionary. Practitioners who have working knowledge of the databases available can keep abreast of the latest developments in their field and use the law as a valuable management tool.

KEY TERMS

Administrative codes
Annotations
Appellate courts
Appellate decisions
Citations
Concurring opinions
Descriptive word index
Dictum

Digests
Dissenting opinions
Federal Reporter
Federal Supplement
Full-dress opinions
Headnotes
Holding
Key number system
Legal digests

INDEX